Out of the Silence

Out of the Silence

A Study of a Religious Community for Women:
The Community of the Holy Name

LYNNE STRAHAN

OXFORD
UNIVERSITY PRESS

Melbourne
Oxford   Auckland   New York

OXFORD UNIVERSITY PRESS AUSTRALIA
Oxford   New York   Toronto   Delhi   Bombay
Calcutta   Madras   Karachi   Petaling Jaya
Singapore   Hong Kong   Tokyo   Nairobi
Dar es Salaam   Cape Town   Melbourne   Auckland
and associated companies in
Berlin   Ibadan

Oxford is a trade mark of Oxford University Press
© Lynne Strahan 1988
First published 1988

National Library of Australia
Cataloguing-in-Publication data:

Strahan, Lynne, 1938–
   Out of the silence.

   Includes index.
   ISBN 0 19 554898 1.

   1. Community of the Holy Name (Melbourne,
   Vic.). 2. Monasticism and religious orders
   for women, Anglican. I. Title.

255'.98

Designed by Guy Mirabella
Cover image by Brian Dunlop from *The Book of Durrow*
Typeset by Setrite Hong Kong
Printed by Impact Printing, Melbourne
Published by Oxford University Press,
253 Normanby Road, South Melbourne

CONTENTS

ACKNOWLEDGEMENTS

I wish to thank Louise Sweetland of Oxford University Press and Carla Taines for their support. I also particularly thank Robin Grove, who gave dedicated and inspired editorial assistance, and, above all, the Sisters of the Community for their tolerance, humour and honesty in responding to my questions about their lives.

A SIGN TO THE WORLD

When I first confronted the task of writing the history of the Community of the Holy Name, I expected to write an orthodox chronicle, based primarily on the treasury of documents that I imagined the Anglican Church and the Community would have lovingly amassed, and concentrating on the Community's contribution to social welfare. Mostly in Victoria, but also interstate and overseas, its work is evident, magnificent, but unacknowledged except among the few. The fact that the Community is Anglican makes it exceptional in several ways. For one thing, it has given it a distinctive practical edge. Because the religious life in the Anglican Church is less organized, extensive and monolithic than in the Roman Catholic Church, the Community has not been able to afford a tidy specialist concentration. Throughout the past century it has had to respond to any call that came its way, staffing schools, hospitals, children's homes, reformatories, hostels, retreat houses, with triumphant amateurism and enviable determination, and in a spirit of selfless, often painful dedication.

The first Anglican order to be founded here, and one of only four such women's communities in Australia, it has always been isolated, intensifying its sense of identity and its awareness of its own heritage. There is a complicated and continuing connection with the spirituality of the Oxford Movement, the revival of religious life in the established Church in nineteenth-century England, and the Church's attempt (not without an eye to its worldly reputation and the challenge of other sects) to provide a response to urban poverty. All this seemed to promise a documentary source so ample that the problem would be one of culling from abundance. Unfortunately, the Anglican archival scene is not like Miss Havisham's time-locked and crowded mansion, except perhaps for the dust.

I began with the Community's first enterprise, the Mission to Streets and Lanes, which began in the 1880s. Its present venue in Napier Street, Fitzroy (Melbourne), is not unlike the places the Mission was founded to serve, and looked like a place with intact and orderly records. However, its documentary holdings were disappointing and stirred early qualms about where I might find the raw material for a history. Correspondence, which injects quirky life into the reconstruction of the past, is absent. The Mission Council's minute-books and odd records relating to the Babies' Home at Darling and to the Caulfield Auxiliary, chance survivals, exist; but minute-takers of any age seem involved in an unspecified conspiracy to obscure as much as they reveal.

Annual reports display the same decorous conspiracy. Those who compiled them in the early years of this century saw themselves as guardians of reputation. Still, their financial accounts can be presumed to be fairly accurate, since such councils always have their quota of proven businessmen. Likewise their statistics, though often sketchy, may encapsulate some dramatic point: the tally of abandoned children, or the toll of a typhoid epidemic. In the end, however, annual reports are political documents; they reveal what they are designed to reveal, and obscure with aplomb what they do not intend to expose. Occasional brochures had been kept, primarily for ceremonial occasions or solicitations for funds, and sparse in information.

In the records of the Mission Council, therefore, the Community itself appeared as a shadowy chorus, less important than the

charitable ladies of the auxiliaries with their sewing circles and
Maytime fêtes. Apart from references to the awe-inspiring authority of Esther, the Mother Foundress, and a kind of collective
praise for the sisters as a totality, one does not glimpse much. *In
Our Midst*, the sisters' own magazine, showed more of the spirit
that sustained them. It was designed to have the human touch,
and provide some factual amplification of their work. As well as
that, a feminist streak is observable in a pious yet strong series
on 'Remarkable Women', and some items suggest how the
sisters, although running with the system in the main, infused
compassion into the punitive social attitudes of the time. But
once again the references to controversy are obscure, the wardens'
reports—especially those of the aptly named Canon Godby—
tend to be unhelpfully moralistic, and the descriptions of visits
to the House of Mercy at Cheltenham and the Children's
Home at Brighton and festive occasions at those places are
often coated with icing before being tied with tinsel. Valuable
record though it is, *In Our Midst* is primarily a publicity organ,
conveying deeper strains only inadvertently.

Melbourne's central granaries for Anglican history, the Diocesan
Registry in the catacombs beneath St Paul's Cathedral and the
elegant Mollison Library in Trinity College at the University of
Melbourne, were also disappointing. Neither place has the full
range of Anglican church-journals. The *Church of England Messenger*, which gave continuing if mild support to the sisters,
eschewed controversy, and the elaborately scripted index to the
paper at the Mollison Library has no entry for either the
'Mission to the Streets and Lanes' or the 'Community of the
Holy Name'.

Enquiries at the Community House, the Cheltenham headquarters of the order, showed that the sisters too had been
somewhat cavalier about the evidences of their past, although
treasures were gradually uncovered. Some of these were letters.
Esther's letters from 1912 to 1922 to a prospective novice,
Blanche Patterson, survive, and concern a matter that became
a theme of great poignancy: the reaction of families to the
announcement that a daughter intended becoming a nun. On
the families' side, responses ranged through hostility, heartbroken
acceptance and incomprehension, while on the daughters' side

is the determination to pursue a vocation despite the traumas that steadfastness involved.

In a later phase of CHN's existence, the new Superior, Mother Ida, visited England in 1938 and again in 1948 when she was accompanied by her chosen successor, Flora, on the well-worn pilgrimage route around the English communities. The letters from both these trips helped formulate themes that had begun to emerge: the symbolic strength of the English connection; the importance—touched with thoroughly feminine fashion-consciousness—of the habit; the life of prayer in the historical context; generalized symbols, such as love of nature and the nurture of animals and children.

Pilgrimage also produced Sister Bertha's diary, written in 1927 when she accompanied Esther on her last visit to England. From this, one gets a more human—sometimes comical—view of the foundress's mythologized personality, and a sense too of the indomitability that lasted to the end of her life. The unflaggingly bright entries in the diary are decorated with sepia postcards of inns and ruins and time-bleached pressed flowers: a combination of language and image which makes it a minor, perfectly consistent relic.

Some of the documentary material had nothing in common with the kind of written evidence that I was accustomed to, except for being written on paper in English. A superseded version of the Community's Customary, printed in a tiny grey wafer of a booklet, might have described the rituals of an exotic tribe—or were they simply girls' school rituals carried to the ultimate extreme? Esther's long commentary on the Rule revealed her as more a literal-minded formalist than a mystical illuminist in theology. An account of the New Zealand Order of the Good Shepherd, absorbed into CHN in 1957, could be seen as a wistful attempt to record the short-lived achievements and to preserve the fragile identity of the small beleaguered group which had moved into the shadow of a much larger mentor, and to create a small compensating mythology for them. Necessarily, some of the facts were avoided and some of the pain was muffled.

Meanwhile, 'The Book of the Dead' seemed to require, as first approach, protection against the intimidating mortality of the title. These thumb-nail biographies of deceased members of the Community were characterized by frustrating factual omissions (dates of profession are often preferred to dates of birth), and they lack what the professional historian might dub significant detail. On the other hand, they often give information on family background, experience before entering the Community, and more general matters like the movement of sisters between CHN's branch houses.

More importantly, depending on the author of the obituary note, personalities are described. Although there are none of those bolts of prose which seem to light the whole of a person in a flash, the invisible writing can be as perceptible as the words that are there. Occasionally, the author digresses into an unprovoked meditation of her own which poignantly reveals her own spiritual ambience and hints at her relationship with the dead sister. Such moments are fraught with the anguished reticence of an atmosphere which encouraged secrecy and discouraged intimacy.

Where they exist, the superiors' addresses to Chapter (the convocation of professed sisters) are a central source; but they bristle with references understood by those who were being spoken to, ambiguous to the mere reader. Moreover, the addresses naturally assume a familiarity with rules and procedure not normally possessed by an outsider. To the stranger, their language is often inscrutable, although to the initiate they are charged with meaning, for the emotional overtones express a world-view that I sense but do not share. In this scenario the outside world and its familiar pressures impinge but are metamorphosed; the ideal and the real constantly and painfully interact; the conflict between good and evil is an immediate event. Though crucial to an understanding of the Community and the role of its superiors, these addresses emphasized the foreignness of the historian's task. I wondered if I would ever manage to inch beyond the borders of the charmed circle I could glimpse.

The amassing of random relics continued. Two press-cutting books promised much, but petered out. The earlier one, dating from the 1880s, showed more interest in the tribulations of the Sisters of the Church in England than in the controversy which

went on here over the establishment of CHN. To go with
them, Sister Louisa presented a carefully garnered cache of
records: a time-line of important events in the Community's
history, with the proviso that it was as accurate as she could
make it. As well, there was Sister Frances's prayer-book, containing lists of women who had entered the Community, with
the names of those who had left erased; a bundle of letters and
postcards, a sheaf of anecdotes, stray items from the press.

A few envelopes and exercise-books relating to the particular
sisters came from the Community's cupboard of archives. One
contained photos of a child with a hydrocephalic head, and
others of adults, probably relatives. A book with a marbled
cover held accounts of one sister's visionary experiences, others
were filled with meditations on the religious life. These survivals
were fortuitous and atypical, sometimes bizarre, and their existence was overlaid by an awareness that the Community discounted the relevance of an individual's personal effects, which
were often destroyed before or after death, and frequently not
accumulated at all.

Its collection of photographs is the Community's most consistent public record, and underscores the importance of the
visual in these lives. Some are group photographs: the beautifully
defined features of the sisters' young Chinese clientele in
Cumberland Place in the squalid inner-city of the early days; an
arrangement of children on the verandah of the Children's
Home at Goulburn before the trek to church; a jolly group in
the kitchen at Ellerslie, the Community's home for the elderly;
the oratory and community-room in New Guinea, replacing
finery with spartan intensity; the Archbishop of Canterbury's
visit in 1950, with clergy to the fore and the sisters waiting
their turn in the wings.

Old-girls/boys from the House of Mercy and the children's
homes have sent photographs which are preserved in motherly
fashion. Many are wedding-groups; where instead of the usual
secular party, black-garbed sisters flank silver phials of brides.
Several photos show self-consciously eager young men in the
stiffness of uniform—portraits taken before their embarkation
to the First World War. Of those who didn't return, one was
Lawrence Oldfield, the adopted son of the foundress.

The faces of individual sisters stood out. Louisa with children, and Lydia with lambs. Esther, who often looks distant and ascetic, sat in a wheelbarrow with two children and a dog. Rae was pictured in academic gown, and Maree on a motorbike. Ida looked like the general of the nunnish troops around her. Flora's jonquil-like face radiated the quality suggested by her name. Retrospectively, the omission of Faith, Superior of CHN from 1960 to 1981, seemed to fit the elusive abstract quality of her personality.

Two secondary sources exist. Norman Marshall's history of St George's Hospital is a conscientious and sometimes lively record; but when one sister asked my opinion of it, she capped my noncommittal response with: 'Yes, you could tell we wouldn't talk to that man.' I wasn't honest enough to admit that I hadn't noticed. The history of St George's was also perplexed by a lingering reticence in a few sisters to refer to the Community members who had dramatically decamped to Adelaide when their position at the hospital was challenged in 1937. On reflection I was amazed to realize I had overlooked its determinedly secular stress.

The other is Sister Elizabeth's biography, *Esther, Mother Foundress*, published in 1948. It does give life to this figure who seems disconcertingly to have been both eminently practical and paramountly spiritual; however, it is marred by the author's preference for the pious, and her assumption that the reader will be familiar with events such as the row that erupted when the original deaconesses revealed their determination to take full vows. It appears, too, that hagiography dictated some materials should be suppressed.

I had always intended to talk to members of the Community as an adjunct to the documentary sources, but my attitude to oral history was firmly prejudiced. It seemed to have become a fashionable substitute for the drudgery of wading through documents, and to have elevated gossip, particularly working-class reminiscence, into historical fact. Besides, my previous experiences of oral history had not been encouraging.

The first sister I talked to was Agnes Mary, then eighty-seven and a half, the Community's librarian and custodian of its history—physically impaired but sharp-minded, passionate in her love for the Community and its life. I met her the first time I visited CHN, Cheltenham, in May 1984, when my ignorance, preserved on tape, was embarassing; she guided me patiently through major events in the Community's history, describing facets of its work. My bias was almost completely toward social history, with an inherently patronizing deference to the Community's spiritual life. At one point, Agnes Mary emphasized the notion of community; my inward response was to award her scant attention and hold my social-welfare preoccupation more tightly.

As I ploughed through the archival sources, I toyed with ideas for the structure of the book, first the rather mechanical solution of dismembering CHN's activities into categories of work, with chapters on structure, foundation and change, then the even more drearily artificial chronological method of dividing the past into more or less arbitrary slabs like a true historicist. Meanwhile, I began to find the living history in front of me more and more meaningful. Patterns began to form, dead personalities fleshed out, symbols and symbolic situations emerged. I realized that the Community was a living organism of immense and exciting complexity, a growing crystal, as few human groups and fewer institutions are. Its life-cycle was uniquely intact, displaying peculiar symmetries, stunning disharmonies, phases of growth and attrition as if it were a sole-standing tree that recorded its vicissitudes in its physical structure.

The fact that the Community has reached its centenary at all is a matter for justifiable pride. With numbers that never exceeded about sixty at any one time, its record in carrying out mission and court work, running schools, establishing and managing hospitals and children's homes—especially while fostering and maintaining the religious life—is formidable, even breathtaking. But in another sense the rounded score is irrelevant, because the Community seems to embody its history with a complicated interaction between past and present available to few groups or institutions. A religious community has a unity of existence that distinguishes it from a school, a town or a board. Other institutions and other groups may have unity of purpose, unity of place, a coherent identity, but for CHN these unities are different in both quality and kind. The core of meaning is of another order.

There have been difficulties, failures, cleavages. Sisters have died or departed the Community. Most of the institutions once run by CHN have gone or transferred to other hands. The past seems irrecoverable and the future precarious. Yet the core of meaning lasts unchanged, and within it all the elements that have made up the Community still exist. It is as if the atoms have merely been transposed into a different relationship with one another.

Apart from my sense of a quality of existence that couldn't be embraced by chronological or categorical devices, a teasing awareness of metaphor and myth began to develop. In the context of the Community, language, the most powerful and complex symbolic system, gained haunting resonance. Not all the sisters are shrewd users of words. Some admit discomfort or ineptitude with language, others are extremely articulate; but the speech of all of them is impregnated with symbolic assumptions and symbolic meaning. Words recur: veil, hair, bonds, freedom, responsibility, friendship, community, loneliness, longing, time, feasts, darkness, happiness, growth, stillness, quietness, silence, spirituality, garden, rule, black, talents, gifts, vision, calling, vocation, authority, self, love. Visual symbols also abounded: the cross, the statue, the icon, the altar, the habit.

I realized that the book should be constructed musically, and that the process of change, dissolution and reconstruction—the shifting patterns all breaking away from, passing through, along and around the core—could be encompassed only if it were seen flowing into the present. The sisters themselves are the living lines by which the Community is linked to its past. In them, my source became limpidly and beautifully clear.

I confess with pleasure that I fell into a unique 'oral-history situation': a self-contained group of forty women either living together or connected by strenuous bonds, without the usual distinctions between individuals' private and public lives, the eldest almost ninety, the youngest thirty, and thus spanning several generations in reaction to the one, difficult and (to the world) inexplicable situation. The ethos that informs the lives of these women means that the observer must confront and try to understand what is, mundanely speaking, a most peculiar interaction between the real and the ideal, between practicalities and essences. The observer must also learn the relevance of concepts which attach positive meaning to suffering and death, and accept the transforming reality of belief in eternal life.

The willing suspension of disbelief which literature enjoys has sometimes to be applied. For instance, in August 1985, Faith, a former Mother Superior of great intelligence and complexity, suddenly died. The sister who was alone with her when she collapsed says that the room was crowded with sisters. She wondered why they were doing nothing to help the stricken woman until she realized that these were the spirits of dead members of the Community. She added that some people might misunderstand the story, and wanted to assert the experience as an ordinary spiritual event.

In the face of experiences such as this, my agnostic position is both disadvantage and advantage: it is hard to put myself into the skin of such happenings, or even into the framework of belief; but scepticism enables me to scrutinize its authentic elements and exercise the faculty of reasonable doubt. In the matter of the religious life, however, one could not adjudicate at all if one believed that the world is entirely held within its material manifestations, or saw the unlikely and the impossible as simply interchangeable.

In such matters, one's whole swag of assumptions must be drawn into the light. I came to write this book believing that I didn't have an attitude to the religious life, except that it was an anachronism, quaint, if not self-indulgent in a world marching catastrophically beyond such optimism. After a while I realized that I had a store of forceful if unspoken attitudes to the subject. My upbringing had been in the Presbyterian vein, with caustic comments on priests and nuns, and a code of activism as the only means of expressing virtue: a moralism of tautology—the duty of good works, and the obligation of duty. Education reinforced the child-grown prejudices, when I gathered the Reformation had banished the chicanery of Roman Catholic practices and released legions of monks and nuns from bondage to live a more sensible life. Luther and Calvin were our heroes, which almost inevitably disabled my desperate attempts as a university student to become a Roman Catholic convert. As for Anglican nuns... like several CHN sisters before they came to the order, I had scarcely heard of such.

In talking to me, several sisters emphasized their ordinariness, both individually and as a community. No doubt their insistence is partly because all spiritual pride must perpetually be guarded against, but some were genuinely astonished—even disbelieving—when I declared how unusual they were. An extraordinary situation can stir the slumbering titan of Difference in the most matter-of-fact type, but none of these women is ordinary—even granted the fact that probably no one is.

They live with an ideal of human behaviour which, for most of us, is swamped in the everyday. Scrutinizing themselves and their actions, not morbidly but rigorously, through the confessional and in many other ways, spotlights both weakness and success. This makes the competitive pressures between them peculiarly poignant. 'Nobody's perfect', several of them said with wistful realism when confronted with compromises, mistakes and failures. Few are formally well-educated, and yet they are capable of enviable shrewdness, intelligence and objectivity. They are an amazingly individualistic bunch. Indeed, the struggle against the circumscription of their life-pattern has not produced a weave of dull conformity, but a tapestry glowingly complex.

The Cheltenham estate of the Community of the Holy Name is an oasis in the Legoland of the suburb. All round are neat, repetitious oatmeal-brick houses, treeless nature strips, traffic lozenges and grids of sensible streets. The only nearby establishment to match the estate is the shopping complex of Southland, and Southland in windowless bleak concrete provides a staggering contrast—as appropriate a shrine to commercialism as the sisters' domain is to the nature of their calling.

Community House is approached along a gravel drive lined by agapanthus which at points burst away from their drive-lining habit into small lakes of Della Robbia blue. Beyond them, black triangles of cypress expand and contract with a sawing movement and winnowing sound. Between the agapanthus and the cypress, golden poplars spread maypoles of shimmering leaf. The grass in this space is wayward but not unkempt, broken by a stone-bordered garden bed, the leaning totem of a fallen branch, an odd plinth of red brick without an inscription. Sombre seclusion and mysterious space produce a perplexing feeling that this is both familiar territory and alien, a realm in which every atom is imbued with significance.

After taking a slow curve, the drive loops into an oval as the garden opens up in front of the Community's main residence: an austerely handsome Spanish mission building completed in 1936—two stories, with arched windows on the ground floor, terracotta tiles, white walls, an intimate portico. On the left, a white-walled chapel repeats many of the Spanish mission features, topped by a modest bell-tower. In 1949 a south wing was added to form a courtyard around a galleon of an oak. The building of the library and St Julian's, the former infirmary wing, has completed the cloister effect. The sisters first arrived on this spot in 1892 and over the years have added new parcels of land, the last bought under Faith in 1967, so that the property now covers twenty-five acres.

The grounds at Cheltenham sometimes seem to have the emptiness of a wind-swept beach. They are unnervingly vast, seeming to provide a physical touchstone for every emotion, and to be governed by an inevitability that goes beyond design. Stretches of bristling grass contrast with mown avenues and enclosures where plants are placed with the care of children designing sand-castle surrounds. There are broken views and uninterrupted views; a medium view incised by a comforting intrusion of the human, and a grand view suggesting an unending beyond. There are gardens where space seems reduced to the size of an urn. Every element seems placed for meditation, or at least a thoughtful pause: the seat under the crab-apple, the wheel-barrow abandoned near a mound of cut grass, the circle of seats around the paved garden with its central cross. Even the buildings have an air of being part of a wonderful organic growth in which the difference between the created and the manufactured is erased.

Proliferation is tolerated, even encouraged, while order is sustained without pernicketiness or formalism. Giant trees are left to lie where they fall; or if a tree must go, the stump,

coloured and textured like raw silk, remains. Variety of shape
and colour composes a medieval miniature: lapis lazuli, lime-
green, sage-green, saffron, scarlet, green-tinged white, white-
throated mauve, purple-spotted pink, in the intersecting shapes
of a round rose-bed, a lily patch, and a vague-shaped plot that
is a free-for-all of flowers. There is a clear preference for the
subtler annuals, the cottage or old-fashioned flower, the one
that is known and loved so well that nobody quite remembers
its name. Sweet peas overhang pansies, English daisies nudge
up to cornflowers, foxgloves brush against columbines, a star-
shaped dahlia beams over the star-heads of hydrangea while
spindles of lavender reach towards drifts of flags. Small plantings
of one flower move randomly into groupings of another. Some
treasures are secreted away as if they are intended to be overlooked or viewed separately from the panorama. A fuse of
nasturtiums blazes at the foot of an elbowed tree, seen only by
the garden-browser who stumbles on them. The making of this
garden has been a co-operative matter between prodigal nature
and human nurture.

With the end of Sister Mary's reign over the garden when
she died in February 1983, many sisters have their own plots
and tend them in garb as individual as the plants they grow:
one in a long habit, another in slacks and blouse. Some of the
sisters, like Helena who worked in a plant nursery before she
joined the Order of the Good Shepherd in New Zealand, are
knowledgeable about flowers; others, if not learned botanically,
have long green fingers. When questioned, Maree speculates
about the name of a flower, and admits ignorance; but her
gladioli are among the first and tallest of the summer, and her
children's story, *The Garden I Live In*, uses the landscape at
Cheltenham as the central metaphor of a Christian parable.
Dandelion-starred in summer, frost-bound in winter, with
autumn's leaf-burnings and a snood of blossom in spring, it is
also Eden and Paradise, the cycle of the seasons as a paradigm
for the seasons of other living things. Sister Lois who has been
disabled by a leg injury still delights in showing local children
how to press flowers.

Alongside exasperated references to absconding girls, the
House of Mercy day-books record the planting of a row of

hydrangeas or the arrival of a visitor with a special cutting. In the obituary entries in the 'Book of the Dead', the sisters' relationship to the garden—often an activity of their retirement years—is recorded. But even as a postulant, Sister Constance Agnes soothed her restlessness by counting, she recalls, ninety water-lilies on the pond at Community House. In London in 1927, Sister Bertha notes in her diary that she has 'bought some garden seeds at one stall to plant in Australia', while from Wantage in 1964 Faith describes a small enclosed garden planted with a spectacular array of wallflowers—'the scent on a sunny afternoon is almost overpowering'—and observes that their intense hues are probably the result of the gauze-filtered English sun. The night before her own death, by the bed-side of a sick sister, she enthuses over violets whose scent is to the nose as music is to the ear.

Some parts of the garden at Cheltenham are totally English-looking: the herbs, scented geraniums, rhubarb and cucumber; others are peculiarly Australian: the informal shapes of the bottlebrush in front of Retreat House. Sometimes, English and Australian merge. Beyond the chapel, where the grounds extend into park-like vastness, a ridge of bay foreshore, strung with tea-tree, floored with sand and stapled with threadbare grass, ends at the Calvary Cross. Beneath it, an English rockery garden massed with cottonreels of bright flower; on the far side, a wall of crazed stone holding metal tablets that record the dates of birth, profession and death of the sisters, each bearing the valediction 'Jesu Mercy'.

The symbolism of flowers, the cycle of the seasons and the ages of humanity, nature benign and munificent, but also a blossoming riven with evanescence: these themes are strong in the Community, punctuating discourse and calling out a joy and gentleness in individual sisters which sometimes stand in contrast to their more acerbic qualities. At Christmas sculpted lilies of the Annunciation are placed in the refectory by the unpretentious statue of the Madonna and child, evoking Mary's particular association with lilies. She is the lily of the field, pots of lilies decorate her room, lilies spring up in her empty tomb. In Lent, the chapel is stripped of its usual tall blooms. Through the rest of the year, however, Community House will glow with flowers. The Superior's office, with business-like desk and filing cabinets, has posies in containers; the long dark table in the vestibule always holds a spire of flowers positioned beneath the austerity of Esther's photograph.

The rose of Sharon and the lily of the valleys: one unexpected survivor among the Community's documents is a folder of meditations given before and after professions on St Andrew's Day 1933—discursive reflections emphasizing the spiritual significance of the rose and lily, both Mary's flowers:

Gather the rose. . . The warm living beauty of the Rose of Sharon. . . Lotus or tulip of great size and beauty and colour clothes the hillsides. The same glowing beauty, the same purity, truth, humility. . . Rose of Sharon taking to it added beauty of lily of the valley. . . Each one of us is to grow up as a lily among thorns

Sister Eleanor's 1934 address to confirmees listed the glories of the created universe, through to 'Flowers, always a succession of them—every year fresh blooms. . . the flowers from the parent bush'. The nun both is and is within the 'enclosed garden', the 'garden barred': while these notions of immurement and *noli me tangere* have been replaced with a more matter-of-fact attitude towards the Community's place in the world, the ancient resonances are hard to dispel.

The feelings of separation and enclosure at Cheltenham are so intense that the visitor may forget how normal much of the life there is, and the fact that many sisters move actively in the world encountering its tragedy and disorder in brutal forms at times. The interiors of the house are similarly permeated with a sense of the unfamiliar. In looking round the rooms and corridors, one is impressed chiefly with the iconographic weight of objects and the immaculate order. It is hard to realize that the objects have the same significance as family heirlooms, and that the control is housewifely management on a larger scale, though prosecuted with a finesse that shows both the clasp of religious ritual carried over into domestic economy, and the husbanding of material resources as required by the vow of poverty. The imagery of home and family is strong in the Community.

The room called 'Courtesy' (correct furniture, plump cushions,

flowers in a swallow-braided bowl, and etchings) has been the
main setting for my conversations with the sisters, but there
have been other places, each with its distinctive aura: the
bustling silences of the refectory; the haunting verticals of the
chapel; the Community Room, with stucco angels on the fire-
place, oval table spread with precisely arranged books and
magazines, television set, and circle of chairs set ready for
evenings when the sisters gather; the room called 'Hospitality'
whose most precious treasure (to be handled only with gloves)
is the 'Book of Remembrance' illuminated in searing colour and
with rhythmical inventiveness by a sister of the Community of
the Epiphany stranded in Australia during the Second World
War. We talked, too, in the infirmary, St Julian's, with its cosy
oratory and air of medical efficiency; and in the lofty Sisters'
Room at Retreat House, beneath the cubicles which were once
reformatory cells and now accommodate those who come seeking
the silence and the silence's companion, spiritual refreshment.

Some of the places have been away from Cheltenham. The
sitting-room at the Mission House near Fitzroy's high-rise estate
has an air of homely informality distinguishing it from the
formalized spaces of Cheltenham. Another place was St Anne's
Nursing Home where Sister Louisa was found early in the
morning, dressed in the old-style habit, dispensing chocolate
biscuits from her personal cache and ready to admit that she
doesn't like the new ways. Sister Ruth who lives separately from
the Community came to my house, which fortuitously happens
to be the former vicarage of St Luke's (Anglican) Church,
North Fitzroy, another setting where past and present interact.

The imprint of these places has marked our conversations,
but the visual dimension includes the appearance of individual
sisters and their body-language. In the Community's history,
gesture and movement have been ritualized to cover stance,
bearing, the placing of the hands, the carriage of the head, the
length of a step, the disposition of sisters when they walk in
groups, the timbre of the voice. The now-out-of-date Customary
regulated the demeanour of the sisters within the Community's
environs:

those dedicated to the Religious Life, being ever mindful of their
vocation, must avoid noises of all kinds, whether of voice or movement,

and be dignified in posture. They must walk quietly, without swinging the arms; the hands, when in repose, should be folded and covered by the sleeves of the habit; the legs must not be crossed when sitting.

The strictures extended to their behaviour in public: 'As far as courtesy allows, the Sisters shall refrain from talking in public conveyances and in the more crowded thoroughfares.'

The rules and embargoes, however bureaucratically prudish they now seem, provided a pattern of reference by which an ideal of behaviour could be made visible. The rigidities have been relaxed over the past fifteen years, but only gradually and unevenly. The degree to which a member of the Community methodically preserves the old rites or ostentatiously abandons them, the point at which a turn in conversation prompts a sudden lift into spontaneity, are notations which externalize the interior and the intangible. Sister Faye's hands were held under the central panel of her habit until the intensity of recounting the resolution of a problem brought them into emphatic flight. Sister Agnes Mary's shrewd eyes filled with tears when she spoke of the equality of goodness that might be found in married and celibate lives. Sister Lyn manipulated her veil as if it were a picture-hat reluctantly donned by a gamin for an unwelcome garden party. Sister Margaret Anne—whose views, social and spiritual, are to the left of most of the Community— accompanied her comments with forceful, untrammelled gestures. The sisters who form an enclosed group within the Community almost invariably reproduce the inflections of earlier times.

Beyond the code of mannerisms, the overall appearance of some sisters mirrored their personalities with an exactness that bordered on witticism. Sister Helena, who described herself adamantly as the Martha type, gave the impression that she had indeed been responsible for countless posy-makings, bed-changings and dinner-bastings. Sister Aileen, who over the years developed stratagems to enhance the physical well-being of the children in her care, beamed with a youthful indomitability of spirit. Sister Penelope, who has led street protests in Kensington and who spoke devastatingly of the atrocity of apartheid, was a spare figure exuding a bleak and purified toughness. Yet there was sometimes an ironic disparity between my expectations and the reality I encountered. Sister Clare, whose adoption of the hermit life made me expect austerity and remoteness, presided calmly and convivially over the tea-tray and showed a familiarity with world affairs that many who live in the thick of the world could not emulate.

To the uninitiated, there is an awesome fascination in talking to someone who rarely talks. Replaying the tape of my conversation with Sister Francine, the other of the two hermits who live at Cheltenham, reminded me of the civility, trust and love I have encountered at CHN. Sister Francine, who is much more remote from the world than Sister Clare, responded to my not always delicate probing with humility of spirit and willingness to explain herself and her extraordinary life. The sisters have almost invariably been honest to the extent of their capacity, and their capacity is sometimes formidable. They have described experiences of suffering with dignity and without self-pity. The inwardness that is essential to the Community's ethos leaves no one untouched; and yet the conversations have been garlanded with laughter. There has been no shortage of humour or irony glinting like quartz.

A range of responses can be detected apart from the actual words. Pauses signify difficulties in finding accurate self-expression, strong emotional reactions to the recounting of traumatic experience or when questions inadvertently touch the quick of some personal fear. Only rarely do they represent attempts to avoid an open response. Even the most seemingly straightforward sisters let fly with statements that surprise.

The tone and pitch of the voice are also indicators. The softness of many sisters' voices diminishes from gentleness to inaudibility. The more extroverted flavour their words with earthy directness, then quieten to unexpected subtlety. Some words are chosen with the care of an embroiderer selecting a colour; others run on with the heedlessness of a child jumping puddles. Emphases, omissions, repetitions are significant. Some emotions and experiences—the nascent sense of vocation, the driving immediacy of conversion-experiences, the difficult harmonies of prayer—defy satisfying articulation.

My own relationship with the Community has become complex and humanizing in ways I could not have anticipated. I have been offered an astonishing degree of confidentiality. The youngest sister at CHN, a talker whose mind flashes and darts finch-like as she tries to verbalize her intense and radical views, told me that this openness was sparked by their knowing I would not judge them. Additionally, I tend to be unconfidential about myself, which often taps the well-springs in others. As well, it seems that in the religious life there is often not as much solidarity as the outsider expects; in fact, personal stresses can be starker and more disillusioning than elsewhere. Several sisters emphasized that the most difficult thing about the Community was community living itself.

The timing of my contact with CHN was also important, though I did not plan it this way. The death of the former Superior, Faith, has produced much painful heart-searching. A feeling of guilt at having 'destroyed' her is abroad, and is partially relieved by being voiced. There is also the knowledge that, with the intention of several sisters to become enclosed, a change is imminent which may prove to be the most drastic in the Community's history so far.

Most of the clichés about the religious life are obtuse and misguided. The consensus—to which I ignorantly belonged— dismisses and demeans such ventures. I have found more normality *and* more spirituality than the conventional image allows, and an impressive self-awareness as well. In tracking down that strange sense of mission called 'vocation', I have found some background similarities and some symmetries of behaviour, but mostly I encountered a sense of mysterious life. The sisters of the Community of the Holy Name may seem to be an archaic survival, consciously set against the drift of the world, and perversely accepting crippling limitations on themselves. Yet there are other dimensions of freedom than those defined by worldly values, and these possibilities are ignored at the risk of limiting the idea of freedom itself.

In considering some issues currently causing turmoil within the Community, and the resolution of a major problem of her own, one sister said:

I think [the experimentation] needs to happen, otherwise we'll never be *free*. I think you can't love others without loving yourself. You need to understand yourself before you can do that. It takes a lot of working through... I would never have believed anyone to say that God can give you all of this freedom...again it's the Community I have to be grateful to there, because they have been flexible in themselves... Without their generosity it wouldn't have been possible for me to come to this [self-understanding].

Questioned about the Community's chances of survival, another sister saw a further dimension of freedom: 'I see it as a bigger thing than just us, because I believe that religious life has a purpose...a contribution to make over and above the individuals who make up this life, and because we're fringe-dwellers in a sense...we've got a freedom.' As people committed not only to existence but to meaning, their freedom may reach beyond that modest claim. As 'fringe-dwellers', they are able to foster authenticity, and to harry fundamentals in a way that is not possible for those in the mainstream. The exceptional can be more fully human than the commonplace. To this extent, CHN is, like the solitary life within the Church, 'a sign to the world, as well as to the Church... Those who appear marginal are in reality central. They live a form of life whose very meaning is an affirmation of unity'. The need to reconstitute and redefine themselves may even have brought new vitalities. As Alan Harrison, an urbane English specialist in the religious life, put it to the Community in 1984: 'for the first time in centuries religious *can* be *free*, free of all the clutter, free of all the junk, to be what religious life was *intended* to be right from the beginning...free to be prophetic.'

2

TO COMPEL THE OUTCAST TO COME IN

This little beginning, moreover, may grow to that which is greater than itself, and supply to the Church an organization by which the dwellers in the streets and lanes may be compelled to come when the gracious Lord has made ready the feast of His love, and waits only for the guests to come in.

Annual Report, 1888

The proposal for an inner-city refuge to be run by the Church of England was first put in March 1885 by the Bishop of Melbourne, James Moorhouse, to the clergy of the parishes of St John (Latrobe St), St Paul (Swanston St), and St Peter (Eastern Hill). The scheme was then propounded to 'a meeting of ladies' at St Paul's, where a Council was appointed to secure a site for the home and to supervise subsequent mission work. The Bishop of Melbourne presided over the Council, and responsibility for the spiritual direction of the Mission lay with the Chaplain, H. H. P. Handfield of St Peter's; all the other office-bearers and committee-members were women. The impetus for the project had parallels in England, where the established Church belatedly realized that it had become irrelevant if not repugnant to the vast riff-raff of the urban poor: 'It has long been felt that a special organization was required to meet the moral and spiritual wants of a large district in the heart of Melbourne, and this effort is made to effect it' (*Annual Report,* 1887).

After several meetings and visitations of available properties, the Council selected an establishment at the centre of

Melbourne's most destitute area, 171 Little Lonsdale St, 'a substantially built house of brick & stone, containing a shop and bakery on the ground floor, and five rooms on the upper storey'. The reality was more ramshackle than the description suggests. Nevertheless, the price of £700 was to be paid in instalments, over two years. With the bishop's approval, a deposit was made and the Council unanimously resolved to finance the matter expeditiously: 'ladies of the Council undertook to use their utmost efforts to raise the [first instalment of] money required on June 2nd'. They succeeded, and within a few weeks the tenant had vacated the premises. The secretary of the Mission Council proposed the establishment of a sub-committee 'to arrange that the whole town and suburbs of Melbourne should be divided into districts and thoroughly canvassed for subscriptions'. The first two years of the Mission's existence were to be dominated by financial considerations and the need to convince often unforthcoming members of the Anglican Church that the cause merited their support.

The Council intended that deaconesses commissioned by the bishop should 'visit in the lanes & courts, & bring the message of the Gospel to the poor and fallen, & by the force of their sisterly sympathy "compel" the outcast to "come in"'. The aim was to reach 'a class of persons who were not reached already by the ordinary parochial organizations. The rescue of fallen women was especially contemplated, and this was a class of the community that called for a special effort.'

A night-refuge or temporary shelter was to be provided, while the deaconesses, garbed in 'simple distinctive dress. . . as people set apart for spiritual duties', would urge reformation of life on the beneficiaries of the Mission's facilities. Bible classes and mothers' meetings were to be held and other missionary activities prosecuted, with the assistance of parochial organizations:

For the main work of the Mission, however, Parochial organizations are too feeble. Melbourne is the centre of business—it is also the centre of pleasure. It can hardly be that and not also be the centre of the evil which lurks behind the greatest of great cities. For the special purposes of the warfare to be waged against this evil, there is needed the devotion of a special enthusiasm, especially organized, and specially equipped.

The hierarchy felt that the Anglican Church in Australia laboured under disabilities that made home-mission work even harder than in England. A belief persisted that the colonies were places of plenty and opportunity, untainted by the inequities of the old world. Ameliorative action was therefore not needed. Further, there was an unwillingness to recognize that other branches of the Christian Church were wealthier and more vociferous. In January 1885 Bishop Moorhouse had described the situation that confronted him:

I assure you. . . that I have still in my Diocese some of the neediest places in the British colonies, and also that it is not possible for me at present to obtain for them sufficient aid in Melbourne. People at home sometimes forget that there have been no endowments here & that thus in a new country we are much poorer than the poorest Diocese in England. I have been doing everything in my power for the last eight years to stimulate my people to take up new work, & overtake arrears. . . Our home Mission fund has been increasing each year & we have raised it to £600. And yet all is absorbed & we need much more. . . I dare say you hear that Melbourne is a rich city, but you must remember that the rule of the old country no longer obtains here. Our richest men are Presbyterians. Again most of our Cornish & Welsh miners are Wesleyans. The Church of England lives here in the fierce light & constant strain of keen competition.

Moorhouse's wan assessment was confirmed by the slow pace of developments within the Mission. While the ladies of the parishes, especially the wealthy congregations south of the Yarra, busied themselves with sales, theatrical entertainments and other fund-raising schemes, tenders for alterations to the Little Lonsdale St building all exceeded the architect's projections, and the Council decided that work should be postponed until further money was available. There was another setback in the middle of 1886, 'when the larrikins broke in to the premises & made havoc' in a frolic costing nearly £6.

Progress was also impeded by the failure of self-denying women to proffer themselves to staff the Mission House, although

Moorhouse who had returned to England wrote describing a visit to the Deaconesses' Home at Rochdale 'where there is a lady who would be willing to come out & work in Australia'. His candidate failed to materialize, and the Council contracted a tenant more in tune with their aspirations in Mrs Davies, a 'Bible woman in St Paul's parish' who soon became 'indefatigable in her labours among the people'. Several members of the Council undertook the depressing task of visiting in the lanes until full-time angels of mercy took their place. However, the native-born showed a marked reluctance to commit themselves to the selfless life, a resistance which provoked the taut question, 'are there no Australian daughters who are willing to give up the world, and answer the Master's call "Follow me"?'

Still, there had been a highly profitable concert under vice-regal patronage, while clergy, previously lethargic in appeals to their flocks, promised to be more energetic. The architect had also agreed to work without payment on alterations to the Little Lonsdale St house, converting the ground floor into one room and whittling the first floor into four apartments. Ownership of the building, newly roofed, painted and papered, was to be invested in the official trustees of the diocese, Messrs Alf Woolley and Henry Henty, together with the Bishop of Melbourne. But while it was possible to raise capital funds, attracting money to keep such an enterprise afloat required a shrewder psychology and a well-developed gift for hectoring. Yet contractual work on the building proceeded rapidly, and in April 1887 the Council was able to met for the first time in the deaconesses' home. Three months later the Mission House was free of debt and ready for use.

Within a year, activities there centred around mothers' meetings, with an associated fortnightly clothing-club, and a weekly Girls' Excelsior Class 'for the benefit of young girls exposed to evil influences, especially when loitering in the streets of an evening'. Girls over sixteen were instructed in needlework and singing, but much time was spent on 'amusements'. 'Tidy habits and good behaviour' were encouraged. The speedy establishment of religious services was intended. These were small beginnings, but they served a handful of mothers, some of whom were depressingly irregular in attendance, and about twenty girls.

Staffing continued to be a problem. In April 1888, a Miss Mitchell applied to be admitted as a probationer deaconess, an offer accepted for six months with the proviso that the Mission would not be responsible for her obviously delicate health. At last, in July of that year, a more positive portent came through 'A letter from Miss Silcock a lady who was expected to arrive in Melbourne in July and was anxious to be employed in deaconesses work'. This unsolicited approach was to be the turning-point in the Mission's fortunes, and to have unforeseen results for the religious life in Australia.

A meeting with Miss Silcock was effected, and Canon Handfield announced that he was satisfied with her qualifications. With the bishop's consent, she was appointed a probationer for six months on an annual stipened of £60, her salary being raised from subscriptions in the surrounding parishes. Employment of a third worker depended on further generosity in the parishes. Meanwhile, other applicants were rejected because, although qualified as communicants, the women were disqualified by lack of 'means'. Like so many nineteenth century charities, the Mission in its early years was characterized by this phenomenon of middle-class women ministering to their distinctly lower-class sisters.

The indifference of the bulk of congregations was supplemented by criticism of the Mission's methods. Agitation for a chapel at Mission House provoked the suggestion, tinged with self-righteousness, that the poor should go to the existing churches. The reply was unequivocal: experience in London's East End, a community similar to that which clustered around Little Lonsdale St, showed that the Church had to reach people who were unattracted by or hostile to opulent buildings operated seemingly for the spiritual massage and personal reassurance of the more fortunate classes.

Within months, the fragile stability of the Mission workforce was disrupted by news that Miss Mitchell's health would not allow her to continue, and that Miss Silcock, who had repaired to Australia in the first place to recuperate from a severe illness, required several months' leave of absence. However, another probationer had been appointed, and one more was available when the Council could afford to vote her salary.

Soon after her return from leave, Emma Silcock first appears in
Mission documents as Sister Esther, a form of address that
reflected her background as a novice in the Anglican sisterhood
of the Community of St Mary the Virgin at Wantage, England,
and her determination to proceed from the parenthetical status
of deaconess to full religious vows.

The nomenclature was soon customary for the full-time workers
at the Mission.

From its beginnings, the Community was subjected to criticism
on theological grounds. The annual report of 1888 felt constrained to explain the apparent departure from Anglican practice
in Australia that was represented by the appointment of deaconesses, drawing attention to the existence in the primitive
church of 'women devoted by the Bishop to serve the Church
by ministering chiefly to their own sex', and the revival of this
principle by the establishment of the London Diocesan Deaconess Institution. References were made to the deaconess Phoebe,
praised by St Paul as 'the succourer of many'. Although the
three sisters who resided at Little Lonsdale St had not taken
'special vows', the chaplain of the Mission referred to them as
'the beginning of a religious community'. 'It seems that something
more than the ordinary parochial machinery is needed to make
the Church properly aggressive. The organised ministry of religious women will perhaps supply the force that is needed.'

Despite its internal problems, the Council was gaining confidence in the work it had set on foot. By its second annual
meeting, its members felt provoked into challenging the
Darwinian social philosophy of a contributor to Melbourne's
forceful *Argus* newspaper, and their reply was resounding:
'Christianity meant redemption—not the survival of the
fittest—but the expenditure of care and cost, that the lost
might be recovered, & those whom the struggle doomed to
extinction might be redeemed to a better hope'. A year later in
pursuit of this ideal the Mission was considering its first expansion
outside the inner-city area, aware how hard it was to find
'suitable places for the reception of women rescued from an
immoral life', and the advisability of establishing a home in the
country for 'such cases'.

The country home might be unattainable at present, but

the Mission could point to the reservoir of female power which enabled its work to go forward. As reported by the press at the annual meeting, the new Bishop of Melbourne (Rt Rvnd Field Flowers Goe) had strong words to say:

Many persons thought it was desirable that women should be entrusted with political power, & that they should have the privilege of voting for members of Parliament & even of sitting in Parliament. He had not much sympathy with ideas of that kind & believed that men & women should always work on parallel lines, the great virtue of parallel lines being that they never crossed one another. Nothing could elevate a woman more than to engage in work such as the deaconesses were occupied with.

The urgency of their task was hammered home in a press statement that drew outraged attention to an entire street near St Paul's 'where every house was an evil house' and 'showed the need of special endeavours being made by the church to grapple with the evil'.

Although Anglicans as a whole seemed sluggish in response to the Mission's pleas, individual donors were generous in backing particular projects. One person had already given £200 towards the longed-for home in the country. Providing accommodation for the nameless women who were often denied places in the city's over-burdened facilities was indeed a pressing need—especially when the moral climate hardly allowed distinctions between destitution and criminality to be clearly seen:

So full were the Homes of Melbourne in the early part of the year that three women had to be taken to Geelong, and were kindly received into the Refuge there. Sad it is to say that several had to be turned away, as there was no Home for them to go to—every place was full; and two poor women had to be taken to the Gaol Hospital to die. It will thus be seen how much we need our Home at Cheltenham.

In early 1889, Sister Esther reported on a visit to the Female Refuge at Geelong, made at the request of Canon Chalmers who had suggested that the sisters might become involved in work there. She advised that 'The institution was considered unsuitable under present management for the Church to authorize its being taken over, though possibly it might be able to do so at some future time, if the Geelong Committee were willing to hand over the building.'

That connection, however, lapsed; and the chance to establish a female refuge came closer home when in October 1889 the Mission Council approved purchase of 'a piece of land in some convenient suburban place...for a Country Home in which women may be received in order to remove them from a[n] immoral life'. Added to the bequest already made for the purpose, gifts from anonymous donors raised the amount available to £350, and promises of a further £450 had been made. For a total purchase price of £500 the Council bought land in Cheltenham: 'eight acres...partly stocked with fruit trees, having a good paddock, and space for building', and set about planning a 'Country Home for Fallen and Friendless Women'. The architects were to be Hyndman and Bates, and accommodation was planned for two deaconesses and twelve women. The estimated cost of the building was £2000, of which only £126 was in hand. A committee of gentlemen was to be formed to raise money for the project, 'leaving to the Ladies of the Council the more arduous task of collecting subscriptions to carry on the support of the Home'.

The Mission had moved to expand its activities at a time that was socially appropriate, but financially unpropitious, for the fabled boom of the 1880s which had transformed Melbourne into a wedding-cake of pilastered façades, crenellated roofscapes and lofty porticos, had proved to be a phantom party. Due, largely, to the unscrupulous manipulations of the powerful and predatory, the boom had burst with the collapse of the financial market in the early 1890s, and a severe economic depression set in. While some of the more desperate disposed of themselves by suiciding in the opulent privacy of mahogany-lined rooms, the main burden fell on the poor, who sank from subsistence to despair. Charitable institutions struggling to answer their proliferating needs found themselves unequal to the task.

What was this 'Marvellous Melbourne' the *Herald* scornfully asked in December 1888:

We will see how far we can carry our pride and conceit through the back lanes and alleys...that world within a world; a world on the other side of the walls of our magnificent streets, and yet so separated, so apart that going among the dwellers is like making acquaintance with another people.

The city's population had doubled between 1880 and 1890. Packed tenements, sweat factories and hovels lowered over mean traffic ways made almost impassable by the swill of garbage and sewage, while the human refuse that inhabited these places was pictured with even more gusto. The young men were deplored for their insolent attitudes and jaunty demeanour. They were 'idlers', if not worse, and the sodden unkempt derelicts got even shorter shrift. The sympathy, tinged with fascination, was all for the women and children—women with pinched or bloated faces, victims of drink, opium and profligacy; the young prostitutes, and the girls who cried with excusable blasphemy 'I do not believe in any Hell beyond this life, my own life is such a Hell upon earth'. Most wretched were the children, consumptive youngsters, waifs whose painful neatness testified to a mother's desperate attempt at decency, ragamuffins who were barefoot, half-naked and dirty. Conditions, it was claimed, were even worse than those of English cities, and charity not nearly as well organized.

Having described these horrors with some relish, the *Herald* article went on to praise the early efforts of the Mission—materially limited its work in the streets and lanes might be, but it was strenous in devotion:

Among the latest efforts are those of two ladies, who, in order to reach the dwellers of the slums, have become residents in their midst. They have taken up their abode in the Church Mission Hall...and from thence cary on these operations. Morning, noon and night, they work among the denizens of the surrounding purlieus, extending their labours to factory and hospital visiting. All their energies and thoughts are devoted to the welfare of their neighbours.

During the hours of the day they visit from house to house, they bind up the wounds of inmates literally, not figuratively, for their rule is to tend the body as carefully as the soul.

Sister Esther and Sister Ellen (the former Miss Okins) had joined a regrettably select band of those who worked in the slums, rather than dispensing charity from the cushioned enclosures of the suburbs.

As bearer of values and vulnerable figurehead in her father's house, the nineteenth-century woman was precariously placed to venture outside, except under the canopy of marriage. Before and behind her, family relationships were tensely codified, channelling sexual energies into the work of an empire that marched outwards under a prolific but puritanical queen. Once elevated to moral guardianship of the home, and crowned with her own purity, the young woman who lapsed had nowhere to go but down. She became 'fallen', a perpetual reminder of the heights she should have occupied, and an excuse for prurient interest in her lost maidenhood and the shameless male responsible for filching it. The social system found it convenient to lump together those who infringed the law, and those runaway daughters and abandoned wives, mistresses, derelicts, who had no secure legal standing. These all came under the control of the law, so that the female 'refuge' became a reformatory.

By mid-1890 there was still little progress towards the building of the 'Country Home'. Money came in slowly; the government was reluctant, and Church members were sadly lukewarm. The social welfare system was a ramshackle vehicle kept going by movements in different directions. While significant contributions towards capital costs were usually made by the government, many institutions such as hospitals, refuges and children's homes were substantially dependent for maintenance on annual donations from subscribers whose contribution could give them considerable power in management. Government finances oscillated according to political circumstances, the power of particular individuals, and the appeal of specific causes, so that private operators were consigned to an unpredictable mixture of dependence and independence. The Mission sent letters to the *Argus* and *Daily Telegraph*, and a circular was to be distributed to all clergy for presentation to their congregations, with the ominous follow-up that 'a Lady of the Council' would 'call on each clergyman to receive their answer'.

Activities at the Little Lonsdale St house had in the meantime expanded. Clergy from St Paul's now conducted weekly prayer-meetings, and a lending-library of 150 books had been accumulated. Places had been found in refuges and asylums for the homeless. Children had been baptised on Mission premises. Visiting the sick was assisted by the honorary services of three doctors, hospital places had been secured for poor women in cases where the sisters could nurse them no longer, and a medicine cupboard had been stocked with 'necessaries for the sick' from the proceeds of old clothes sales (at which token amounts were charged, on the principle that more value attached to a purchase than a handout, no matter how modest the charge).

Lunch-time visiting of factories near the Mission had burgeoned into the creation of a Busy Bee club for 'factory & servant girls', which provided lectures, readings from Shakespeare, music, recitations, cooking lessons, and an evening meal for threepence. Sunday evening services had been instituted. A children's choir had been formed and was training for the ceremonies at Christmas and Easter. A savings-bank scheme was inaugurated. The Excelsior Girls' Class begun by Miss Woolley in 1887 had expanded with further volunteer help into a kindergarten group and a class for small boys—at which one sister taught free-hand drawing, and the atmosphere of instruction was sometimes leavened by hearty bursts of singing. The serious, proselytizing nature of the Mission enterprise was offset by occasional treats, magic-lantern shows, the performance of uplifting cantatas, a trip to Mordialloc for the sewing class, a visit to the zoo by furniture-van for the boys.

A more harrowing need was reflected in the bishop's suggestion in July 1890 that a soup-kitchen should be set up at Mission House 'as there seemed much distress in Melbourne'. He offered £10 to start the project, and further funds came through an appeal to the *Argus*. 'A Lady who wished to be anonymous' was responsible for the viability of the scheme which planned to operate only during July and August 1891, but was reopened in the winter of 1892 'on account of the great amount of poverty prevailing'.

The sight of rough men crushing through the doors, and willing to be so crushed, in order to obtain a basin of soup, convinced those who witnessed it of the need which was supplied... Women and children fetched away soup in cans and jugs; only a few strong-minded of the weaker sex preferring to eat with the men.

In one ten-week period a huge dispensation of 830 gallons was recorded. In 1893 the soup-kitchen was not open for meals; instead soup was distributed twice weekly 'to families in distress'. The next year, the trough of the depression, the service was 'confined to sending out portions to be carried home, as it was found the plan of allowing meals to be taken at the Hall was not desirable'.

During the depression normal Mission activities continued as far as possible, but the emotional pressure intensified. 'Appeals for aid have been very distressing.' In the face of overwhelming need, the sisters sent a letter to Council in October 1893, asking 'that during the present depression they should only receive £30 instead of £40'. Council at first refused to make a formal reduction, stipulating that any return of salary should be 'received as a free gift from the Sisters'; but they later reversed their decision because, apart from 'the low state of funds. . . two applicants who wished to be admitted as probationers' had to be provided for.

The Mission's finances did indeed decline as the depression grew worse. Already, at a special meeting in November 1890 the secretary had drawn attention to a shortfall of £29, stating bluntly:

Some few of our Council, one especially, have toiled with unremitting diligence to collect money, but these few have only been feebly supported by the Council in general. It is now five years and a half since we commenced the great work we have in hand. We have since weathered many difficulties and seen the Mission fairly started. Shall we now allow it to fall off for lack of funds?. . . I have no fears for the future of the Mission, except for the lukewarmness of the Council.

This stern message apparently failed to strike home. In August 1891 the secretary was forced to advance money for stipends and wages, until the deficiency in funds was remedied. Many annual subscriptions failed to materialize, and Sister Esther presented a report to Council pointing out that it was unrealistic to rely on donations, and outlining some of the difficulties of maintaining the Mission. The harmony of the Council could not have been helped by hearing again that some members were languid in their 'sense of responsibility as to the raising of funds for the maintenance of the Mission'. A rash of resignations at this time may have been the result of such members feeling themselves caught between reproach and incapacity to turn the financial tide. The strain affected the treasurer particularly, who 'felt her position a very trying one', and who advised deflecting some of the burden by getting the government to increase the maintenance grant. She was soon forced to repeat her frazzled urgings to Council, as subscriptions continued to dwindle alarmingly, while expenditure soared to £66 per month.

From the beginning, the Cheltenham project was a drain on the Mission's almost dried-up finances. Expenses for the six months to February 1891 were nearly £62, while income from grazing and the sale of produce amounted to little more than half that amount. Another practical problem was lack of water. Raising money with one hand while draining the land and investigating wells with the other, the Council somehow managed to get its building programme under way. The architect had revised his plans, and the lowest tender of £1350 had been accepted for the work. By the end of February 1892 the building, amazingly, was finished and approved, though there was some anxiety about dormitory windows which looked too 'prison like'. Furnishing was left to the deaconesses, who enlisted the generosity of the public. The question of a water-supply still had not been resolved, but a dispute about the name of the home was settled by adopting the cumbersome title 'The House of Mercy in Connection with the Melbourne Diocesan Deaconess' Home and Mission to the Streets and Lanes'.

It was opened in June 1892 by the vice-regal Countess of Hopetoun before an audience including many of the subscribers to the Mission. By October, eight girls were living at Cheltenham, occupied in washing and gardening, and clothed through donations of leftovers, a swag of old shoes, or yarn and muslin for aprons. Canon Handfield reported on a visit of inspection:

Sister Christina seemed to have good control over the inmates who were happy and docile. At first they had resented the strict rules as to cleanliness & tidiness, but there was a marked improvement in this respect & the whole routine appeared to combine firmness & kindness in a way that could hardly fail to win them to better ways.

Although, thanks to the efforts of its supporters, the House of Mercy was free of debt, the Council's financial problems continued. By March 1893 there was a substantial shortfall in quarterly receipts, partly mitigated by a profit of £17 from the laundry at Cheltenham, and a sale of produce that netted £12. Council members were urged to 'try to obtain home orders for washing', and receipts from the labours of the laundry-workers climbed.

While the Council was trying desperately to stabilize its finances, a disagreement arose as to the parochial position of the House of Mercy. At first, it had been intended that the refuge should enjoy the same extra-parochial status as the Mission House, whose management and internal organization—like those of Trinity College and the Anglican hospitals—were under the care of a warden appointed by the bishop. But parishioners of Cheltenham, Mentone and Dingley had petitioned against this arrangement. Believing that a divided responsibility for the affairs of the house would make his position untenable, the warden threatened to resign 'as no man could honestly carry out the rules as they stand at present if he had to ask permission of the clergyman of the parish to enter the Home where he was supposed to rule'. At a special meeting in October 1893, the Council strongly recommended that the House of Mercy should be extra-parochial, and the employee at Cheltenham would take his instructions from Sister Esther direct. This apparently trivial matter represented a dispute on authority which had been anticipated years before in England where Dr Pusey insisted that Anglican sisterhoods should be centralized to minimize interference from parochial clergy. Melbourne resolved in favour of a similar arrangement.

The authorities were immediately impressed by the House of Mercy: 'in many respects...a decided advance upon those Refuges and Rescue Homes already in operation'. Certainly, the house's disciplined certitude was a contrast to the shambolic misery that pervaded the Melbourne Benevolent Asylum, and its inmates were treated not as exemplars of original sin, but rather as victims of circumstance:

It is in leisure hours, and in search of amusement and recreation—perhaps as a refuge from unhappy homes—that opportunities and temptations to evils occur, and girls may be saved from crime and misery by a kindly helping hand held out to them.

A year after the first occupants moved in, another need was voiced. To attempt more than was being done in the House of Mercy seemed quite unrealistic, 'yet we find it necessary again to contemplate enlarging our borders...[to form] a Temporary Home for Children, Waifs, & Strays—in connection with this Mission. Sad cases of neglected children are frequently met with by the Sisters.' Esther was empowered under the Neglected Children's Act 'to take charge of and apprehend children, to be dealt with according to the aforesaid Act', but there were no facilities to house the children. The spectre of Anglican apathy was again raised, and the Inspector of Charitable Institutions himself predicted curtly that 'the Church of England would soon cease to have any members among the poorer classes if it allowed the neglected children to pass out of its hands'. Other denominations, it was pointed out, provided for needy youngsters of the Anglican persuasion as well as their own.

By March 1894, the worst year of the depression, with subscriptions continuing to decline (by £89 over a two-year period), the Council decided to ignore the ogre of debt and to proceed. Individual Council members were urged to undertake a little lone-hand fund-raising, and the annual cost of running 'a small house' for children was estimated to be £200. When a donation of that amount was made by a single patron, the Mission Council took the providential cue and rented a house in Wilson St, Brighton. Appeals for additional funds were made through the press, and circulars were sent to clergy and bodies affiliated with the Church.

When the Bishop of Melbourne opened the 'Church of England Home for Neglected Children' in its temporary premises in June, one deaconess (Sister Ellen) and eleven children were in residence. The first child to enter the house was described by the *Church of England Messenger* as 'a waif and stray, having no name, and no excuse for his existence'. Sunday schools and the Girls' Friendly Society rallied to provide cots for the children. Despite the fact that the year was one of 'great depression and anxiety', Council's annual report concluded 'the Home has been opened under bright auspices'. A year later, twenty-six children of all denominations were in residence. The annual report for that year gave harrowing profiles of some of those who had been taken in:

(I) Waif and Stray. Parents not known, had been left with a strange woman who would not keep child any longer.
(L) When admitted was half starved, been sleeping in gardens.
(L) Parents bad & drunken, child turned out of doors, slept out, taken from parents for child's protection.
(A) When admitted was unmanageable by parents, developing into worst forms of larrikinism, frequenter of Chinese quarters.
(N) Mother lunatic, father deserted.
(V) Father deserted, when admitted was reported as totally incorrigible.

The cost of this reclamation work was high. To maintain the home, a formidable £400 would probably be needed each year, and the Mission was characteristically overcommitted already. 'Five Special Ways of Helping the Home' were urged on supporters: prayer, assistance in forming an endowment fund, commitment as an annual subscriber, exerting an influence on potential subscribers, and the making of children's clothes. 'May we not commend to their notice some words of the Great Head of the Church who once said:—"Inasmuch as ye have done it unto one of the least of these my brethren, ye have done it unto Me".'

Pinning down the facts of Mission finances would take a skilled unraveller. Accounts fluctuate, emphasizing frugal management at one time (four shillings a week per child), and outstanding neediness at another. It is often hard to remember just how few workers were involved. Apart from a cluster of (dedicated) day-to-day helpers, in 1894 the deaconesses attached to the Mission numbered five, and the Children's Home was only one of their responsibilities. The general education of the children was divided between the sisters and the local state school, while religious instruction was undertaken by the sisters and St Andrew's Church, Brighton. A Ladies Working Party had provided clothes for thirty youngsters; two doctors agreed to donate their services; Sunday schools, private schools, Ministering Children's Leagues, all lent a hand.

In its first two years, the home accommodated forty-five children, of whom all but eleven were girls, and the majority 'Fatherless or Motherless'. Some were found foster-parents or adopted, others went to 'situations'—a euphemism that usually meant domestic service. The dry statistics of Council minutes and Mission annual reports are given individual reality by the monthly newsletter that began in August 1895 as *Mission Notes* and a year later was renamed *In Our Midst*. Sentimental though the magazine often is, it does show the social philosophy and the religious attitudes behind these purposeful beginnings of the Mission's work. The social critique was muted and reformist, the theology positive and simplistic. Contributors aimed to rouse conscience through a style which mixed the picturesque and the romantic with the sordid and the practical, and seldom forgot the need to get something *done*.

The children at Brighton were a stirring focus for rousing the generosity of the faithful. They appear in January 1897 as 'eager bright little faces, many of whom had never before had a Christmas worth mentioning'; and on other occasions as giving entertainments to raise money for the Boot and Stocking Fund (November 1897), or embodying true loyalty at Queen Victoria's Jubilee:

each child on stage was decorated with flags, in which, it is needless to say, that the meteor flag of the British Empire was predominant, and the National Anthem was sung with a heartiness that we trust may be typical of the spirit of the rising generation throughout these colonies. (October 1897)

So the campaign went on, to loosen the purse-strings as well as pluck the heart-strings, and frustration only stimulated more strenuously sentimental anecdotes. The departure for adoption of Jessie, 'a chubby curly-headed child of five, with splendid health, and plenty of smartness, and a pretty way of speaking', was opportunity for another sermon:

we would fain keep all in this safe shelter of the Church's Home, but that cannot be while beds are lacking and funds are low; therefore we can but do our best, and send them forth as well equipped for the battle of life as may be. If our friends will help us in this direction, perhaps we may find room for new claims, for verily the cry of the children is ceaseless. (October 1900)

The sisters were cheerfully unabashed in their mendicancy: 'we are always in the same state as Oliver Twist—insatiable—and now Sister Ellen wants some Turkey twill' (April 1897). The approach of Christmas brought extra garnishings of exhortation:

we beg to remind our readers that we have thirty children at Brighton, and thirteen girls at Cheltenham, who are expecting to have a good time. Whether they do or not will depend greatly on what is sent us for this festival. (December 1896)

The sponsors' generosity might flag at times, but work with children was universally appealing as an idea. Labour among 'fallen women' provoked more complicated reactions.

Not surprisingly, the metaphor of cleanliness ran through early reports on the House of Mercy. For a visitor in 1896, the gleaming bees-waxed hall, the iron-partitioned cubicles ('safe in case of fire'), the calming atmosphere of the chapel, all spoke virtue. The orderliness of the house was matched by the appearance and demeanour of the inmates, neatly done out in a uniform of 'blue and white galatea, cap and apron', busily washing, mending, embroidering and ironing. Other visitors stressed the naturalness, order and submission that prevailed. Signs that the place was a reformatory were barely evident; instead an atmosphere of culture and religion was assisted by the rural aspect of the site, with its view of hilly profiles and serried market gardens. Cavanagh St in Cheltenham was 'one of those red-ochre roads, bordered with the greenest of grass...golden gorse and briar roses', while the reception room was 'ablaze with flowers'. The sister in charge, 'a born home maker', took the place of the mother in the ordinary domestic sphere, and the fresh faces of the girls proved how truly changed they were from the painted harridans of court appearances. Attention again focussed on the laundry, the physical and moral centre of the reformatory programme: the 'wet' laundry with its huge coppers and troughlined walls, the 'dry' laundry with long ironing tables and 'bright coke heaters' for the irons.

Behind this pleasing interpretation of the scene, the architects had been given the necessary directions for the revamped dormitory block:

Partitions of cubicles and cupboards & Housemaid's Cupbd & c to be covered with 24 gauge corrugated iron on both sides all well screwed down with lead washers and with a 3" lap to iron. Cubicle & other similar doors (as specified) to be covered both sides with 24 gauge flat galvanized iron.

The daily routine, sometimes described as a 'regime', was divided between work, meals, prayer and relaxation, allowing little variation except for extra prayer sessions during Lent, or some planning of Christmas festivities. Supervised by the sisters, inmates were responsible for all work in the house and kitchen, and the laundry and ironing rooms remained the major source of income for the house. Elementary teaching and religious instruction went on; books were read at meal times, usually of an instructive bent, though occasional entertainments like *Pickwick Papers* were allowed. Individual activities were confined to the short time after tea, when the girls gardened, or operated the irrigation pump, or selected 'their own needlework' for sessions in the dining room at night.

The major ceremonies of the Christian year were felt to have special significance for 'those upon whose outward form sin has in many cases set its mark'. Emphasis was placed on visual teaching for 'hearts so dark, intellects so untrained'—a combination that gave the magic-lantern a special place in the educational programme. Caught between the iron laws of heredity and the inescapable coils of environment, the girls might seem theoretically beyond recovery; yet belief in the innate goodness of humanity was set against a manichean acceptance of social fate, and it was noted how often these poor girls preferred 'heavenly or specially spiritual poetry' in their choice of music. Determinism was not permitted to have the final say.

Those who realize what a dreadful history of evil each girl who comes here brings with her, and who know what constant and unremitting work and prayer is necessary, before the bad part is rooted out, and the hearts opened to the light of heaven, may well be thankful and take courage, as they look over the list of former 'Mercy girls'. (August 1898)

Sometimes the transformation was near-miraculous. Take the apparently irreparable case of Sophia, the child of a heathen father and a mother who was 'a mere cork on the waves of circumstance'. Companion of loose talkers and thieves, Sophia once immured in the House of Mercy became a thorn in its side. With some relish, *In Our Midst* describes the process of regeneration in a morality tale called 'Working Out the Beast'. Sophia was tamed in the end, received as a Christian, launched into the world 'with excellent qualities for a servant, cleanly, industrious, intelligent'. She became so rigorous in her faith that she left her first situation when her employer forbade her to go to early morning communion. Marriage and the baptism of her first child at the Mission Hall completed her rehabilitation.

Even the failures could be put to good pedagogical use. Such was Annie, a rejected adopted child whose resistance to good influences was aggravated by her having acquired 'all the faults and trickeries of the typical boarding school'. Her condition occasioned a homily to parents who might think to rely on expensive education, rather than proper instruction in the home, a chore that fell naturally to the mother (April 1901). In fact, *In Our Midst* never quite achieved its independence from prevailing social attitudes, and so could see the female as the repository of an innate goodness—and then castigate her for falling to the level of her male companions. Altogether, it was in a quandary over the relative powers of original sin and social conditioning. There was also an unacknowledged difficulty in assessing the genuine effectiveness of the Mission's work—whether the apparent improvement in many of the sisters' charges represented a lasting transformation, or simply a temporary gloss.

It was honest enough, however to report the more awkward facts. Some offenders were so hardened that they preferred gaol to institutions like the House of Mercy, while to the sisters' dismay others were returned to the dubious care of unpromising mothers. Like the rest of society, the Community was involved in both bolstering the family and consenting to its dismember-ment when things went wrong. Again, the picture of demure acceptance and hard-won containment at the House of Mercy lay uneasily beside recognition of persistent rebelliousness in many of the girls. Particularly intractable cases were felt to require two years of the regimen before regeneration could be accomplished, and the sometimes fruitless nature of the work produced a defence against those who counselled work towards more hopeful ends:

Some people discredit...the work we undertake at the House of Mercy, saying it is hopeless to attempt to reform such characters as have been warped and drawn out of their right way. But the Sisters did not think their work was thrown away when fourteen of the 'old girls', all doing well, and two already married, came down during the Christmas week to see them and their old home.

Marriage was the apotheosis, although some blighted matrimonial outcomes (generally the fault of the men again) showed what a lottery that condition could be.

Despite the often dispiriting nature of the work, hope was the keynote. The whole person was the target. The house was seen to be organized around recognition of 'a threefold organism of body, spirit, and mind', with concerned attention to each. 'Nothing dirty, nothing ugly' was to be allowed; if possible, contact with the good and the beautiful should be constant. Commonsense, avoidance of sentimentality, patience, and silence, combined to make the right approach, and constant ac-tivity closed the doors of temptation, for 'The best way to exor-cise the Evil One is surely to give him no room to lodge in'.

Although the initial stated purpose of the house was to succour 'fallen women', the age of inmates was tenderer than the label suggested. By 1898 seventy-two women had been accommodated, fifty-two of whom were under the age of twenty,

the remainder under thirty. Of these, twenty-one had returned
to their families or had been placed 'in respectable situations';
ten former House of Mercy girls had married, four had died,
twelve had lapsed 'back into drink or evil courses' and nine had
disappeared without trace. The ratio of reclaimed souls was not
all that encouraging. Their mentors, however, never gave way
to the hopelessness experience might warrant, and continued to
act in the belief that 'With religious training, habits of obedience,
truthfulness and self-restraint are instilled'. As well, positive
emotions of a less penitential kind were encouraged. Strenuous
efforts were made to stimulate the spirit of fun in the House of
Mercy, and they were often inventive. Queen Victoria's Jubilee
occasioned a series of tableaux in the dining room, festooned
for the event in ivy, lights and flags. The presentations ranged
from 'Fatima and Bluebeard's seven wives with their flour-
whitened faces suspended from the roof by means of white
cords', to 'Rule Britannia', in which the indomitable lady 'arrayed
in robes of steely whiteness, stood on a car composed of a chair
and the opossum rug, bearing a toasting-fork for trident and a
dish-cover for shield' (August 1897).

Jollity also pervaded activities at the Mission House, but a
serious purpose often underlay the apparently random gathering
of amusing anecdotes. In 1898 when 171 Little Lonsdale St had
sunk into dilapidation, with 'cracked walls, unsound foundations
and leaking roof', and plans for a £616 rebuilding programme
had been prepared, *In Our Midst* ran a series of items only the
hard-hearted could ignore. 'Wanted: A New Mission House',
was the title of the October editorial. Another contributor
underlined the message with an appalled description of 'Where
Our Deaconesses Live':

Ever since I have pondered over the scene, and wondered if we could
not make a united effort towards the rebuilding of the Mission House,
and do something to protect the health of our missionaries... Summer
is almost here, and one dreads to think of the consequences for those
brave women who are compelled to live there.

Mission House cats contributed their autobiographical accounts
to portray how rushed and varied a day in the life of a Mission

House inmate might be. The combination of cajolery and homily was successful, and in 1899 the new Mission House was opened, and clear of debt by the following year.

The ethos of the Mission's work speaks loudly through *In Our Midst*. One reads of the rescue of yet another young woman who had fallen into evil clutches, or 'one more "mitherless bairn" that nobody wants; another victim to the cruel selfishness of man, and a social system which cries aloud daily for reform' (October 1896). Right attitudes were encouraged through such occasions as old clothes sales, where the buyers 'do not lose their self-respect, are able to choose garments of the required size for Tommy and Kitty, and all of the time...have the warm, philanthropic sentiment in their minds of doing a good action and helping others'.

Along with the inculcation of appropriate moral feelings went a call for proper political loyalties, including affectionate pride in 'our country with few records of the past, but surely with unlimited possibilities for a glorious future'. This combined with a fiercely uncritical empire spirit. When Queen Victoria died early in 1901, the orgy of public mourning reached the Mission Hall itself, plunging it into funereal black leavened only by the inspiriting colours of the British flag—though the sisters found themselves needing to dampen Boer War enthusiasm in parents who were inspired to afflict their children with names such as May Florence Mafeking.

As well as constantly striving to raise funds, the magazine campaigned for the religious life in Australia and the work of women in the Church. Anglican sisterhoods were still regarded darkly, and the sisters themselves were felt to be in a condition of dangerous flirtation with Rome. In February 1897, there was instituted a series on 'Remarkable Women', designed to show how nineteenth-century deaconesses stood in a line reaching back through the ages of the Church. It began with a rousing profile of St Hilda, Abbess of Whitby, 'the highest of a band of women—numerous enough in early times, one of the many "weak things of the world", chosen to "put to shame the strong"'. The catalogue of weak but unbreakable vessels included 'St Rhadegund Queen and Deaconess', a French abbess of the sixth century, 'the Sister Augustine', an early nineteenth-century German stalwart whose sufferings and achievements

spread over two instalments, and various other inspirers. Closer
to home were Harriet Starr Cannon, an American pioneer of
the religious life, and Harriet Monsell, Superior of the Community of St John the Baptist, Clewer, who was presented as
one of those 'strong and vigorous' personalities who accompany
'all movements which have brought about changes of importance
in the world's history'. Then a two-page editorial on Miss
Honnor Morten appeared in March 1898. 'What a lesson for us
in Australia—in Melbourne': Miss Morten, who had just been
elected to the School Board of London, was a noted feminist
figure. The overall message was unmistakable: exceptional
women had the power to overcome trials and obstacles, and to
create new structures of practical and spiritual force:

it is not of [domestic] work we would write—but of the progress of
women in various spheres of labour outside the domestic area...
Women are now taking their rightful place in the work of the world
again, and an increasing number among us feel that the possession of
the franchise is but the complement of the duty which women owe to
their parish, their country and the State. (June 1897)

The area of women's work that seemed most significant was
the astonishing proliferation of the steely flowers of Anglican
sisterhoods in England. It was probably Sister Esther, a product
of that movement, who penned the drum-roll of editorial comments on the Lambeth Conference which boomed from *In Our
Midst* in November 1897. The failure of assembled churchmen
to refer to deaconesses, sisterhoods and other religious communities was deplored, and compensatory tribute was paid:

Those of us who can remember the early days of the movement, and
who have seen the immense deal of work done by Sisters, can only
give thanks to Almighty God and take courage. Fifty years ago a few
women were struggling on to obtain recognition of the Religious Life.
To-day, there are more than 3000 Sisters in England belonging to our
Church.

Unfortunately, it mostly *was* in England that candidates for the
life of self-sacrifice were forthcoming. Over the next few years,

the plea for more probationers was renewed so constantly in the columns of *In Our Midst* that it became a somewhat hectoring refrain. Sometimes, the deficiency was felt to lie in inadequate publicity: the Mission 'only needs to be better known to rouse the interest of those who wish to reach the "lapsed and perishing classes"'; at other times, it seemed that Australian women themselves must lack the needed zeal:

We are asked sometimes why we have not more Sisters to help us in working for the Church. We wonder why it is, and sadly are forced to the conclusion that it is because of the want of self-denial and the love of one's own way. (June 1897)

Someone has suggested sandwich-boards with Sisters inside, to perambulate Collins Street during the fashionable hours, and the more important suburbs occasionally. (February 1899)

Nevertheless, though numbers grew slowly, the work went forward, and the Church was proudly identified as standing in the vanguard of the liberation of women—within certain carefully controlled bounds.

The last half-century has been one of enormous progress in civilisation and science. One of its chief features...has been the opening of almost all the professions to women, though nowhere has woman so truly found her sphere for work as in work for the Church... In England, at the present day, there are more Sisters in the Church than before the Reformation. (November 1900)

In 1890, in a ceremony 'sanctioned by the Archbishop and eighteen of the English Bishops', Ellen Okins and Christina Cameron had been admitted as deaconesses—a landmark for the Anglican Church in Australia. On the festival of the Annunciation, 1891, nine lay associates, 'ladies, communicants of our Church, [were] solemnly admitted by the Chaplain...to assist the Deaconesses in any way in their power'. By 1900, the Mission had a staff of six deaconesses and one probationer. Four years later, the origin of applicants was examined and alarmed attention drawn to dependence on candidates from interstate: 'We close this report with an expression of our feeling of shame.'

By 1907 the tally showed only a modest increase to eight sisters and two novices, although several requests for admission had been refused because there was no room to accommodate probationers at Mission House.

By then, however, the formal status of the sisterhood had changed. Despite hostility and suspicion, Sister Esther fulfilled her intention formed as a novice in the Community of St Mary the Virgin at Wantage, and was professed under full religious vows in the diocese of Ballarat in 1904. Over the next few years, that provincial centre and its sympathetic archdeacon were resorted to by other aspiring religious, until in 1912 the Diocesan Deaconesses' Home came out of the shadows and was given full recognition by charter as 'The Community of the Holy Name' under Archbishop Lowther Clarke. In adopting the name for her community, Esther had asked for the reaction of their English counterpart, CHN Malvern Link, and had received from the Superior there a positive and friendly response: 'I say to you in all Christian love: Go on and prosper, and may God abundantly bless you and the Australian Community of the Holy Name'.

3

IF I PERISH, I PERISH

I also and my maidens will fast likewise; and so will I go in unto the king, which is not according to the law: and if I perish, I perish.

Esther 4:16

The effects of the depression lingered into the new century, and the Mission continued to endure considerable financial strain. By 1907, however, the Council could congratulate itself on twenty-one years of constantly expanding endeavours. The Mission House in Spring St was now the focus of a variety of charitable and religious activities which combined tight-laced attitudes with a free-for-all spirit. A loyal entourage of mothers flocked to meetings where the sweetener of afternoon tea was followed by a dose of religious instruction. 'Esprit de corps' had been developed among the boys by the formation of a football team sporting vivid guernseys—purple, because that was the bishop's colour. Soon, there were twelve keenly competitive teams, ably marshalled by Sister Agnes in whom was detected 'a wonderful understanding of the boy nature'. Afternoon services and classes for young children continued, with weekly classes for female prisoners, and visits to the cells of Anglican inmates 'for private conversations'.

Temperance work through the Band of Hope was perhaps the least hopeful area, but the Mission concentrated on encouraging abstinence in children 'to prevent at least some drunkenness in the coming generation'. Meanwhile, new avenues continued to be explored. A girl's gym class met at the Mission House, and a newly formed boy-scout troup exchanged letters with a group in England 'to remind the boys that though divided by the ocean England and Australia are one in love of King and Country'.

Pressure on the Mission's other activities was intense. At the House of Mercy there was 'scarcely ever a vacancy', and alterations to enable thirty girls to be accommodated were postponed several times through lack of funds, only to be further retarded by a building strike once they were under way. Eventually, the new wing opened in October 1907 with a debt of £200, and by March the next year furnishing was still incomplete, a shortcoming that provoked *In Our Midst* to the blunt admonition: 'The Roman Catholics reap largely by the apathy of our friends. They have ample room for all the girls we are unable to take for want of funds, and strange to say, the Protestant public is quite content that it should be so.' Besides the spectre of Anglican apathy, the moral tone of the house continued to be a problem, as the 'class of girls' to be dealt with had plummeted to new depths of intransigence.

More positive was the purchase of land next to the Children's Home, an event that both improved life for the children and summoned up some fantasies of empire-building:

the children are rejoicing in a large playground, and the cow in a more luxuriant paddock, while the Sisters even now are not satisfied, but are casting longing eyes over to the meeting-house, and dreaming of the time when all the land up to Male Street will have changed owners, and a beautiful church will top the hill in Wilson Street, Middle Brighton.

Another development simultaneously created difficulties and opportunities. The sisters had resisted several requests, particularly from the formidable Association of Presbyterian Elders, that they should take religious instruction classes in addition to those they already ran in St Paul's School, the Toorak College for Girls and, at the other end of secularism and security, the Brighton State School. In 1907 the Council agreed to take over St George's Day School, 'at the request of the Hornbrook

Ragged Schools Association'. The sisters, three of whom were registered teachers, also undertook management of St John's School, LaTrobe St. These new initiatives put added pressure on the Mission House, where 'This cold winter has brought many cases of poverty and suffering to the notice of the Sisters'. Given that the novitiate was increasing at tortoise pace, *In Our Midst* was prompted to suggest what might be done by those whose dedication fell short of total self-giving: 'The sisters and their workers need a rest and a change; can you offer to stay a month at the Children's Home, and help to wash and dress and care for in every way the big family at Brighton, or won't you go to the House of Mercy and fill a gap there for a time?' (September 1907).

The new year began on an exhausted though long-suffering note that soon deepened to a hint of despair, as the Community was made to face a problem that would bedevil it for decades. The fragile balance of its work-force was dangerously unsteadied if a single worker was removed. The temptation to expand into new areas of work aggravated the difficulty. When Sister Anna, a member of the Community for fourteen years and one of its trained teachers, died, the instability was highlighted:

We have to face the loss of a Sister, and in our small Community such a loss is hard to face... There are rumours of fresh undertakings; another School is offered, but without more Sisters—and it takes nearly three years to train one—we cannot do more than carry on the work we have in hand. If only some Australian girls will come and offer themselves, all may be well. It has been suggested that we try for recruits from the old country. But surely this is an error.

Regardless of the shortage of teachers, numbers in the Hornbrook School swelled to 'more than overflowing', a squeeze that suggested the school be demolished and rebuilt 'on a much larger and more ambitious scale'. The rewarding nature of the work was evident when the 'Hornies' were examined by former functionaries of the Education Department and came through with flying colours. The flying colours included liberal applications of red, white and blue. On Empire Day, patriotic hymns were prescribed, and marching, with masses of ribbons in the magic colours; it was 'a pretty picture to see the earnest little faces of Syrians and half-caste Chinese all joining in "Three cheers for the red, white and blue"'. The Mission, which since its early days fostered a connection with the communities of the Syrian and Russian Orthodox churches, and tended the Chinese whether or not they were promising candidates for conversion, often drew attention to these multi-racial elements with pride— and a tinge of surprise at the human variety in their midst. Educationally, too, they could feel a proper satisfaction that 'pupils are not converted into conventional copies, but each is helped to develop individually'.

The sisters' position at the school remained one of labour and responsibility without ownership until 1911, when both land and building in Cumberland Place were gifted by the Hornbrook Ragged Schools Association and legally transferred to the Mission. That year was marked by two other major developments: the gift of land in Spring St adjoining Mission House, and the bequest by Florence Hughes, an earnest barracker for the sisters' cause, of Ellerslie, a 'valuable house and land in Kew', as a rest-home for the sisters. The Kew bequest was to signal the Community's entry into hospital management.

The Church of England had for several years admitted its poor record in the care of the sick, and recognized how much more the Roman Catholics did. In October 1911, Synod resolved to back 'the establishment of an Intermediate Hospital in connection with the Church of England in Melbourne', and Kew Council, alert to the potential of the imposing mansion the Community had inherited, requested that Ellerslie should be converted to the purpose.

Early in 1912, the premises having been passed by the Board of Health, the house was registered as a hospital, to be named St George's after Esther's favourite saint. *In Our Midst* greeted the development enthusiastically:

the new Hospital will be in a very convenient position for the Eastern suburbs, where at present the need for such an institution is greatly felt... [It] is to benefit those who cannot afford to go to Private Hospitals, and who do not wish to be the recipients of charity in the Public Hospitals. (April and July 1912)

A month after Ellerslie was registered, the British Medical Association Council was informed that the Church was to establish a second such hospital in King St in the city. The *Church of England Messenger* applauded this sudden quickening of Anglican spirit, but joy at the two-pronged advance was short-lived. Although the BMA had approved the scheme, individual members of the medical profession pronounced the city site unsuitable. Their thumbs-down may not have been entirely unbiased, for private practices were lucrative and intermediate hospitals threatened to intrude. In April 1912 the *Australian Medical Journal* gave qualified approval to the establishing of a network of hospitals which would bridge the gap between the over-worked, infection-ridden public hospitals, and the punishingly expensive private hospitals: 'intermediate hospitals...are not intended to be, and never should be allowed to become competitors with private hospitals...they should fill a gap which at present exists between such establishments and public institutions.'

Their advocacy was based on the grounds that many of the middle class could not afford the private hospitals' fees of five guineas a week, so that a growing proportion of Victorians were relying on hospital relief. This was parasitism; and some medical commentators promoted the application of a means-test to ensure that those on moderate incomes were excluded from public hospitals. Trying to determine if a patient deserved public medicine had the catch of ensuring that sometimes a hospital bed became a death bed. The government, for its part, encouraged the establishment of intermediate hospitals to reduce its own expenses, to salve the sensibilities of those who felt shamed by 'charity', and to curb the proliferation of public hospitals—many of them set up by local worthies as a self-promotional exercise.

The Church abandoned the King St proposal. St George's was confirmed as an intermediate hospital, and in October 1912 its rules were submitted to Council and approved. CHN's management was ratified, a medical council was projected, and fees (variable according to the circumstances of the patient) were set. In the interests of maintaining the position of its members and exerting its own power, the BMA stipulated changes which gave it control of the proposed medical council, and set terms on patient admissions to try to ensure no person who could conceivably afford private hospital fees should slip through the net and gain first-class treatment at second-class prices. The ability to advance a moral philosophy and one's own professional interests at the same time was an enviable achievement.

The fabric of Ellerslie required substantial alterations. Most of the ground floor became four-bed maternity wards and a labour ward, with kitchen and domestic quarters in a basement at the rear. Staff quarters, a general ward, operating theatre and recovery room were on the first floor, and the whole provided accommodation for twenty-eight patients. Money for alterations and equipment was raised by the issue of debentures and a scintillation of linen, kitchen and pantry teas in the smarter suburbs. £300 was also advanced from the McPherson Bequest, and there was a substantial anonymous donation. St George's was opened on 29 October 1912, in the seemingly obligatory vice-regal presence. The venture which had been so swiftly carried through was heralded by *In Our Midst* as 'the third branch house of the mission'. The first Australian-born sister, Agnes Row, became sister superior, but as she still lived at the Mission House the daily management of the hospital fell to Sisters Cecil and Ruth, assisted by a small staff of probationers and registered secular nurses.

St George's, Victoria's second intermediate hospital, took some time to establish itself. In the first year for which figures are available, 1914–15, 148 patients were treated and a £126 loss was recorded. However, from the beginning the sisters reported 'the right kind of people have been coming', patients who responded to the mixture of good medical treatment and human sympathy, and who left behind complimentary testimonials. Yet staffing was a perennial problem: 'The ideal to aim at is to have Sisters of the community who are also nurses. . . Why is that so few nurses are willing to embrace the religious life?' The genesis of many sisterhoods had, after all, been in the rehabilitation of nursing in the nineteenth century.

Despite the war, a year after the hospital opened many of its problems had eased. The electric tramway passed it now, making it more accessible, and the warden was able to report: 'The days of anxiety for the finances of the Hospital seem to have ended and there is every reason to hope for its rapid extension and usefulness as it becomes more widely known.'

Another initiative took longer to come to fruition. A logical extension of CHN's work for children was the provision of a home for babies—a scheme that had been forming in the Community mind for several years. In 1912 the sisters publicly expressed a desire for this addition to their work, their hopes having been raised by a gift of land adjoining the Children's Home and the formation of an 'influential' fund-raising committee. Sister Esther advanced the argument with her customary vigour, at the same time rebutting the curious idea that the enterprise would encourage a surge in the numbers of illegitimates:

it seems extremely difficult to find a resting place for an infant derelict. We at present have to refuse all applications for children under two years of age, and after a painful interview the mothers go away to try elsewhere for a shelter for their babies, and the Sisters wonder, when they read of a little dead body being found if it was the baby they had held in their arms a few days previously... Some people speak loudly against such a Home, declaring it to be an invitation to vice. But, alas! the vice is rampant, and the babies are being slain. Surely it is better to try to save a few.

The case for establishing a babies' home gained strength from the sisters' experience of gaol visiting, particularly the desperate calls on condemned women. Such scenes were described with a powerful sense of drama in the biography of the Mother Foundress:

What a poignant moment when a Sister received a baby from the arms of a mother about to die a shameful death... Sometimes young girls were encountered who were serving sentences for infanticide... hardly more than children themselves, they had become half-demented through pain and fear and bewilderment. Now they were suffering detention during the Governor's pleasure, a sentence which might have been passed more fittingly on those who had brought them to this, the callously irresponsible father of the child and the coldly self-righteous folk who had turned them out when their plight was known

...it was a matter of great rejoicing to Sister Esther that when the House of Mercy was built the sentences of some of the younger ones were commuted, and the girls passed altogether into the Sisters' care.

Some rigorous moralisers frowned on the sisters' propensity for gathering up the illegitimate, thinking this looked like condoning the laxity that had brought both mothers and babies to such a pass. But if providing care for babies would encourage illegitimacy and, in its wake, infanticide, such logic itself was barbarous. The sisters' philosophy oscillated uneasily between acceptance of the prevailing moral codes, and revulsion at leaving unassuaged the human devastation they saw. They could not agree that the unborn should carry the stigma of the previous generation, and for them the doctrine of original sin was hard pressed by the evidence of natural innocence. They were also caught uncomfortably between observing social injustices and hestitating to tamper with the social order itself. The question of large-scale and co-ordinated state intervention was rarely raised, while the achievements of private philanthropy were applauded. There was a natural temptation to concentrate on practicalities rather than theory, and the practicalities were intimidating. In 1913, the Children's Home was obliged to refuse admission to many youngsters, and thirty or forty babies were turned away. 'Only a few weeks during the year have we had an empty bed in the house, and it has been suggested that a notice be put up to the effect that none need apply until the building of the Babies' Home will give a little more room.' Continued inaction produced anguished disappointment.

More and more babies seem to need a home every day. They increase alarmingly, for the destitution is now great, especially in the nearer suburbs, and many young mothers, some only children themselves, have no option but to bring the babies to the Court, as they cannot possibly rear them.

The question was raised: Did the record number of infants committed to state care represent an upsurge of 'war babies'? The answer appeared to be negative, but the constant stream of 'little derelicts' could not be ignored, and Anglicans lagged behind other denominations in providing charitable services.

Churchgoers' apathy was not the only cause. According to those who repaired to Treasury with their begging-buckets, war and the recent drought had dried up government funds, and the war was also held responsible for long delays in granting permits for a babies' home, since Board of Health officials had been diverted to war service. Those who remained to deal with the increased workload did not always understand the sisters' intentions: '[they] seem to think, by their requirements, that we are going to cater for sick children. We hope not; we wish for healthy babies, and rely on our cows in the paddock and plenty of commonsense treatment.' That, however, would be supplemented by a novice 'specially trained in baby management'.

Inaction and scepticism among many of the Mission's supporters continued to keep the babies' home 'only an imagination'. The Charity Organisation wondered if it was necessary at all. But the sisters pointed out that the 'Babies' Home will be only an extension of our existing House', and by 1915 almost half the estimated cost of £2000 had been accumulated, thanks to the core of faithful enthusiasts. Twelve months later, after a wait of more than seven years, persistence won out, assisted by the death of a recalcitrant owner who had resisted all inducements to sell. The building was purchased for £1800, and renovations were under way. *In Our Midst* could barely suppress its triumph:

For many years past the Sisters have looked with longing eyes at the house which stands next to the Children's Home, on the left. It has been empty for six or eight years. The boys of the neighbourhood have invaded the garden...doing all the mischief possible... The new house is admirably suited for the object in view. Verandahs run round the sides, and one can almost see the little cots there.

The original modest proposal for twelve babies immediately expanded to 'at least thirty'. When the home was opened on 2 September 1916, the Mission Council congratulated all who had rallied to the cause of optimism and compassion in defiance of the snipers: 'the whole place was paid for, and most of the furniture as well'. The house was soon full, another of CHN's versions of the old woman who lived in the shoe.

Demand, however, continued to outstrip available facilities, and in the last year of the war *In Our Midst* lamented that 'there seem to be more babies needing homes in Melbourne than ever before'. It announced a 'Baby Saving Week'. Corporate action by the Mothers' Union was suggested to raise funds 'to secure accommodation for young mothers and babies when they leave the Women's Hospital, and are faced with. . . the question of how to live'. Instead of chastising abandoning mothers as 'unnatural', the challenge was to nurture 'valuable assets of Australia' and replace 'some we have lost in the war'. CHN was not about to retreat because of charges of being busybodies: 'Possibly our readers may say: "Why don't the Sisters mind their own business?"—in fact we hear it said. But the babies are worth fighting for, we think, and the Sisters are in the position to know the sad state of affairs. If they kept silence they would be blameworthy.'

Despite the rustle of criticism, the work for children attracted plaudits and soft-hearted accounts of visits to Brighton. The babies were confident and fearless 'because well loved'. Particular pathos attached to a 'few weeks' old mite whose life had but lately been despaired of'. Fed through an eye-dropper, the little creature had been saved. Elsewhere, toddlers gambolled, performing acrobatics for the visitors. The picture of lively well-being was reinforced by photographs of chubby smiling youngsters disposed about the entrance or gathered like daisy-chains in the gardens of the home.

The biography of the foundress gave an even rosier tint to the picture-postcard images of the past: 'Quaint little mites they look, in their befrilled pinafores and button boots, or dressed for an outing in prim little frocks and immense sailor hats, the smaller children winsome in fur-trimmed bonnets and many-caped pelises.' But the stereotyped idyll stood at odds with Esther's own reminder that 'as a rule, the children who come to us are not normal in any sense, and they require the greatest care, not only in detecting and removing post nasal [?natal] troubles, but in rooting out moral defects, and results of bad feeding and environment'.

The delay in establishing the Babies' Home was only one of the difficulties for which the war was partly to blame. Even the

'The office of superior is less an honour than a burden': the Mother Foundress when she was professed in 1894 and shortly before her death in 1931.

'Nunnish garb was tantamount to defection to Rome, and a more neutral deaconess uniform was adopted . . . sober, curlian, Victorian dress': the first three, Sisters Esther, Christina and Ellen, c. 1890.

'Behind the scenes all these old sisters like their starched table napkins and their nice silver': Sister Winifred, c. 1920.

'We must rise betimes too, and meet God early': Sister Maree in Brunswick Street, Fitzroy, c. 1960.

build-up to war had in small ways affected the Mission's work. When the government in 1911 initiated compulsory military training for boys over twelve, Mission Hall activities lost some of their liveliness with the withdrawal of the older group. However, the mood was buoyant, convinced, and unswervingly loyal. Empire Day 1914 was celebrated with particular fervency at the Mission schools ('all nationalities...all are one, all are British subjects'), and when war was declared in August a clamorous editorial came from *In Our Midst*: 'we...may well be proud of the British blood that flows in our veins...our consciences are clear; we are on the side of the defenceless and weak, and so must go forward without panic or excitement to do the duty which lies before us'.

Inevitably, though, more jarring effects were felt. The Mission lost its cross-bearer, a member of the choir, and others; the House of Mercy girls began to devote their scant leisure to 'making garments, shirts, cholera belts and nightingales for the soldiers', and even the street-wise 'Hornies' began to squirrel money for chocolate for the troops. The thought that the Mission would have to curtail its activities was brushed aside with an affirmation of faith in 'church-people'—a confidence which flew bravely in the face of long-standing evidence of their lukewarmness.

By January 1915, the tone was anxious, subdued, almost elegiac: 'behind the opening gate of the new year we may expect trial, disappointment, suffering, which are now hidden'. At least funds were stable, and the generous provision of goods, especially for the children's Christmas treat, proved that 'our friends have not failed us'. The minutes of the annual meeting that year praised the healthy attendance, and the chairman expressed 'the deepest thankfulness that the Mission was able to carry on in spite of unparallelled difficulties. Through the devotion of the Sisters & others who had helped, especially Sister Esther, this had been accomplished'. Although war and boom are often equivalent states, the same report drew attention to the doleful condition of the Mission's clientele: 'a large number of men in Melbourne out of work, and a large number of men refusing to work, and the Sisters are finding more than the usual number of cases of deserted wives and families'.

The mail from Europe brought constant reminders of old boys and friends turned soldiers. One Mission boy admiringly reported the courage and humour of grievously wounded Turkish prisoners under his guard. 'Keen to go to the front', he proceeded to the Dardanelles. Another, who had determined to kill a 'Fritz' to avenge his brother's death, found himself overcome by a more humane impulse, so that 'when I got to him I never had the heart to'. A cable reported the arrival in Egypt of Sister Esther's adopted son, Lieutenant Lawrence Oldfield, one of several who were not to return. Occasionally, the experience reported was remote from war: one Australian soldier, who had formerly been a theological student, described his visit to Canterbury, enclosing with the letter 'an ivy leaf, also a bit of stone from the wall. It was coming off, so I just took it, and didn't do any harm—this bit of stone may have heard St Augustine's voice'.

Two years into the war, as the voluntary workers the Mission relied on to top up its efforts were siphoned into war work, the stresses on the home front could not be denied. St George's School was 'suffering from want of helpers. The claims of the Red Cross have, for the present, overshadowed the needs of our little ones'. On the sisters the strains told heavily. One sister was in charge of a lively complement of thirty-eight children—'all sizes and ages'—and was required to teach the entire primary school curriculum. In mid-1917, illness in the Community forced the hiring of a temporary teacher assistant. And at St John's School the situation was just as bad: 'the proverb "Hope deferred maketh the heart sick" is experienced when one contemplates the want of things'. The tribulations caused by the war spread beyond the schools to the House of Mercy, where 'there is only too abundantly evident a most disastrous slackness of parental control... The increase in numbers here is probably due to the presence of so many soldiers. Parents are asking the Sisters to take charge of girls whom they describe as incorrigible, and whom they cannot keep away from the camps'.

Plunged into a thicket of difficulties, In Our Midst abandoned its earlier faith in the good-will of 'church people', and directed a furious rocket into the complacent company of the faithful:

Possibly our steady respectable Church of England life needs a bomb-shell or two to wake it up. The question has often been asked, 'Will the war deepen the religious life of the world?' God grant it may... If the old Church cannot get nearer the people, she will perhaps be swept away as having failed in her mission.

The strain of the war years showed in the sick-lists of the Community. Esther, who bore the major burden of responsibility, and in whose imagination the Community's most prolific flowerings germinated, was periodically out of action. When the thirtieth year of her work with the Mission came, Council considered a proposal that 'a fund be established—bearing Sister Esther's name—to provide a Home where, in case of sisters becoming ill—they might rest & receive proper attention'. The time was unpropitious, but as a stop-gap gesture the mother foundress was presented with £50, and requested to 'use the money in taking a holiday'. By the beginning of 1918, the situation had become so grim that the closure of the schools for the January break was seized on as a pathetic palliative:

The new year 1918 must be full of hope for us, for the preceding one has been hard to face. In no time since the beginning of the Mission has there been so much sickness among the Sisters, or so many difficulties to face... Most of the Sisters have been working at high pressure, and are now seeking rest during the month of January when the schools are closed.

Patriotic elan had given way to an exhausted and despairing resignation. 'We, knowing our case to be just, can only work and wait, and trust in God to bring the longed-for peace to this distressed world of ours.'

In six months, however, the wait was over. Spirits revived and, with their revival, consideration immediately flew to the future, where expansion, curtailed by the war, could be unrepentently in the air once more: 'we can again look to our future needs. Where is the Boys' home we need so much?' Supporters were reminded of the parlous state of St George's School where desks were scarce, and shortage of funds prevented development.

The Community's numbers had barely increased during the past few years, and now that the war was over severe attention was again given to the vocational condition of Victoria's womanhood. In 1918 a pleased announcement was made that two nurses training at St George's Hospital 'desire to throw in their lot with the Sisters', while another quartet, including two teachers, also intended to join. On the debit side, the failure of the Mission of Repentance to net a single novice was deplored. With peace, the focus naturally fell on 'the young women who have been working so unselfishly and nobly during the war', and the Community's propagandists were not above exerting a little pressure, and pointing out that the bugle-call of the Holy Ghost should be answered throughout the Empire: 'We have seen the self-sacrifice of our soldier boys... Surely their sisters are not going to hold back from work which is crying out to be done, for God, the Church, and the suffering weak and poor'.

But the Community and Mission hardly had time to gather their united proselytizing breath when a new disaster descended. An influenza epidemic struck, winnowing the survivors of the war and spreading through the crowded environs of Mission House; 'the edict went forth that all churches, halls and schools were to be kept closed' (April 1919). Pitiable cases were described, whole families cramped in ramshackle rooms where none could escape the infection. An appeal through the *Argus* raised £100 for the sisters' work among the victims. Indefatigably, the sisters moved in, cleaning and ordering rooms, providing food, hospitalization for the worst cases, and temporary shelter for children left without parents. Attempts to secure a convalescent home were often thwarted by stony-hearted landlords who refused to rent premises to 'flu sufferers. But a house in the providentially named hamlet of Paradise was finally secured, and pure air, abundant food and milk, seemed guaranteed—together with buckets of blackberries and field mushrooms. A stream of convalescents returned, 'invigorated, strengthened, and more fitted for their various duties'.

Temporarily spared, the Brighton homes then succumbed to the epidemic. Forty sick children, babies, and helpers, were tended by sisters sent from Mission House, together with nurses from St George's Hospital. The homes rapidly assumed the pathetic aspect of a sick-ward. When the cook collapsed, the situation seemed to have reached desperation point. Rescue came in the form of ministering angels from Brighton and Red Cross provision of 'a bountiful supply of suitable food'. As the epidemic abated, the children were removed to a house in the Dandenong Ranges, while the homes were disinfected and cleaned. Three months later, the children returned, and 'it was good to hear the shouts of approval that they were "home again", and there was no institution flavour about it either. Our children really do love their Home'. An outbreak of measles a few months later did underline their vulnerability to infection, congregated together as they were. But with this last assault, the furies of war seemed finally to have exhausted themselves.

The armistice was punctiliously observed at all houses of the Mission, but hopes that the experience of war would deepen the public's moral awareness appeared to be misplaced. Perhaps Australia had not experienced enough of the suffering which redirected all but the most insensible to first and last things—or so the suggestion went, overlooking the disproportionate human loss the nation had endured: 'We in Australia have felt the effects of war as little as any nation, but is it right that the Australians should grow more and more indifferent to the great issues of life, death and immortality?' (October 1919). Given that CHN's preserve was primarily the female population, 'the bad habits of the "flapper" and the rising generation of young women in Melbourne' were felt to be particularly reprehensible. Girls were corrupted at a devastatingly early age ('A wine shop on the way home from school. . .'), and In Our Midst's eyes flew once again to that body of self-sacrificial ewes who were uniquely responsible for the moral tone of the younger generation:

It seems, just at present, that the most urgent need of Australia is not gold, but good mothers, who will teach their children reverence to God, their elders, and their own selves. . .for self-respect and cocktails on the sly cannot coincide. . . It is the mother who is responsible for the moulding of the child's character. It seems to onlookers that mothers are not playing the game.

On the Mission's thirty-third birthday in 1921 the survey of the moral scene was gloomy:

Considering all things, not much progress has been made. Institutions have been founded, it is true. It can no longer be said with derision that the Church of England has no Homes for children and girls, and does not work among the most degraded; but, at the same time, it makes one sad to think of the 'might have beens'.

The despondent tone was deepened by the closure of St John's School after seventeen years under the sisters' management. It was the first time that the Community, attuned to frequent, balmy requests that they expand their efforts, had to watch the attrition of their domain: 'We have experienced "tearing up stakes"—old associations and old affections, all must go, a new order of things has come' . Just three years later, despite reminders to the Anglican populace of the 'need of Church Primary Schools' to preserve children from the secular or the Roman way, St George's Hornbrook School was relinquished—because, as Esther reported to Council, it was far from the homes of the children now, '& it was undesirable to bring them into that neighbourhood'.

There was also the disappointment of not being able to participate in the management of the Boys' Home which opened in early 1920. Apart from other considerations, it appeared that the provisions for the home went beyond what the Mission's constitution allowed. The Mission in fact was unable to provide for boys the care from infancy through adolescence that it offered girls. Meanwhile, however, girls needed that care more than ever, it seemed. Many observers continued to blame the war for social problems whose origins perhaps lay deeper: lack of discipline and self-control, strident self-will, cheap and superabundant amusements, deficient parents worst of all; the results could be seen in hordes of skittish girls 'in the crowded streets, at picture shows, in dancing halls', and the House of Mercy was always bursting at the seams.

Pressure on the latter institution had intensified with the establishment of Children's Courts in 1914. Many of the girls dealt with by these courts were technically children, yet in the eyes of their mentors 'too advanced in evil to be admitted among the young children at Brighton'. So the fallen woman for whom the House of Mercy's ministrations were intended had been replaced by the wayward girl, younger each year, and completely lacking the incentive for improvement. Given the

deep-seated rebelliousness of the charges, the surface docility
with which they accepted events, such as an informal visit by
the Countess of Stradbroke who watched the girls at work in
the laundry, may well have covered much darker emotions.

A compassionate but perhaps minority view was put by the
Dean of Melbourne at the thirty-eighth annual meeting in
1924:

He thought there was no more 'original sin' in a girl of the submerged
class, than in ours, but think of her environment and temptations.
Slums make the slum dwellers, & citizens make the slums. The slums
of a city are the price paid for its prosperity in the lives of those who
are broken by it.

Esther seemed to align herself more with the strictures of Canon
Snodgrass, 'the Wandering Warden' of CHN, who made a
grand tour of English institutions and reported gratifyingly that
the House of Mercy was equal to any of them, except in its lack
of modern conveniences such as electricity in the laundry; 'but
Sister Esther thought the more primitive methods of Cheltenham
possibly produced a more suitable wife for the ordinary working
man'.

Shifting his attention to the human furniture of the establishment, Snodgrass described the situation with horrified distaste:

The girls now are not only immoral, but unmoral, they see a thing,
want it, take it, and are most surprised when the sinfulness of such an
attitude of mind is pointed out to them. As one said to me a short
time ago when I was pointing out to her the sinfulness of theft, 'I was
never told that by anyone before'. Many of them are astonished when
one rebukes this unbridled acquisitiveness.

Lack of moral discrimination made the likelihood of their retrieval
even more remote than if they had been consciously evil.
Another deeply shocking aspect was the new preference that
many showed for gaol rather than committal to the House of
Mercy:

Years ago it was different. Girls would be overwhelmed at the stigma
attaching to a gaol-bird, or at the shame of their relatives and friends;

and would do anything to avoid it. Now, however, they seem
to regard it as a distinction or 'badge of honour' amongst their
depraved associates.

Another development which converted life at the House of
Mercy from the difficult to the almost impossible was the practice
of sending there girls whose behaviour was so outrageous that
other institutions refused to keep them. 'We have had as many
as six of these girls at a time, and their insolence and utter want
of respect for any kind of authority are trying for the sisters to
deal with.' Snodgrass recommended regular and strenuous prayers
for the sisters' survival. One of his associates in turn described
him as virtually a procession in himself.

The church ought to insist on fresh legislation... In the police courts
young girls who thoughtlessly yield to temptation, shoplifting, petty
larceny, and the like, are put on probation or committed to the care
of some Home...most of these cases should be segregated for a time
at least, and given an opportunity, amidst an atmosphere of love and
sympathy, to learn what they have missed, and to gain self-respect,
and a desire to live a different life.

This article from the *Church Standard*, approvingly summarized
by *In Our Midst* in May 1929, represented a cautious admission
that the problem lay in the way offenders were treated. The
critique rarely extended to suggesting that the real problem was
not the moral inferiority of the lower classes, but inequities in
the social system and the distribution of wealth. Practical ideas
for improvement were a hostel for those released from gaol, and
a court, based on one in Chicago, where delinquent parents could
be called to account. A more daring suggestion was to enlist
'the practical science of psychology': 'The present classification
of crime solely by legal categories is hopelessly unscientific'.
These views were a lone and somewhat timid attempt to tackle
the causes of delinquency, rather than simply to deal with the
results. Generally, over the House of Mercy's fifty-four year
history, treatment not prevention was preferred, despite occasional
avowals to the contrary, and nineteenth-century mores survived
like untarnished relics well into the twentieth century.

An unquestioning adherence to moral precepts did not prevent changes in method, though these were only cautiously adopted. In 1929, Snodgrass reported a shift from strict reformatory methods, based primarily on a belief in the redeeming effect of hard domestic labour, to a more lenient mixture of work and recreation: 'now music, and musical drill, singing and indoor games are encouraged, whilst basket ball and other outside recreations form an important part of daily life there'. The days when visitors rhapsodized over the steaming cauldrons, brimming troughs and relentless flat irons of the laundry were being superseded, but not quite. Nostalgic visitors were liable to recall the 'splendid happy industry' of former years, and contrast it with the unglowing present 'when perhaps you have found it difficult to manage and keep just one maid in these days of independence'. The nostalgia for a supply of tractable servants suggests what really underpinned the halcyon scene of scrubbed wooden surfaces and lines of perfectly washed clothes.

Shifts in the moral tone of the house were anxiously reported. Improvements were gratefully recorded, the chief indicators of good times being the number of inmates confirmed and the frequency of visits from rehabilitated 'old girls'. But standards, it seemed, were slipping and there were earnest deliberations about the possible causes. More damaging even than the effects of war was 'our Godless state education'. Expatiating on the causes for the steady lapse of the young into heathenism and amorality, Snodgrass took as an authority 'one of our foremost judges', who blamed the increase of crime among seventeen-year-olds on

the cruder communistic and socialistic propaganda in our midst, which is 'white-anting' even our children; for I was appalled to hear the large numbers of children that are attending the so-called communistic Sunday schools, which inculcate these doctrines and ridicule God, religion and all constituted authority.

He omitted any reference to the effects of the oncoming depression that may have drawn the most vulnerable members of society into rebellion and rejection, although there was an admission that general unsettlement was the prime cause of deterioration of the social fabric. The young women of the

1920s who flocked heedlessly to picture shows and dance halls, intent on 'self-gratification', and who later appeared at the Mission House with illegitimate babies in their arms, were the subject of particular censure.

The apparent decline in morals prompted self-questioning on the sisters' part. They were forced to admit a falling-off in calibre in their charges in terms both of character and age. And since the courts committed girls for shorter periods than previously, the good influence of a stint at the House of Mercy was curtailed. Still, the sisters believed that they had an advantage over the secular institutions, on the principle that 'Goodness is contagious, thank God, as well as badness', and the power of a noble example might sometimes impress even the most hardened. Despite their vigilant and sincere efforts, however, there were occasions when 'a wave of naughtiness and disobedience seemed to be engulphing the House'. Perhaps this was due to a higher than usual number of intractables. Such outbreaks at any rate were emotively measured. Though the statistics themselves are inconsistent, they do suggest that the numbers of girls committed to the house rose significantly during the 1920s.

An even more alarming development was the report in 1928 of a growing incidence of venereal disease among prospective inmates:

A sad change...has come over the class of girls who now come to the House of Mercy. Years ago, the girls, though incorrigible and unmanageable at home, were usually innocent of the grosser forms of depravity; but now, case after case passes through the Sisters' hands which cannot be admitted to the House of Mercy owing to venereal disease.

The decision was taken not to accept such cases. Girls were referred to the Mission House and sent for examination to the Queen Victoria Hospital. If infected, they were then passed to other institutions, allowing the House of Mercy to maintain 'a free bill of health in this respect'.

At the same time, the pressure of court work was increasing. Two sisters were 'now wholly engaged' in it and received many first offenders on probation. More agreeable was the praise that came from court officials. At the 1927 annual meeting a magistrate from the Children's Court spoke glowingly of 'the most loyal & valued aid from the Sisters in caring for girls whose lapse was most frequently due to a past dreary & lonely life. The other alternative—state control—proved a soul-less cold thing'. Two years later, the plaudits came from several quarters, including a formal expression of gratitude from the City Court, stressing the humane and comprehensive nature of the sisters' approach, 'preventive & redemptive rather than punitive... double work of rescue & character building'.

In other aspects of the Mission's work, the problems were practical and material, rather than moral and emotional. Success in reformatory endeavours tended to be fragile and transient, and was often a matter of simply maintaining control, whereas St George's Hospital was reported to be 'most flourishing' and was quickly approaching a state of financial respectability.

By February 1920, only £500 of the £1200 taken out in debentures for rebuilding remained to be discharged, and the Council determined that a £4000 extension 'may be undertaken as they cannot now comply with all demands'. Pressure was particularly strong in the midwifery section, because of a post-war baby boom and the decline in home births. At the thirty-fourth annual meeting that year, the hospital was free of debt, and £80 was held in the new building fund, swelling to £300 a year later. Replanning the hospital, with conversion of Ellerslie to nurses' quarters, was felt to be a partial answer to the needs of the outlying suburbs and 'the incessant pressure on the city hospitals'. As the toll from motor-car accidents grew, one medical authority observed that 'St George's must inevitably become a casualty centre as there was no public hospital within sixty miles in an easterly direction'.

The rebuilding programme was felt to be the responsibility of the whole diocese, and attempts were made to stir the corporate conscience by arousing a little competitive spirit and pointing out that the Brisbane diocese had raised a whopping £80 000 for its Anglican hospital. At the same time, the government's obstinate refusal to supply a grant because of St George's 'denominational' character was deplored, especially when it was considered that 'the spiritual basis upon which Sister Esther and her Sisters worked was the secret of their success'. The Community's seriousness about its hospital commitments was manifest in attempts to upgrade its members' own professional qualifications, and for several years a CHN sister had been in charge of the nursing department.

Although the government refused to subsidise hospitals run under religious auspices, it was not shy in setting the terms under which such institutions could operate, and in 1923 the Board of Health required 'very costly additions and alterations' to St George's. Perturbed by estimates of between twenty and thirty thousand pounds, the Council decided to build a new maternity block and to retain Ellerslie for general and surgical patients, a recourse that reduced the estimated outlay to £7000. However, even the quote for the truncated scheme soon whizzed up to £13 000, thanks to galloping inflation.

Competition between hospitals in the fund-raising stakes was intense, and central institutions such as the Womens' and Children's Hospitals, with their conventionally touching appeal, often did better than local enterprises. Council was disappointed that its efforts through the *Argus* netted only about £2000, but solicitations by the Mayor of Kew and energetic fund-raising by Sisters Ruth and Cecil, whose loyalties were firmly embedded in the hospital, brought the sum to £8000—which, combined with a £3000 mortgage on the Mission Hall, enabled building to begin.

The new midwifery ward of twenty-three beds opened in 1925 by the governor's wife, Lady Forster, who was flanked by a guard of honour of 200 of the 1400 babies born at St George's, was an instant financial success. The hospital was reported to be full, and the overdraft had dwindled to £335. Despite the still-modest qualifications of the sisters in charge, the Board of Health soon registered it as a midwifery training school offering a six-months' course for nurses with the general certificate, and it was recognized by the Royal Victorian Trained Nurses' Association. It was soon the third largest training school in the specialty, exceeded only by the Queen Victoria and Women's Hospitals, and its reputation lay not only in its size but in its connection with experts in the obstetrical field. Praise for the hospital's standards, heightened by the selfless dedication provided by the sisters, was often combined with pleased repetition of the old adage that 'a woman going into the hospital was not accepting charity'. Self-respect, another term for middle-class pride, was salvaged.

Success, however, tended to produce its own pressures. By 1927, monthly revenue amounted to £500 and the overdraft had been discharged; but a surge of births required additional trainee nurses—then housed in makeshift quarters including a tent—and improved accommodation for them was stipulated by the Board of Health. Plans for a bungalow with eight bedrooms and a sitting room were approved in August 1929, and the building was finished a few months later. The nurses revelled in their superior quarters, but a chastener remained in the Board of Health's continued restrictions on the number of trainees. Ellerslie itself was barely altered since its conversion from a residence in 1911; but like a grand old dame still decked in outmoded fashion, there was some attraction in its archaic glories.

As St George's began to record monthly profits of around £150, once again success generated the pressure for further expansion. A new X-ray block was called for, at a cost of £3000. The project was completed within months and ready for use by early 1931, despite the bitter and intensifying signs of the coming depression. The query remained whether a much larger hospital was required. In Our Midst was able to quote the bluntly pragmatic assessment of a member of the medical profession:

The boon to the people who have come to live in these delightfully elevated and healthy suburbs, in not having to be thrust back when sick into the comparatively grimy and noisy city atmosphere is inestimable if you will grant this by extra accommodation; and the facility offered to relatives and friends not having to make journeys and pay fares to the city to see their sick is a great appeal.

In its early phases, the Mission's other venture into hospital management, St Ives private hospital in East Melbourne, had also prospered. St Ives had been leased in 1917 from Dr Morton, who offered the establishment to the Mission on flexible terms, and by 1918 it was 'more than paying its way'. At the annual meeting that year, the archbishop had reported enthusiastically

on 'a considerable sum of money...spent in improvements &
alterations to make it second to none. He had always felt the
need of a Church of England institution of this kind, & now we
have one it must be kept up to date'. After temporary closure,
the hospital had reopened in 1919 with a new theatre and
improved facilities so impressive that they prompted an *Age*
reporter to urge the proliferation of such superior medical care—to
which the equally heart-felt reply was 'May Heaven forbid! At
any rate, let them not be managed by the Community of the
Holy Name'.

The first burst was impressive. Two years after the salubrious
alterations, the well-heeled sick were flocking in; quarterly
receipts showed a profit over £330, £1470 had been paid to Dr
Morton, and the hospital's only liability was £100 owed to St
George's. The glossy picture obscured some shady factors, though,
and the sunny period of profit-making was short-lived. Some
members of the Community may also have felt uneasy at the
plutocratic bent of the work. The Mission's efforts since its
inception had been single-mindedly directed to the poor and
defenceless, the reprobate and the misled. St Ives represented a
move in a vastly different direction, and rumours of some
inhabitants' luxurious tastes were legion. A comparison of
expenditure for St George's and St Ives showed massive differences, with hefty charges for servants and laundry in the latter
institution. By the end of 1922, in the face of evidence that its
liabilities were overtaking receipts, its closure was discussed.
The public documents of the Mission avoided exposing these
embarrassing problems, but in the inner sanctum of Council
they could not be ignored. Council agreed with Sister Esther
that closure would reflect unfavourably on the Church, and
accepted her offer to take over the hospital and its lease for the
remaining five years 'in the name of her Community or her own
name & run it without a committee as she considered the
present management unworkable'. The lease was duly transferred
to Emma Silcock on 20 December 1922.

The archbishop asked for the strictest secrecy about the
transfer, 'as otherwise it might do much harm'. The warden
capped this injunction with a resolution 'That the Council
wishes to express its unfailing confidence in the Sister Superior

& hopes that she may be spared for many years to direct the community she has founded', a flourish which suggests a mixture of guilt at the discharge of the burden, and the possibility that the sisters had attracted some criticism. On the other hand, Esther may have been asserting the Community's preference for independent control, and a hope that ownership of the hospital might provide income for the Community in lean times.

Despite some judicious glossing in public statements, the Mission's finances were always unstable, and in some areas of activity frequently lapsed into the red. A hint of this precariousness surfaces in the hectoring tone with which church people were solicited, and the ambition—much emphasized but never realized—of raising the number of annual subscriptions to cover expenditure, leaving exceptional profits for improvements. In the privacy of its meeting room Council recognized that apparently healthy balances could quickly become debilitating losses. From time to time, members assured themselves somewhat unconvincingly that a £100 deficit was normal. But the coincidence of resignations from Council and periods of financial stringency suggests that need and dissension went together.

Even positive achievements such as the rapid construction of the maternity wing at St George's often took place against a backdrop of uncertainty. When the wing was almost completed in 1924, Council was left with nearly £4000 to raise in a month, and the possibility of loans from individual Council members was canvassed. Another recourse was to shuffle off a further deputation to the government which still adamantly refused to give grants to hospitals flying the religious flag. The chief secretary was more sympathetic, but no more forthcoming in practical terms, when he was approached for a contribution to building works some of which had been decreed by the government itself. The ultimate solution, raising a mortgage on the Mission House, could only be a last resort. Although the hospital was solvent within a few years, and could report that its facilities, especially the maternity wing, were constantly 'overflowing', the pressure to expand still further meant that without ongoing government assistance the hospital's financial situation was endemically flawed.

The Mission's general finances were constantly unsteadied by the desire to perfect its existing works and to enter new territory. This instinct to extend and improve was especially insatiable in the Community's work with children. The first interstate move in this area was made towards the end of 1921, when *In Our Midst* reported that one sister was working in the Newcastle diocese. Within months, a request for more sisters was made, and by the end of 1922 Sister Alice was in charge of a children's home in the commodious surroundings of a former bishop's palace.

The sisters were soon firmly established in Newcastle, operating homes for babies (Lochinvar), children and older girls (St Elizabeth's Home for Girls, Mayfield), and had earned hearty praise:

The Newcastle people are most generous, and are all very kind in welcoming the Sisters, from the Bishop to the poorest of the poor. At present there are five Sisters in New South Wales, and others are asked for. How we want more young women to come and offer themselves to work for God and the Church, no one knows. (July 1926)

In partial answer to that forlorn plea, the possibility of postulants from Newcastle was pointed out. Although there was no panic of vocations from the senior state, the sisters were loyal to their interstate commitment, and at the end of 1931 extended their sphere of influence in New South Wales to Goulburn, where two houses were relinquished to the Community.

Back home, expansion was also persistently in the air. The annual meeting of 1924 was told of the need for a girls' hostel in association with the Children's Home, 'so that girls could be kept on after 15 yrs of age in suitable surroundings'. The enlightened reason offered was that this would spare them the usual menial fate, allowing 'a much better chance of finding their true vocation. The Sister at present in charge of the Home was a great believer in "Vocation" both religious and material, and that if a girl was called to serve God as a teacher or typist, she should not be compelled to take up domestic work'.

This bold and compassionate enterprise was soon associated by masterly serendipity with another scheme. The obvious place

'This little beginning, moreover, may grow to that which is greater than itself': the first Mission Hall in Little Londsdale Street, Melbourne, 1888.

Community House is approached along a gravel drive lined by agapanthus.

'Waif and stray . . . half starved . . . child turned out of doors . . . mother lunatic, father deserted . . . we beg to remind our readers that we have thirty children at Brighton . . . who are expecting to have a good time . . . this festival': Brighton Children's Home opened in 1894.

for a hostel was next to the Children's Home, and were not the babies wilting in that unnecessarily bracing seaside spot? The need 'of moving them to a warmer inland climate' was projected, and by the end of 1926 all the Council's energies were directed towards the new Babies' Home. In January 1927, *In Our Midst* announced a £10 000 appeal, rebutting in advance those who saw Brighton as the perfect location:

What! is not Brighton a healthy spot for babies? Eminently so for yours or your friend's, but not for the ill-nourished, half-starved anaemic babies, the children of the very poorest, that are brought to us. A more sheltered spot away from the ozone-laden air is more suitable. The committee have a splendid house and grounds offered to them at a reasonable price.

The house the Council had in mind was Yarrayne, a rambling Edwardian mansion festooned with trellises and gables, in the south-eastern suburb of Darling, and purchase was approved by the archbishop in May 1927. The annual meeting that year was reminded of the substantial good an insignificant outlay could achieve: '£25 would keep a child in happiness in the Home for a year. Only £900 was required to free the Home from debt'. When it opened that year with thirty striplings in residence and many more applying, propaganda and clarification could be simultaneously dispensed: 'The new Home is already showing its provincial usefulness—a baby arrived from Mildura and another from Portland a few days ago. We must emphasize the fact that it is a charity; some people seem to think by offering to pay for the babies' maintenance they can have a first claim on any vacant bed'. The former Babies' Home meanwhile held two clerks, two apprentice dressmakers, two domestics and one schoolgirl, together with two inmates who worked on the premises, and the whole experiment was deemed to be 'justifying its Existence'.

Although the financial situation at the Babies' Home was strained, and the hostel had not yet reached self-sufficiency, permission was given at the end of 1928 to build the Chapel of the Holy Innocents at Brighton. The sisters were skilled at praying buildings into existence, and money for the chapel was gathered within three months through the formidable powers of the sister in charge, Ida, assisted by a hearty donation of £200 from 'an "old boy" who had done well in New Guinea'. Designed by architect Louis Williams, with a rose-window designed by Christian Waller around the motif of a child's head, and an altar presented by the chaplain of CHN, the chapel was consecrated on 20 August 1929 by Bishop Reginald Stephen. A procession of twenty-four sisters, forty-one children, fourteen girls all in veils and tunics, and several boys from St Martin's and St John's Boys' Homes, trailed behind Sister Esther as she opened the chapel door with a gold key.

Preserve their innocence, strengthen them when ready to slip, recover the erring, and remove all that may hinder them from being brought up in Thy faith and love. Grant, O Father of all, that Thy Holy Angels as they always behold Thy face in heaven may evermore protect Thy little ones on earth from every danger both of body and soul.

The dangers to body and soul were not confined to the children. In 1923, the annual meeting was informed of a portfolio of difficulties facing the Mission:

particularly during the last year, when there had been an unusual amount of sickness... The Sisters now number 22, & 3 out of this number had been compelled to rest for many months...the cause is ever the same, over work, and this entails fresh anxieties to the Sister Superior, whose health is far from reassuring... There must come a time when it is impossible for them to carry on, and the doctors blame them for overtaking their strength; yet what can they do, somehow or other the work must be carried on.

Consideration was given to establishing a memorial to Esther while she was still alive. While emphasizing her vigour and unflagging spirit, the company was now observing a figure about to move into the orbit of mythology: their spiritual mother, Sister Esther, still 'strong, courageous and faithful', said the Dean reviewing her life-work of thirty-eight years:

When the hour was growing late, she seated herself at last at the piano and brought this memorable evening to a close by leading the whole company in their singing of the National Anthem. As the last of the guests passed into the night one's eyes rested on her who had won their hearts and helped to shape their characters in days long past, while there came to one's mind those words of the Wise Man—so often inscribed on the stony memorial to a beloved and *departed* parent, but never more applicable than now—a human monument to a loved and living 'Mother':—

'Her children arise up and call her blessed'.

The danger was not confined to the Superior; the meagre work-force was vulnerable altogether, with as little protection in material terms as the poorest of its customers. 'There was an urgent need to provide for the Sisters when they were unable to work.' When the insurance companies rejected an attempt to secure composite cover for them, Council agreed to establish a sick-fund, each member agreeing to collect £5 to that end by September 1924, a deadline which coincided with Sister Ida's being 'dangerously ill at St Ives'. Some relief was provided by invaliding sisters to the warmer climate of Newcastle, and by the gift of a rest home 'on a most picturesque spot of Mt Dandenong. About fifteen Sisters were able to come up, and we created quite a stir at Croydon as we entered the omnibus at the station'.

In recognizing the mortal frailty of the generator of its work, the Community felt an anticipatory sadness and apprehension. Esther had a long history of physical fragility, and for all her indomitable spirit had several times been reported incapacitated during the war years. Now, the strains were more evident. When she fell ill in April 1925 it was suggested that she should take three months' leave, 'spending some or all of the money, given her last year for her Sick Sisters Fund, as it was imperative in the interests of the Mission that she should regain her health'. She seemed much recuperated after three months in Ceylon, where several English sisterhoods had branches. In 1927, she went to England with Sister Bertha on the trip that many surmised would be the last she would make to her homeland—a voyage begun in weariness, but continued with the old omnivorous energy and enterprise. Two years later, she was reported to be seriously ill.

Awareness of the foundress's tenuous state of health highlighted the implications, given the new works undertaken, of
the Community's modest growth. By 1929, more than forty
years after its inception, CHN still numbered only twenty-five
professed sisters and five novices, although several aspirants
hovered in the wings, and 'All were Australian girls!'. Although
the Community was tempted to expand into every field that
bore a 'to let' sign, restricted numbers meant restricted works:

To the Rev. Mother's great sorrow, she has had to refuse, once again,
a request from one of our most respected Victorian bishops to begin
work in his diocese... This makes the fifth request from different
bishops she has had to refuse for the same reason—lack of experienced
Sisters. (December 1929)

Will and ambition, however, did not flag in the face of seeming
impossibilities; given the bevy of the aspiring, 'she hopes, in a
couple of years, to be able to extend the work to other dioceses'.
    The economic situation, which was beginning to affect all
aspects of the Mission's work, added to the pressures and uncertainties. Increased requests for admission to the Children's
Home resulted in heart-rending refusals, although the reassuring
sign was that all the girls in the hostel were employed and
'gradually becoming self-supporting'. Generous financial help,
particularly from the country, for work among the unemployed
was being received, but need threatened to outstrip supply. In
October 1930, Esther reported 'a very large number of applicants
for food & having spent £100 in relief during the last few
weeks'. Before long, the relief fund was exhausted, while seventy
poverty-stricken mothers appeared at weekly meetings hoping
for succour. An uneasy equilibrium was maintained, and at the
annual meeting of 1931 the warden praised successes utilitarian
and humanitarian:

He spoke of the great work of the Sisters, & their personal attention
to distressing cases, & how much better they were dealt with, in the
love they put into their work, than in the indiscriminate giving of the
state & public bodies.

Within a few days of that meeting Esther was dead. Among the conventional obituaries to her more conventional side, one tribute isolated the splendid radicalism of her unquenchable spirit:

Shakespeare showed his greatness by knowing when to defy the rules of drama. Sister Esther, staunch Churchwoman as she was, was great enough to know when Christ would give dispensation from Church laws.

In photographs, she looks like the Community's icon: sad, penetrating eyes with lids like the shells of bivalves, small mouth that unites firmness with compassion, straight nose between waxen cheeks, unmarked forehead, her face shaped into a drop pearl by its natural configuration and the constriction of the habit. In her image, curvilinear like the Annunciation lily, the most dramatic dualities of existence seem concentrated: the contrast between the obscurity of the habit and the translucency of the face; the combination of delicacy and strength, sympathy and severity; juxtaposed darkness and light. When the warden and his wife did the round of English communities in 1925, an unnamed English bishop had enthused about the whirlwind achievements of CHN and its foundress. 'I should think the Mother Superior was one of those gifted women who sees great visions—whom God raises up once in a generation to revive our faith in His power and in His Church.'

4

THE HIDDEN LIFE

Is not the Hidden Life the ideal of the true Sister, and where can she find it sooner than in extreme simplicity, a quiet exterior, and in deep humility.

Bishop Butler

In his oration at Esther's funeral in September 1931, Archdeacon W. M. Hancock, Warden of the Mission, referred to the double nature of CHN's endeavour. It was direct heir to the nineteenth-century sisterhoods, and thus dependent on and imitative of many of their traditions: 'Sister Esther was a child of the Oxford Movement, the spiritual daughter of such men as Keble and Pusey, Butler and Church and Liddon'. It was also in the Australian context a unique creation, both adaptive to and formative of local circumstances, and all the more remarkable for its almost impromptu launching: 'The foundation of the Community of the Holy Name is distinguished by the simplicity of its unpremeditated beginning... The crowded days—and nights—left no room for introspection, for wondering at the uniqueness of their position'.

Esther herself, however, was tartly aware that her visit to Australia, which lengthened into permanent exile from England,

had had surprising results: ' "O you Australians!" she would say
to her sisters, "I did not ask for you; you grew on me like the
hump on a camel's back" '. And she was not above pointing out
that other sisterhoods were a good deal less self-determining
than her own. 'Here in Australia we are pioneers', whereas
'The Kilburns [the Community of the Sisters of the Church] are
branch houses of the English Order'. Exactly where CHN stood
in relation to other religious communities, and to society at
large, became even more preoccupying as the twentieth century
went on.

In committing itself to welfare work among the poor, the
Church of England in Australia was responding to the renewed
spiritual impetus and aroused social conscience of its mother
church. There were close parallels between the English and the
Australian experience. In England however, as here, Anglo-
Catholics were a minority and provoked much opposition from
those who caught the whiff of popery in their doings. Even
before the first sisterhoods were established, poet Robert Southey,
an ardent advocate for the creation of these self-denying communities, was constrained in 1829 to rebut the anticipated
charge: 'There is nothing Romish, nothing superstitious, nothing
fanatical in such associations; nothing but what is righteous and
holy...' But Southey looked to the Methodists and Quakers,
rather than the established Church, to realize the ideal. When
it turned out to be Anglicanism which gave rise to sisterhoods,
the Church hierarchy was intensely ambivalent. Following
Newman's secession to Rome in 1845, and the consequent
crisis in the Oxford Movement, Anglo-Catholics fell under
even darker suspicion, and sisterhoods were obliged to establish
themselves gradually and as it were invisibly, in the face of
often powerful opposition among church authorities. 'The Bishops',
writes one historian, 'accused the sisterhoods of being virtually
non-conformist bodies, and the Anglo-Catholics, from being
ardent defenders of the establishment, became virtually its opponents'. In Australia, there were sympathic prelates, such as
Bishop Moorhouse under whose aegis the Melbourne order of
deaconesses was formed, and Archdeacon Stretch of Ballarat
before whom Esther made her vows in 1894; but in general the
hierarchy preferred to play down the fact that the Community

existed at all. CHN's most valuable support came from a small band of committed clergy, congregations such as St Andrew's, Brighton, who had seen the sisters' work at first hand, and the enthusiastic women of the auxiliaries. When theological justification was advanced on the Community's behalf, it tended to be in terms of its conformity to the history of deaconesses within the Church. Monastic precedents were by-passed, and the sisters' good works attracted approval while their mode of life was glossed over with disavowal or embarrassment. Both in England and in Australia, the sisterhoods to a great degree exemplified 'the hidden life', the unbidden resonance, the unsung oblation.

On both sides of the world, however, communities shared the same springs of spirituality: 'a Christianity which was at once eager for holiness, and creative of it. . .immediately and in practice'; a commitment both doctrinal and practical; a spiritual revival which associated itself with political and social reform. They developed the full meaning of liturgical prayer, the use of the breviary and offices, and the more advanced practice of mental prayer, alongside frequent communion and regular confession.

Meanwhile, in both countries practical impetus came from the evidence of urban social distress on a scale too large to be served by individual charity, and crying out for organized assistance. At the heart of the sisters' practical activities was this involvement in social welfare with, especially in England, a professional emphasis on nursing. In 1840, after a visit to the Lutheran deaconesses, Elizabeth Fry had founded an institute to train nurses. The raised status of that profession was integral to the movement towards expanding opportunities for middle-class women to work outside the gilded and often tarnished cage of marriage. But even Florence Nightingale admitted that the Church of England had done nothing to provide her with openings for dedication, much as she might have looked to find her centre in the Church:

[It] has for men bishoprics, archbishoprics, and a little work. . . For women, she had—what? I had no taste for theological discoveries. I would have given her my head, my hand, my heart. She would not have them. She told me to go back and do crochet in my mother's drawing room; or, if I were tired of that, to marry and look well at the head of my husband's table. You may go to Sunday School if you like it, she said. But she gave no training even for that. She gave me neither work to do for her, nor education for it... What training is there [in the Church of England] compared to that of the Catholic nun? there is nothing like the training which the Sacred Heart Order of St Vincent gives to women.

Only the rise of sisterhoods in the second half of the nineteenth century challenged this blistering indictment.

Given that the colonies were habitual borrowers of ideas, the language of practical spirituality in both countries was almost identical. What Australia lacked was the call to revive monasticism, which English Tractarians such as Pusey had delivered so ringingly:

We need missions among the poor of our towns: organised bodies of clergy living among them; licensed preachers in the streets and lanes of our cities; brotherhoods or guilds which should replace socialism; or sisterhoods of mercy, for any office of mercy which our Lord wills to be exercised...we need clergy to penetrate our mines, to migrate with our emigrants, to shift with our shifting population...to secure in Christ's name the Deltas of our population which the overflowing, overspreading stream of our English race is continually casting up.

The nationalistic fervour and the conservative political tincture were also, in Australia, translated into a less dogmatic mood. But over all, the programme of works conceived in England could be transposed unaltered into the Australian situation. When a committee of laymen headed by Gladstone put forward a proposal for the creation of the first English sisterhood, the 'works of mercy' it listed might have provided the blueprint for Esther and her scanty flock of deaconesses:

1 Visiting the poor or the sick at their own houses.
2 Visiting hospitals, workhouses, or prisons.
3 Feeding, clothing, and instructing destitute children.
4 Giving shelter to distressed women of good character.
5 Assisting in the burial of the dead.

Only the last of these obligation did not apply directly to CHN, although in fact the sisters were often called upon to officiate at death beds in the teeming back lanes of inner Melbourne.

In both countries the sisterhoods had frequently to combat vigorous parental opposition to a daughter's choice of the conventual life, although nothing in Australia equalled the fury generated at East Grinstead in 1857 after the funeral of the first member of that community to die. In an event matter-of-factly called the Lewes riot, J. M. Neale and the surviving sisters of the community were set upon by an enraged mob who believed that the dead woman had been lured into the community against parental wishes, stripped of her money, maltreated and deliberately exposed to scarlet fever, in order that after her death her goods could be appropriated. The sinister fanaticism of the sisterhoods loomed large in the Protestant mind. Although no incident as extreme as public pitched battle was witnessed in Australia, many CHN sisters suffered the bitter and prolonged opposition of parents. Esther's own encouragement to Blanche Patterson over the years when she was experiencing such a conflict shows the fortitude required to pursue a vocation when it threatened to sever ties of blood and love.

Like her predecessors and contemporaries in England, Esther was cast in the mould of the great mother superiors, a combination of spiritual intensity, iron will, persuasive power, and undeviating practicality. In a world often unsympathetic and sometimes hostile to grandly spiritual claims reminiscent of a period of radical Christianity which more sedentary Christians preferred not to acknowledge, the sensitive plant was likely to be an early casualty, and toughness and realism were necessary qualities for survival. As against the candleflame delicacy of popular expectation, J. M. Neale described Harriet Monsell, first Superior of the Community of St John the Baptist, Clewer, as 'the most sensible woman I ever met'.

The Sisters of the Church, with their initial foundation as a lay charity, and their emphasis on activism in the social sphere, especially in work among children and the unemployed, had much in common with CHN. Their founding Superior, Emily Ayckbown, who established the community in 1870, had the mettle to resist pressure in the most uncompromising manner.

In 1895 she was confronted by a triple-pronged attack from the Charity Organisation Society, a bevy of seceding sisters, and the Protestant Alliance. The brief of charges included financial mismanagement, cruelty, and the careless misappropriation of illegitimate children. When the Archbishop of Canterbury was drawn into the imbroglio and proposed to enquire into the community's affairs, offering to act as their visitor provided that the sisters acceded in advance to any decisions he might make, the Superior promptly removed his name from her list of patrons. The names of all other male patrons were similarly expunged, and the Superior, a forthright tactician, announced that in future only patronesses would be accepted. The archbishop, who with many senior clergy disapproved of the impertinent independence appropriated by the sisterhoods, expostulated in the privacy of his diary:

The Mother Superior is the most comically audacious Mother in the Universe. After I began my enquiry into the rumours against them as Patron, she calmly dropped her list of Patrons. Now that Lord Nelson has joined me in telling her that her Sisterhood ought to have a fixed constitution and a Visitor, she has told him she must not expose him to so much obloquy, and therefore dismisses him from his Chairmanship.

In 1906, CHN was subjected to far less public, powerful and lurid criticism of its methods, although hurtful enough to provoke a rebuttal in the Mission's annual report. In both cases, opposition stemmed largely from principled objection to the conception and claims of the sisterhoods, rather than from verifiable faults in their performance.

The matter in which they diverged most abruptly from public acceptance was in the question of vows. At least in England there had been a slow gestation period that eased the way for the success of later communities. The first Anglican sister since the Reformation was Marion Hughes, who took her vows on Trinity Sunday in 1841, before proceeding to Oxford to take communion from Newman. The first community was established in Easter week, 1845, in a house near Regent's Park in London, and both it and the second pioneering community went through troubled early years. The second group, in

Devonport, was attacked in 1849 on the grounds that the sisters were indulging in repugnant Romish practices, such as the wearing of crosses. A subsequent enquiry acquitted them of being disguised Romans in a disguise all too easy to penetrate, but some erstwhile supporters discreetly distanced themselves from possible odium. It took half a century of chequered existence and temporary setbacks to prepare the public for anything like full acceptance of the new phenomenon.

Even so, the religious life in the English Church of England grew startlingly. By 1861, there were eighty-six sisters in seven communities; seventeen years later there were almost seven hundred; and by the end of the century they numbered between two and three thousand—an assessment whose vagueness is perhaps explained by some groups' preference for obscurity. Against this upsurge, only three Anglican sisterhoods, one of them an import, operated in Australia, and the growth of all of them was frustratingly slow.

Another difference between the English and Australian situations was the more vigorous desire in the mother country to increase women's opportunities for active work. Even if some of the hierarchy failed to lend their weight, the cause was backed by influential churchmen, and the Dean of St Paul's, Richard Church, gave full-throated sympathy in an eloquent sermon of 1875:

For a long time, among ourselves at least, it seemed as if there were no room for any special application to the service of the gospel of the gifts and faculties of women...it broke upon us almost like a discovery... that among human occupations and employments...there was a large space for the employment of women: there was work they could do, and none could do but they...intelligent, beneficent, fervent labour for Christ—labour serious, habitual, sustained, like the labour of men...we have a right, we have a cause, to bless God that the ministry of women has again become one of the recognised institutions of the English Church.

Although his advocacy had an unmistakable tinge of relegating women to a public extension of the 'practical' housewifely role, his case was serious and fervent, and gave women a distinct place in the Church's renewal. Retrospectively, the claim could be made that 'To a young woman wishing to engage in full time social welfare work, in nursing or teaching, the Anglican sister-hoods offered opportunities which were not easily found in the world in general'.

The growth of sisterhoods in the Church of England after the mid-1840s 'differentiated that Church from the rest of Protestant Christendom', one historian claims, 'and asserted its affinity to the Catholic and Orthodox world'. No such statement could be made of Anglican communities in Australia. Circumspect as all the sisterhoods were required to be, and accepting that a degree of silence was their lot, CHN was far more isolated in its setting than the English orders were, and lacked the moral and ideolo-gical support of a phalanx of parallel communities. In the utilit-arian, secularized society of Australia, where God tended to be regarded at best as chairman of the board, debate on religious questions was sparse and uninspired. Besides, the Anglican Church lacked authoritative establishment status, and faced vociferous competition from the other denominations. On the doctrinal position of women's work in the church, there was little discussion, although Esther was clearly an ardent and uncompromising advocate, and CHN propagandized for itself through *In Our Midst* and its concoction of a dynastic succession of churchwomen who fought their way to celibate status through mighty trials which sometimes included marriage. Blunt though the magazine was about women's potential for dynamic action, it did not draw theoretical conclusions on the woman's role, and was unswervingly conservative in its attitudes towards married women.

The difference in the numerical strength of the movement in the two countries was matched by a gulf in intellectual sophist-ication and passion. The English revival was deep, widespread, and attracted some of the most powerful intellects of the age. J. M. Neale was credibly able to reserve a prime place for the Oxford Movement in the course of Christianity:

I very much doubt whether, in the whole History of the Catholic Church there is anything more wonderful than the revival which the last thirty years have witnessed in the Church of England... Yes: God did indeed know, he foresaw the wonderful outpouring of his Holy Spirit that he was about to vouchsafe to England.

Flooding across the at times arid plain of theology, the revival 'carried a spiritual renewal inescapably with it'.

From such English soil CHN sprang directly; but it was not part of a widespread renewal in the Anglican Church in Australia, nor was it surrounded by an intellectual ambience providing a link between theory and practice, theology and life. Hiding circumspectly for nearly twenty years under the deaconesses' garb, it attracted criticism, but it did not generate a full-scale debate on the place of sisterhoods within the Catholic tradition of the Church. So, while Esther did not deviate from her commitment to the full religious life, there was no body of doctrine or indigenous spiritual movement to confirm the conventual as well as the practical nature of the Community she formed. In its visible form, CHN was pushed towards an emphasis on works.

The slow growth of the Community and the onerous demands made on it also helped to emphasize the practical activities of the religious life, while the Melbourne diocese, aware of social needs, strongly favoured the creation of an institution of deaconesses which could be justified by precedents in the primitive church, rather than a sisterhood bound by conventual ties. When a commentator in the *Church of England Messenger*, November 1883, considered the implications of the Bishop of Winchester's speech on 'Sisterhoods and other Church Organisations', he opined that for Melbourne 'What is wanted among us now is not the conventual ministry, but the parochial'. In sisterhoods, there were possibilities for an independence unavailable to deaconesses who would serve 'under the authority and direction of pastor and bishop'. The concentration on male initiatives to send women sallying forth when and as directed, rather than as they found convenient, was strong. Group organization was preferred to individual effort, because of ingrained female weakness: 'Women differ from men in not being able to work on by themselves without the support and comfort which they get from the sense of association with others'.

Fortunately, along with weakness went a willingness for self-sacrifice, for they were prepared to do unpalatable and risky work—as proven by the Bedford deaconesses who, during a recent panic, had 'nursed the small-pox patients when nobody else could be found to go near them'. In repayment for their spirit of reckless compliance, deaconesses should certainly be given 'considerable privileges' in the Church.

In September 1891 Synod debated the comparative merits and demerits of sisterhoods and orders of deaconesses, without direct reference to the dangerous theological package Esther had placed in their midst, although they can scarcely have been unaware of the direction she was likely to take. Some members thoroughly approved the validity of the deaconesses' position, which represented devotion without pretension, while others looked with horror at the untrustworthy shoals that eddied around the sisterhoods. In moving a motion which would advance the cause of deaconesses and allow sisterhoods to slip in behind their skirts, the Revd George Spencer deplored the antagonism towards them which was, in his view, rooted in:

ignorance or from the idea that it is an imitation of Rome. Deaconesses' work demanded sisterhoods. They are compatible with extreme Protestantism... In England they are thoroughly recognised... There is a general revival of community life in the Church, and it should be under proper regulation and regular synodal recognition.

Adding his approval, Canon Chalmers pointed out that there were five times as many sisters as deaconesses. Although he drew the line at permanent vows, he pronounced in a thunderclap of ecclesial adjectives that sisterhoods were 'Scriptural, Primitive, Catholic, and Anglican'. Other supporters of the motion repeated the hoary truth that sisters, protected by the sacrosanct nature of their calling and their dress, could enter 'places where other Christian bodies would not venture', and cited the Salvation Army as proof of 'the worth of women's work'. Some affirmative arguments had backhanders built into them: recognition of sisterhoods gave no real advancement to 'High Church teaching', while they would at least serve to corral 'well-intentioned and fussy ladies' and keep them from trampling too wildly over the preserves of the parish priest.

The opposition then weighed in vociferously with Archdeacon Langley's move to excise from the motion all reference to sisterhoods, on the grounds that vows were 'positively unscriptural, contrary to Christian liberty and the ideal life', and that sister-hoods were grounded in 'Scriptural despotism...a pure wife and mother [was] as chaste as any nun'. He found a backer in the Dean of Sydney, who sourly expostulated that 'sisterhoods were not all that novels made them out... It was nobler for a woman to live in the world and let her light shine'. The weight of the gathering favoured cautious and apologetic recognition of sisterhoods as well as deaconesses, and the original motion was passed by a healthy majority.

At the 1902 Church congress, the debate was renewed in virtually identical terms. Opponents defended the ordinary Christian from the special claim of self-sacrifice made by brother-hoods and sisterhoods; supporters again went through their appeal to the ancient origins of the 'female deaconate'. Discussion was dominated by a paper from Fr E. S. Hughes of St Peter's Eastern Hill, on 'Brotherhoods', which he favoured as a 'protest' against the values of Andrew Carnegie and Cecil Rhodes: 'there were...signs that warned them in Australia to be prepared to understand and to welcome the revival of the old system of community life'.

Muffled reverberations of the Evangelical/Anglo-Catholic de-bate continued, despite attempts by the *Church of England Messenger* to soundproof the issues and prevent 'party spirit' from degenerating into factionalism. Over the next few years the paper printed occasional uncontentious reports on the 'Sisters' work' which carefully skirted any mention of religious vows and concentrated on the social-work function. The granting of CHN's charter in 1912 went unmentioned, although a short article on deaconesses linked sisterhoods to them, as though by stealth, and the archbishop launched an appeal for funds to engage curates or deaconesses in the densely populated parishes where the sisters most often worked. Although a quiet mention of the granting of CHN's charter was slipped into an article on the Mission's good works (1914), there was no serious discussion of the claims of sisterhoods in this 'official organ of the diocese' over the period of the Community's creation and consolid-ation.

The strength of a minority Anglican attitude towards women's claim for fuller participation in the Church was shown in early 1914, when the archbishop found himself defendant in a Supreme

Court action brought by a member of his Church Assembly intent on quashing a bill that allowed women to vote for members of Synod, Hugh Lathrop Murray of East Malvern: it was not 'ever contemplated that women should be active members of the Church'. This cranky attempt to deny women voting rights comparable with those they had in the community at large was disallowed. Perhaps the groundswell of Anglican opinion was better represented by the Revd Edward Knollys' article in the *Church of England Messenger*, 'A Girl's Vocation' (13 February 1914): only in the rarest case would a young woman make it as a missionary or nun:

for the majority of girls there should be no great difficulty in following their vocation at home. If you have household work to do, it will occupy much of your time; if you have leisure, there are books and friends, and work outside among those less fortunate than yourself. Others with more experience than you have had will help you find you[r] work if you really wish to work, and guide you in your choice of books.

Given the querulous tone of the theological dialogue and the blanket of conservatism many churchmen wished to throw over the condition of women, the Community's operations were often anonymous and obscure. A condition partly forced on the Community, this was also a metaphysical ideal: as evidence of complete willingness to submit oneself to the supernatural, the human face was to be veiled, if not obliterated. As Esther said in her 1914 'Notes on the Religious Life':

Recollection keeps us to a hidden life in God... Interior self-denial is an outcome of recollection... We must not forget that it is our life, and not our work which is important... What is wanted is not your works—but your being—not your gifts—but yourselves.

In a worldly environment that counselled circumspection, the low profile was also an aspect of 'domestic economy', she said. Her injunctions to secrecy are not simply a code of loyalty stretched to extremes; they show canny awareness of the sheer commonsense of stifling the kind of gossip, tantalizing to outsiders, that might threaten the Community's existence:

In all Mission Houses there are occasionally outsiders—visitors who may be in the house. And at times these may be very curious as to the inner working of the Community. The rule forbids any un-reserve. It is no outsiders' business as to what the Sisters eat or wear or think—or what they are going to undertake, and it is the Sisters' business to guard loyally all matters pertaining to the community and never to divulge anything of importance for the sake of gratifying idle curiosity or the delight of hearing one's own voice. We might also take warning as a preceding rule has mentioned, not to speak of any other Sister, or to speak only good.

An unforeseen consequence was that personal tensions were liable to be internalized, and in the developing hot-house atmosphere these strains could be aggravated by being denied spontaneous expression.

The early sisters have left few traces of their individual personalities. There is a small satchel of documents: Sister Frances's prayer-book, Sister Gertrude's account of 'The Northern Houses', Sister Agnes's Australian fairy-tale, Sister Bertha's diary of the 1927 trip to England with the foundress, Sister Ella Mary's account of the Order of the Good Shepherd and the uneasy account of her visionary experiences, Sister Julian's books of broadcasts, 'This is the Victory' and 'Joy Cometh'. But the record is both slender and askew, thanks to human intervention. Julian's radio talks were, despite her protests, vetted by the chaplain of the time, an imposition that deeply distressed her masterful character. Even her letter of complaint about this gratuitous censorship was recently destroyed. Only a few scraps remain of Sister Elizabeth's voluminous commitment to the adage 'I pray on paper'. The effacing of ordinary sisters was all the more effective because the Superiors were the cynosure and taken to be the shining symbols of the Community's existence—so their letters and addresses have been kept; but even the foundress was subject to a scarcely credible act of obliteration from within, when one sister, angered by the closure of St Ives, disposed of most of her surviving writings. Events within the cloister walls are not necessarily conducted with more reasonableness and refinement than those in the secular hurly-burly.

The photographic record, as well, fixes on the Community's

works, and the impression is usually demure, if not prim. Few portrait studies that seek to draw out individual character exist, and those that do are not always accurate. Sister Alice, for instance, is the subject of a photograph in which she looks lenient and yielding to vanishing point. It seems unlikely that she was. Group photographs, however, are more common, and in the informal snaps with children the sisters look like surrogate mothers absorbed in their youngsters, while ceremonial occasions show them muffled in the black habit leaving clergy and visitors as the more striking presences.

In one of the earliest pictures, Esther, Ellen and Christina are disposed about a table. Christina is sewing and Ellen, hands clasped on a book, is gazing at her, both young and vulnerable-looking, while Esther, glasses perched on the end of her nose, reads as if submitting to a formality and disapproving of the self-publicity implied. As producer of the House of Mercy nativity plays (with a life-size cut-out for Mary, none of the resident girls being thought to be pure enough), Kathleen appears with the cast, but beside her strapping young actresses she is a wraith. 'On deck', Bertha stands on a lower level than the foundress who is somewhat comically perched on a ladder, surrounded by ships' funnels; the young sister looks quizzical and sharp, an expression at odds with her subordinate and protective pose.

Later, the symbolic nature of this picture of Esther and Bertha is clarified, for it seems that Bertha, an eleventh child whose mother died after the birth of the twelfth, had a dependency that may have been 'rather embarrassing for the Mother Foundress...a clinging...she put her in her mother's place, the mother she'd never had'. And this was not the only mother–daughter relationship to flourish in the Community's early days; for given that many of the first sisters lived into their eighties, a few even into their nineties, there is also living memory to testify to some of these matters and flesh out a picture of those who made up the Community in its formative years.

The authority of memory, especially when the responses come from the quick as an unexpected question is put, has an authenticity that written assessment lacks, but it is unreliable and untidy. The muslin of some memories has a more generous weave than others, allowing evidence of frailties to slip away;

and yet the tighter weave that catches the adversities and transgressions is not necessarily more accurate. As well, the retrospective glance attempts to find a pattern, and so may fix on a distorting emphasis. For instance, the belief that most of the first generation belonged to 'the upper crust' may have a basis in truth but be exaggerated by an unconscious desire to see the Community taking a different direction in the present.

Memory is also overlaid by the summoning up of the particular, often peculiar relationship between the one who remembers and the one remembered. One sister felt that an older colleague who had impressive child-care qualifications and spent much of her Community life with children, did not in fact like them; but her own very different behaviour may have coloured her views, since as against the regimented, sometimes stingy style of bringing up children in institutions, this sister exerted herself to make their lives as relaxed and home-like as possible, and remembers being rebuked for teaching the children the common name for dandelions—wet-the-beds. The strenuous fight she had to allow the children clothes that were marked as their own was resolved on her vehemently asking the offending sister how *she* would like wearing the other sisters' underclothes in rotation. 'We haven't got the natural inbred trust you find in a family', one sister remarked; there are strong cross-currents inside community life, but no inevitable unities.

The first sisters can now only be recalled when they were old and had relinquished their full powers. Incapacitated and dependent, the softer side of often imperious natures may emerge. A lot of mellowing has gone on; and yet in extreme age inhibitions and sensitivity to other opinions frequently drop away, allowing a unique intensity of character to surface. Not surprisingly, the human failings of the dead are seldom mulled over by those who recall them now: 'a darling', 'a dear', 'a saint', 'loving', 'devoted' are words which recur, with 'outstanding' especially prominent. The wildly diverging personalities that have been contained in the seeming strait-jacket of Community life are gathered under the shade-tree comment that all the sisters have been different, but each has had something unique to offer.

The embargo on speaking ill of the dead overlays the only considerable documentary source on the individuals who came to the Community in Esther's time, the 'Book of the Dead', and this record is often frustrating for its omissions. Its entries, written as reminiscences of old age, depend for strength and flavour on their authors. The knowledge that nobody could be found to write an obituary for one key member of the Community, presumably because they could not bring themselves to be nice about her, puts the process of compiling the book in an odd light. To a degree, the dead are all mythologized; the notes on them are distillations from individual life-stories and a philosophy that gathered all its subjects into a meaningful metaphysical framework; difficult personalities are exonerated by the suffering they endured, just as dominating ones are tolerated for the frustrations they had to contend with. Consulting the 'Book of the Dead' is a search for almost inaudible resonances, always aware that its silences may be more powerful indicators than what it admits.

Despite this, an unexpectedly vivacious picture comes through, most unexpected perhaps in the degree of eccentricity in a Community modelled on the rigid Victorian template. The warrior saint and the church mouse seem to have been the predominant types, with forceful disposition ('a little spitfire', 'a real Tartar') naturally attracting most attention. When private tastes in underwear were still allowed, pink and blue bow-bedecked knickers used to appear on the line. A new bra fitting at Myers was requested by an octogenarian. A surfer in her seventies had 'a puckish sense of humour, a real waggish sense of humour...a tomboy, if you could describe a sister like that'. Another, 'a real old bully...one of those dragons who really loved you not to be frightened of her...a duchess...big, beetling eyebrows', in old age confronted a surgeon with the command, 'Doctor, this leg has to come off. It's so painful I can't bear it. Take it off!' 'Do you know the Creed?' was the first question put to accident victims by a sister concerned with the unfortunates' eternal destination. Sister Mary's 'wonderful telephone ministry' was applauded; 'the bills used to be very expensive'. A novice recalled her first encounter with 'a funny old stick...used to read all night' who got straight down to business: 'Whose penitent are you?'; while a particularly spry body was deemed to be 'masculine to her bootlaces...charging out with a flame-thrower burning the bush'. From being seen publicly as faceless and anonymous, the sisters come into view through their personal

idiosyncrasies instead; features are caught from the dark, like
faces in the glare of a spotlight.

Given the preponderance of strong-willed women and the
unique enterprise that the Community represented, power relationships were complex and could be bitter. With limited opportunities for leadership, aspirants who had a tart sense of
their own quality might be stranded in subservient roles and
react by brandishing the stick in the small but potentially dictatorial arena they had gained. The disappointment of losing a
spot 'in charge' when an institution closed, led one vigorous
wielder to the Florence Nightingale solution of retiring in disgust
to bed.

This problem was exacerbated by the authoritarian mould
in which they were formed, Victorian women carrying their
Victorian expectations like iron-bound hurricane lamps into
the twentieth century. Esther herself was born in the 1850s,
and most of her lieutenants well before the turn of the century.
Although details are not always known, many of these women
also came from middle or upper-middle-class backgrounds, daughters of a bishop, a judge or dentist, prosperous businessman, or
humbler watchmatcher or teacher. A private education, by
school or governess, enhanced these secure origins, as did the
continental touch of travel in Europe and, occasionally, the last
polish of finishing school.

For daughters of the well-to-do to devote themselves to the
task of helping the poor was a pattern on English home ground,
and can make it seem that CHN was bathed from the font in
conservatism of nearly indelible dye. Modern sisters sometimes
comment that their predecessors were dispensing patronage and
exerting the power that goes with a dogged display of good
works. Even if they did not come from good backgrounds, 'they
still behaved as if they did... [They] were English, structured
gentry', who treated the novices like servants. But the severity
of this view is a recent accretion, and overlooks such complicating
facts as the high proportion of the first stalwarts who, as
infants or small children, had lost one or both parents, and the
manifestly chequered careers of families who came to Australia
to recoup their fortunes. An alternative feeling is that, although
'behind the scenes all these old Sisters liked their starched table

napkins and their nice silver', their interaction with their charges
was remarkable for its lack of 'snobbishness' and 'class consciousness'; 'all those early Sisters had that rapport with the Mission
people'. However, the English orientation and refinement are
undeniable; one dyed-in-the-wool anglophile prided herself on
never having set foot in a church that was not Anglican.

Another distinguishing feature of the first generation was its
daunting capacity for hard physical work: 'they were made of
sterner stuff', a 1980s inheritor said; 'it's not just Sisters, it's the
older pioneers'. Tales of the feats of octogenarians who could
clamber up to clear spouting after an already strenuous day, or
dig the garden in extreme heat only hours before death, are
legion. The handyman streak could have comical results. At
Cheltenham, the sight of a senior sister singing at the top of
her voice and swinging an axe around her head sent a guileless
intruder scurrying in the belief that he had sprung a ghost.

Suffering, both physical and mental, was withstood. Surviving
major illnesses, often two or three in succession, or long-term
conditions that would make ordinary mortals wilt, was regarded
as admirable, but not exceptional. A baroque emphasis on the
physical torments of the Crucifixion, expressed in gory icons or
statues with writhing limbs and pain-drawn faces, was not the
Community's way, but the very unspokenness of the suffering
central to the Christian mystery allowed a world of private
suffering that was lurid enough, at times, no doubt. This
transference from overt to interior expression was perhaps attractive to girls whose upbringings did not encourage the unrestricted
indulgence of personal grief. Unwillingness to show emotion in
public or in disappointing circumstances was part of the code;
the tensions generated by this stoicism could accumulate to
show in stress-related ailments (skin disorders, obesity), or the
sudden release of pent-up anger that occasionally resulted in
irritational acts such as the destruction of most of Esther's
writings. Asked to make the traditional posy for a profession
ceremony, one sister concocted a tight little nodule of flowers,
a floral symbol of clenched emotions.

Yet 'sense of fun', 'sense of humour' ('Sister Lydia makes you
want to laugh' or 'Sister was a true bohemian') are among the
traits most mentioned. The physical and emotional closeness of

community life probably revived the spirit of the robust and
heedless in women who were unlikely to have had such close
interaction with their contemporaries since their nursery days.
The patterns of authority and submission were formidable, but
they differed from the patriarchal and linear construct of the
Victorian family, and offered a bracing if peculiar liberation.

The contrasting lights and shades of the collectivity apply
also to individuals, many of whom are described as an amazing
amalgam of soft and hard qualities. The sister who in brusque
nineteenth century fashion cropped the hair of absconders from
the House of Mercy, also spent a three-week vigil at the bedside
of a girl dying of tuberculosis. And the manysidedness of the
emotional picture is matched by the variety of talents most
sisters possessed—part of the Victorian reticule no doubt, but a
boon to a group that had to shift for itself in all its activities. A
skilled accountant might also be a good cook, a pianist was
handy with the copper stick, nifty dressmakers were commonplace, and gardeners abounded, which meant that a haze of
fierce competition hovered over the rose beds. Practical capacities were often balanced by an 'artistic bent'; the Community
harboured many embroiderers and several amateur painters; and
when practicalities oppressed, an aspiring bluestocking light-
ened the mundane round with heart-felt renditions from *The
Oxford Book of Mystical Verse*. Many talents, though, never
developed beyond amateurism because of the edict that special
abilities were to be left in the umbrella stand at the convent
door, and a regime of hard work that disallowed the leisure
needed for potentialities to flower.

Fact shading off into speculation and anecdote garnished with
an air bordering on the surreal are evident in the unfinished
embroidery which is all that survives as the life-story of one of
the three original deaconesses, Sister Christina.

In photographs, she is pictured in her youth, pure in profile,
seemingly defenceless, with Esther in formal pose or with the
short-lived Ellen dispensing medicine at the Mission House;
then in dignified old age, posed beside an even more dignified
poodle, planting a tree with a hefty spade, walking with the
governor's wife, wimple slightly askew, a bunch of keys dangling

close to the ground, a walking stick in her right hand. Even more than these pictures, though, the facts of her life are disconcertingly patchy. The 'Book of the Dead' describes her as 'a lovely girl fresh from the Highlands of Scotland'. The personality is praised as 'warm hearted, generous minded, high spirited'. Her family purportedly came to Australia to settle in St Kilda just before Esther's arrival, but her place of origin is otherwise unknown and no birth date is given. Her father's profession and the family's status are unclear, but the kind of rumour that often passes for established fact in the Community suggests they were comfortable and well-connected, even rich—although the sole evidence for this is the claim that the family had wealthy Western District friends (memories of an old grey holiday house at Lorne substantiate the belief). No siblings are mentioned; Christina's education, religious background, and professional training are blanks, and her age at joining the Community is unstated. Her progress into CHN began at the Mission House where she helped on Sundays, and soon after she moved into the Little Lonsdale St house. When the House of Mercy opened in 1892, she was put in charge, and there she remained for the next forty-four years, after which she retired to Community House, dying there in 1938. Perhaps the most significant fact available is her determined retention of the deaconess status she adopted in 1890.

This account is plain to the point of ordinariness, although her long sentence as overseer of the House of Mercy is a startling term to consider. But as her obituarist goes on, the story takes on fictive colour. Her preoccupation with animals looms large:

Her love of animals was almost an obsession and very often in this connection her head did *not* rule her heart, so that to the care of animals she subordinated her consideration for the human kind around her. It was a small matter to her that the staff should wait anything from ten to thirty minutes for a meal, whilst she rescued her cockatoo to bring up to the tea table—Cocky always sat on the back of her chair... At that time Sister's menagerie comprised 4 or 5 dogs of varying breeds, as many cats, two cockatoos, a parrot, a hutch of wild rabbits, one white rabbit (Mopsy) who had the run of the Laundry at night—a goat (Jock) a large white gander (Rex).

This private Noah's ark was so assertive that visiting priests refused to continue services or even to venture inside the grounds until particularly obstreperous dogs were restrained; and one sister remembers that, as a novice, she had to edge around the goat to go to the lavatory.

The well-being of this entourage was so vital that when the House of Mercy was marooned by floods in 1934 the novices were despatched into waist-deep water on a mercy mission that rescued several ducks ecstatically enjoying the downpour, and some hens, one of whom promptly laid an egg in the kitchen and was placed in the open oven to dry off. The lights did not work and there was no hot water, but Christina observing the drenched novices ordered hot baths all round. 'I've got a very soft spot here', she said, touching her habit near the heart. The recipient of this tender comment took it as a personal tribute, only to discover that the soft spot was a white rabbit. But the love of animals was not entirely sentimental: live pigs bought at the Victoria Market for no life-preserving reason escaped from their sack at Flinders St station, causing chaos before being rebagged and carried off.

Other preoccupations were no less eccentric. Suffering from rheumatism as she aged, she began her day at midday, and that day 'went on half the night, and you'd have to listen to her read'—*Hiawatha* being a particular, much repeated and tiresome favourite. A captive audience of weary sisters and novices were disposed about her while she sat 'in full charge'. Yet she was applauded as 'the most patient and sympathetic of women', who attracted hordes of visitors, including many former House of Mercy girls with often insoluble problems to unload. Her tenure at the reformatory was recalled as compassionate and humane. When miscreants absconded, she washed the girls' feet. Her death too was characterized by a spirit of humility:

She was a brave Soul always, but no more so than on her death-bed. 'Don't let them stand'—she whispered during these last moments, when those of the Community who could, had gathered round her bedside.

Sister Elspeth, born in Queensland in 1882 to a family who

held station properties in Stanhope and elsewhere, educated by a governess, and seemingly without professional training, was, more verifiably than Christina, a lady. Her sister is said to have married the Governor of Tasmania. Her governess, who was niece to Canon Handfield, vicar of St Peter's and chaplain to CHN, was responsible ('presumably') for introducing her to Mission House and Esther, encounters which weaned her from her Scots and Presbyterian background. She joined the Community in 1903 at the age of 21, and was professed two years later. 'Coming as she did from a background of affluence, she soon adjusted herself generously to a way of life which particularly in those days of C.H.N. was far from affluent.' Given that she was a pioneer, professed for sixty-two years, her obituary in the 'Book of the Dead' is terse to the point of mystery.

Her experience in the Community began at St John's School and the Mission churches of St Peter and St Mary, Fitzroy, and extended to 'the training and teaching of novices and postulants' before an ordered novitiate programme was introduced. But her main involvement was as Sister Superior at St Ives private hospital.

In the few surviving photographs, her face is fine-featured to the point of sharpness, like an ermine. The tension suggested by this image is confirmed by the story that she would lap the Melbourne Cricket Ground to work off agitation. She is remembered as one who 'thought herself superior', 'an excellent hostess', an English gentlewoman despite her colonial origins, 'a lady and she knew it', marvellous with people, but she 'really was a snob'. 'She loved the vice-regal people [and] Sir Robert Menzies when he used to come and visit people...finger bowls on the trays...with a jasmine flower floating in the top.' St Ives' brass finger bowls are now at the Mother House at Cheltenham, used for less showy purposes, along with the china that was reserved for vice-regal patients.

I know that peace cannot be got without pain—may be a submission so complete that it humbles to the dust. It was my prayer before I reached this decision that He would humble me to the very dust so that I could rise in absolute submission to His will. 'Oh to be nothing, nothing, only to lie at His Feet—A broken and empty vessel For the

Master's use made mete'. A prayer I say many times a day—God only
knows the sin & bitterness of my own heart—the often almost
despairing sense of failure—but through it all He has given me a
Vision, the way that I must tread, & in spite of all it is the path of
peace—though often hard & thorny, 'O'er moor & fen, o'er crag &
torrent'. Success, even in finding the Light we seek, is not always
ours—nor is it ours in other things. Faithfulness *is*. Some day my faith
may show that things are real—that absolution is the blessed thing I
in faith accept it to be. Perhaps too, I may be given a Vision of the
Blessed Presence that I now cling to by faith—but—*go on I must*, as
bravely & cheerfully as I can—& *some* day the Light will break
through & light it all up for me.

Quoted in the 'Book of the Dead' in an entry longer than that of
the foundress, though written by the same scribe, this letter is
pervaded by a sense of futility as taut as a clenched hand, and a
conviction of faith as incisive as the nails of that hand. Its
writer was a decidedly dumpy, round-faced figure, a haphazard
organizer, and a friend of Squizzy Taylor. As court sister, she
went to a hearing, toothbrush and toilet things in her bag,
rather than divulge a criminal confidence.

Ellen Sarah Mawson, born in Geelong in 1879, lost her
mother early and she and her three siblings were scattered
among relatives. Her dentist father remarried a Roman Catholic
who renamed her Helen and sent her to the Nicholson St
convent, Fitzroy. In her late teens she was influenced by 'deep
but not always wise readers & thinkers' to reject religion; but
after a sister's death 'she found her way back to her real Home
in the Church of England', and became Sister Eleanor on St
Andrew's Day 1905.

Apart from this sprinkling of facts, her life is sketchy; no
mention is made of job experience or professional training
before she joined the Community; the date and place of birth
are filled in after the obituary was written, and the date of
her death passed over. However, the plaudits are many: 'the
most acute brain & the largest heart in the Community of
her day...an intense wit...intense loyalty...humble...self-
effacing...a woman of many parts...outstanding'. She was an
exceptional Mission sister who advised on the framing of legislation that brought in the probationary system. At her own

request, she was transferred to take charge of St Elizabeth's Home—Newcastle, and after its closure headed St George's for four years, 'wholeheartedly—albeit with secret fear & dread', seeing the hospital through its most strenuous building programme. Left to manage its affairs while the Superior was overseas, she had an 'inevitable' breakdown, 'pushing along, pushing along', her heart ultimately collapsed. (The privately admitted fact that she was a haphazard organizer may explain the extremity of her downfall.) She became a patient at St George's, then retired to the Mother House where, 'practically worn out' at sixty-four, she managed the workroom. Her last years were spent in 'weakness & weariness of body', her chief pleasure being the small garden where she reclaimed 'wasteland' and grew vegetables. One summer day she left 'that little corner', put away the garden tools, and died a few hours later.

In the face of apparent contradictions and unexplained omissions, Sister Eleanor's 'hidden life' becomes puzzling, if not obscure. The extremes of 'tenacity' and 'endurance' demanded by the religious life can be seen more starkly, pushed perhaps to a self-punishing degree, in the story of Sister Pleasance. She:

had the defects of her good qualities. Her championship of the weak, the sick & the oppressed produced in her a seeming want of sympathy for the rich & successful... Perhaps the very strength of her character made her wish to do violence to herself... To her it was given to know the hardness of the Cross... There are sacred places in the human soul, better shared according to our measure by prayer & sympathy than described.

'An English gentlewoman' is not an appropriate typecasting for Edith Pleasance Ingle, who was born in Gippsland, Victoria, in 1887. Nothing is recorded of her family except that it was 'large', or of her education except that, while she was 'laundry matron' at the House of Mercy in 1913, she decided to do midwifery to facilitate her entry into the Community. Professed on Michaelmas Day, 1920, she was shunted furiously around the Community establishments, working at St George's St Alban's Home, Newcastle, the House of Mercy (in her old job in charge of the laundry), the children's homes St Elizabeth's,

Mayfield, and St Christopher's, Lochinvar, and Mission House where she acted as court sister. She was said to appreciate the simplicity of 'unspoilt' country children, while her directness and realism were qualities thought appropriate to the manage-ment of boys. Her love of farm and country life extended, predictably enough, to an affection for animals, with the cor-ollary of novices trailing into the night, holding lanterns, in search of strays. A desperate hunt for hand-fed lambs continued from one day into the next, only to be resolved when the wanderers, used to the human touch, returned of their own accord.

A spinal defect that necessitated wearing a brace led to her retirement to the Mother House, where she acted as librarian and, once again, found herself in charge of linen. The demands she made on herself continued unabated. Feeling 'united mysti-cally' to the sufferings of the Asian people, she wanted money given to her for a rubber cushion to ease her back pain to be diverted to the Korean sisters of the Holy Cross. The blackness of life fascinated her and allowed no melioration. She was remembered as 'a gloom and doom prophet... You'd sit up in the community room, and she'd say "Did you hear on the news? Fifty people killed in Cambodia. Ten bank robberies"'. This preoccupation with injustice and devastation had its positive side; she was 'left wing definitely...she didn't belong to the Communist Party, but that's only because she hadn't heard of it... Everyone here thought that they had to be Liberal, and she was always the one who'd put the other side'. The 'wealth of tenderness' hidden 'deep in her character' is perhaps symbolized by a climbing rose she planted that is still flowering after decades.

'If I'd been a boy I'd have been a priest': Sister Julian (Margaret Radford, and daughter of a Bishop of Goulburn).

The Community's first graduate (BA, University of Sydney), and one-time head of training for the New South Wales Girl Guides' Association, Julian represents another tragic version of the hidden life. Born in 1897 in Norfolk, England, 'Victorian out of her context, very much the lady of the manse', she was prevented from joining the Community until two years after Esther's death, by a promise to her dying mother that she would look after a younger brother who later became a doctor. After a difficult novitiate, once professed she was put in charge of Mission Hall activities and opened the Community's Adelaide branch. It provided temporary shelter for female alcoholics and drug addicts, and within four years had helped to produce a nervous breakdown in its supervising sister who returned to the Mission House in Melbourne. She became novice mistress, a job she'd always coveted, but after some years asked to be relieved of the position, and thereafter declined physically and mentally.

Even now, this masterful personality arouses ambivalence, admiration tinged with pity, criticism leavened with understanding. For one sister, the melting point only came when she nursed her at the end. Julian was a snob, intellectually (her degree a badge that distinguished her from the common run), and socially as well; and yet she had 'a complete empathy with those [Mission] people, she loved them. It wasn't just a do-gooder attitude; it was genuine affection and concern'. She loved the outdoors and camping, even if this had to be done sternly 'according to the books'. Photographs show her on Brownie and Cub camps, beaming with joyous informality while she dispenses drinks from a jug. Her appointment as novice mistress was regarded by some as an appalling mistake. She treated her novices 'like Girl Guides'—a convenient explanation perhaps for different compulsions—and regarded others as her intellectual inferiors, to be driven with the same fierceness that she applied to herself. Different opinion valued her enthusiasm, generosity of spirit and a sense of humour that embraced 'enjoyment of the laugh against herself'. They were qualities, salty and sparkling, that she was felt to share with her namesake Julian of Norwich.

The key to any frustrations may well lie in the reported comment that had she been a boy she would have been a priest. Forceful and competent, never in a position that marshalled or reflected her true ability, 'there was no way she could fulfill her deepest longings'. 'In the Jungian sense', said one sister, 'the feminine got a *very thin go*'; with her purposefulness and overview of ecclesiastical fundamentals, perhaps she should have been a bishop rather than a religious; and yet so pervasive was the feminine submission forced on her that she had to accept the emasculation of the religious broadcasts which were one of her main contributions to the Community's existence. The temptation to lapse into scorn and acerbity must have been hard to overcome. In exaggerated form she represents the tensions that many of these first sisters had to hold within themselves, while living in outward circumspection, control and simplicity. A token of the degree to which this was achieved is the tribute brought by a woman who lived near the Community's Kalorama cottage when Julian died: a bunch of real old-fashioned primroses with an attached card that read 'A mountain farewell'.

5

A KIND OF COLONIAL MENTALITY

We'd seen ourselves as perpetually expanding... It was a kind of
colonial mentality, expanding, growing larger, moving over the frontiers.

Sister Faith

In December 1931, *In Our Midst* lamented the loss of the 'late
beloved Mother and Foundress, who loved her Mission folk and
knew so well what Christmas, and all the festival brings, means
to them'. There were other causes for sombreness and anxiety,
for the depression was still deepening. At Mission House, ninety
mothers were on the roll for clothing sales, and the sisters had
set up basic palliative measures such as the establishment of a
milk fund for nursing mothers or those with delicate children,
and the creation of an informal domestic banking system to
help towards Christmas expenses. The time-honoured way of
augmenting right attitudes was to encourage those prepared to
contribute, however meagerly, to their own support and not
sink into the trough of dependency.

Perhaps on the principle that in hard times the need to boost
the spirits with a sprinkling of hopeful cases was even more
urgent, the journal maintained its tone of self-conscious, slightly
exasperated good humour, continuing to serve up variations of
the old recipe, the chief ingredient of which was humanity in
its perplexing and pitiable variety. Throughout the gallery of
the derelict, the deserving poor, the inebriate, the wayward

youngster and abandoned wife, the predominant goodness of humanity still showed through—in spite of cases so harrowing that undiluted indignation was the only proper response. Again, the plight of women and children prompted the most vociferous compassion. Often the children could be helped, 'leaving the woman free to look for some work. Poor thing—she must face parting with them ultimately, for no one wants a woman with two children'. But Mission Hall bazaars and harvest festivals continued to be touted as rowdy affairs, with their swag of pumpkins, apples, jams, and the wily but benign stork arrived at St George's on schedule, while Father Christmas trundled round the children's homes as if depression were a hiccough from Wall St dyspepsia.

Times may have been grim, but CHN was in a stage of consolidation and growth. Although many of the original stalwarts were ageing, the accretions of time, and a steady if not massive flow of novices, meant that the Community had expanded. A few months before Esther's death, Council had been informed that 'At present the Community has no room to cope with the number of young women offering to join', and that a house for novices was needed. In April 1932, it was resolved that such a house should be established as a commemoration of the mother foundress. At the same time, in accord with the growing emphasis on proper preparation for the religious life, Sister Elizabeth was sent to Wantage to train as novice mistress. By June 1933, seven hundred circular letters had gone out soliciting contributions towards the memorial, and a promise of £1000 had been secured, provided that the house was on ground controlled by the Community. (Ownership problems concerning St George's, which had been left to the sisters but vested in the Mission, intensified a feeling that all future properties and gifts should be in CHN's name, 'to avoid all this trouble & confusion'. Such a resolution would also provide a measure of financial security, particularly for the sisters in old age, should that be needed later on.)

In early 1934, the warden observed contentedly that the Community now ran seven institutions in Melbourne, three in Newcastle, and two in Goulburn. It had established itself within the Church as exemplifying the life of profound and unstinting commitment. And when Sisters Louisa, Lorna and Catherine were professed in the Mission House chapel, *In Our Midst* surveyed the packed scene with sober pleasure:

the dedication of the three 'living stones'—surely the most fitting memorial of all to her who under God was the Foundress of this Community, and the first fruits of the Religious Life in our land... Every corner in the Chapel—all too small for such occasions—was filled, and nine priests were in the sanctuary.

More palpable stones were in the offing, however. In September 1934, Sister Alice, who had been elected Superior for the three-year term after Esther's death, retired, having filled with 'gentle tact and unfailing faith' a role that the warden deemed unprecedentedly difficult. Her successor, Sister Ida, a forty-eight-year old woman of unswerving strength of purpose, had been professed in 1911 and in charge at Brighton for the previous eighteen years. She was installed by the archbishop in the Mission House chapel on 6 October 1934, and attended her first Council meeting the next month, announcing 'tremendous plans for the future' with her stout-hearted troop of '40 Sisters & Novices all intent on carrying on with the spirit of the Mother Foundress'. She intended visiting all the Community's houses, and since Sister Elizabeth had now returned from England 'thoro'ly equipped to train novices', the Community's greatest need was a place which would combine facilities for novices and a retirement refuge for older sisters. CHN had ideas of buying four acres from the House of Mercy estate which belonged to the Mission; in the event, the land was given and, with this encouragement, Ida announced that she hoped to have full plans and estimates ready for the next meeting.

In July 1935, tenders for Community House were being called. The annual meeting of the Mission was told that the structure was to be 'a fitting memorial to the Mother Foundress... This house is growing out of the settled determination of the Sisters themselves'. With breathless excitement, *In Our Midst* described the October laying of the foundation stone by Lady Huntingfield, who looked so at ease with her place in the colonial structure that she might have been opening the central post office in New Delhi. The building was

there, in bricks and mortar, right up to the roof. . . . The scene might have been taken from a medieval Pageant, as the procession of Sisters wended its way across the green paddocks, joined by a long queue of white-robed clergy, and together they approach the building and the waiting people to the strains of 'All people that on earth do dwell', the voices of people, Priests and Sisters blending and floating out over the field and highways to the world around.

The establishment of the mother house was lauded as 'the first religious house of the Church of England in Australia, definitely planned and built as a Home for Sisters and the training of novices, and as such will stand as a milestone in the Church of England in this country of the Mother Foundress's adoption'.

By February 1936, Community House was almost finished at a cost of £7700—of which the lion's share of £6000 had been gathered by the sisters themselves—and the building, collegiate and ecclesiastical-looking in its flowerless and almost treeless surround, was dedicated by the archbishop on 26 May, the birthday of the foundress. At the Mission's fiftieth annual meeting, the archbishop enumerated recent achievements: the remodelling of St Ives, the improved laundry at the House of Mercy, the new wing at the Children's Home, and the commencement of the new building at St George's; but he reserved special accolades for the significance of Community House, to generate 'an influence that will become more and more a very important factor in the Church life of the diocese'. The completion of the complex was made possible by the announcement in July 1938 that £3000 for a chapel had been received from the Hughes bequest.

The Community was ordering its house in other ways. Early in 1937, Council was informed that CHN was drafting a constitution to replace the antediluvian document in force since 1912 when the sisters were still on the defensive and suspiciously regarded by low-church eyes. Ida later informed Council that the Mission too should revise its outmoded rules and constitution. In the

face of all this purposeful activity, the archbishop's tribute to
the new Superior seemed a modest statement of fact: 'The Rev.
Mother was a real leader & in her hands the fortunes & future
of the Community were safe'. The flurry of expansionary activity had proved exhausting, however, and Council agreed to
find a way of providing £250 to £300 for a well-earned overseas
trip. Farewelled by a huge gaggle of well-wishers bearing flowers,
Ida accompanied by Sister Elspeth sailed for England in early
1939.

Arriving in London in early March, she moved into a chintzy
flower-decorated room at the Ladies' National Club ('about 2
dozen inhabitants, mostly the *elderly* female'), and set off on the
tourist round. Hyde Park, Kensington Gardens, spring bulbs,
Harrods; at Warham Guild Altar Vessels and Ornaments, where
Sister Marabel's work was in particular demand, prices seemed
prohibitive to colonial eyes: 'a whole crib set, to go with the
Bambino we have is £17.10'.

Outside London, the cathedral crypt at Canterbury seemed
to hold the compacted essence of 'our history written in these
stones'; Keble's church at Hursley 'I imagine...almost as Keble
left it—quite simple and plain'. Salisbury provided another
Oxford Movement echo in Clewer House and the Community
of St Denys, and at Glastonbury 'the first thorn tree grew when
Joseph (of Arimathea) planted his staff (we saw some of its
successors in the ruins)'; there was Glastonbury Tor, the elevated
portico that gave a panorama of the mystical Vale of Avalon,
towers, spires, a weft of fields, and the stilled waves of Wells
cathedral in the distance.

But the true goal and crown of the communities was
'WANTAGE—March 22nd Really here!'. The warmth of the
welcome, the comfort of her quarters (a room significantly, she
felt, called 'Discretion'), and the pleasure of observing such a
large community in chapel and comparing procedures, were
tempered by feelings of dislocation aggravated by again experiencing the conventual life: 'my mind is on you the whole
time'.

The uncertainties of the international situation also impinged.
Newspapers were anxiously seized as soon as they reached the
streets, all church services included prayers for peace, and at
Wantage the nuns were fitted with gas masks. Yet Holy Week

enclosed her in its own peace. Tenebrae reached a powerful climax in the black chapel with a single light illuminating 'the prostrate forms down the aisle'. In the cloister, the sepulchre, three empty crosses, sealed stone, cords and ladder, hammer and nails, pussy willow and chestnut branches ready to burst into flower, awaited the army of flower-bringers who would assemble an Easter garden of potted geraniums, coleus, maiden-hair fern, mossy paths sprung with primroses '& a perfect statue of SS. Peter & John arriving', for the culminating ceremonies of Easter Day:

The Chapel was packed. As the line came out of chapel—(several crocodiles rolled into one!) the Sisters lined up on each side of the corridor & the Mother kissed each one. There was great jubilation & chatter & exchanging of cards & everybody kissed everybody else. I later found a box for me, containing a perfectly wonderful white stole—a gift from C.S.M.V. to C.H.N. for the new Chapel... In the procession a station was made at the Easter Garden where the stone had been rolled away & a light showed the angels, & the linen clothes lying—the Music & everything was simply magnificent.

Being taken aside by the Superior, however, to be told of Prime Minister Lyons' death in Australia, and the accumulating tensions in Europe, was a sobering note that turned her thoughts homeward with a sharper sense of CHN's individuality and vivacity:

I can see that it is wonderful for the Church to have a Centre of the Religious Life such as this—but we too have our part—in our own humbler way... I didn't sleep much last night (which was unusual) but the war—& Mr Lyons—& *your* Easter gave me a lot to think about.

The return to London was made through Oxford, cradle of the Movement, and a string of country churches golden with daffodils and primroses. In the capital, Anglican idiosyncracies flourished profusely as ever. At a service at St Alban's, Holburn, the officiating bishop was robed and disrobed, shifted and shunted from one spot to another like a ventriloquist's doll: 'They did everything it was possible to do—Italian, Wantage would call it'. A retreat at St Margaret's convent, East Grinstead, began with some pantomimic comedy:

it was difficult to keep from having hysterics. The orphans came in—They might have stepped out of a mediaevel picture in their antiquated white cotton sunbonnets with enormous flaps down the back... Vespers began, the orphans singing every scrap, while the Sisters remained mute!... Anything more businesslike than those orphans cannot be imagined, but it was awfully funny.

The bizarries multiplied. On one occasion, Ida found herself ninth in seniority in a gathering of superiors 'mostly ancient', whose habits and headdresses represented every permutation of ecclesiastical fashion, and who came from communities that varied from the strictly contemplative to a small mission band that specialized in the quixotic practice of speaking at village fairs.

Perhaps 'the nearest thing to home we have yet seen' was the Kentish Town Mission House of the Community of the Resurrection, but the Community of the Epiphany at Truro pleased because of its music, more approachable than the 'glorified' Wantage performances, and the more manageable size of the Community which gave 'an atmosphere of "home" that is lost in the larger ones'. The Truro sisters, however, were already dwindling, most of them decrepit, and few novices to replace them. She did not foresee that the same problem would confront most communities within a decade or two, CHN included. Her gaze was on particular traits instead—for instance, the elitist procedures at Clewer where most domestic work was relegated to lay sisters, a class distinction which had been rejected by CHN. Similar divisions even obtained in their House of Mercy where sixty girls either toiled in the laundry or, in fine aristocratic contrast, sewed exquisite lingerie for sale. Or again, there were communities which gave the impression of being placidly wedged in a time-lock. St Thomas' Convent, Oxford, was intriguing in its unworldliness, exaggerated to the point of unreality at times:

On Sunday quite a sane Wantage one was talking to me about telephones—(They have no telephone here) 'Telephone, what would we do with a telephone? And where would we put it—couldn't be in

Mother's room—Think of her being bothered with all the noise &
distraction of that!!... And you couldn't have it in the Community
room—certainly not! And the Portress' Room—what would they do
with it—the Portresses are all old & deaf & wouldn't hear it if did
ring!—! As my mind went home I wanted to laugh & laugh. There
wasn't the slightest thought of ever wanting to use a telephone
themselves & no idea whatever that it might be a convenience to
people to be able to ring them up.

'Childlike simplicity', Ida noticed, was able to coexist quite
well with 'childlike perversity'. The Sisters of the Love of God
at Fairacres, Oxford, represented a further extreme of withdrawal;
they never left the convent, except for medical reasons, even
spending their rest times in the convent garden which had been
agreeably furnished with 'the most comfortable up-to-date little
garden house you could imagine...a revolving affair, & one
can get sun, or shade as one wills... I thought that if all else
failed it wouldn't be too bad to be a contemplative!' Sometimes
the ceremonial simply wearied. The Sisters of Bethany seemed
to bow to one another at every encounter, and to double their
bowing-rate at meals; the nuns of Ascot Priory were suspected
of having reached rarefied crags of ritual observance, as they
coursed about in 'purple habits & girdles & black veils full of
pins—all rather delapidated'.

The overall experience filled her with enthusiasm for developments at CHN, Melbourne, and a conviction that her own
community was set on the right course. It would never be
surrounded by the artistic riches of the Established Church. Yet
Community House, even though there was more to be done to
it, stood up well in any comparison with older English convents;
and unlike many of the English communities which were dwindling, her own was in an expansionary phase. All the same,
there were strengths and resources that CHN still lacked. Its
buildings, especially its facilities for child-care, might be more
recent and consequently more workable, but the English groups
possessed more effective support systems. Most had full-time
chaplains, a situation that CHN longed for. 'I remember how
much work we have—& how small our numbers are,' wrote
Ida, 'but more & more I believe in the special call of C.H.N.
Melb. to do what it is doing & to be what it is'. She anticipated

that Community House would increasingly become the hub of their activities, had 'visions of what Cheltenham can be in the future', and was uplifted by finding how many people thought that CHN was 'a bit marvellous considering all we haven't had'. A visit to the Archbishop of Canterbury at Lambeth Palace was 'one of the *great* moments, and one which we can each take—every one of us—as a direct commendation to God from His grace of Canterbury'.

In the weeks remaining, there was time for a mid-August trip through Yorkshire and beyond, rich with the evidences of a much older Christianity. 'I do love this Northern Christianity— and tomorrow we hope to sleep at Lindisfarne.' Bede's church at Jarrow held an unexpected trove of ornaments and recent embroideries 'all done by a Miss Davies', one of those spinsters whose contribution to the decorative holdings of the Church has been immense. Back at Oxford, Ida picked some sprigs of heather for home from the spot where Pusey had read and meditated.

Even in the peace of the Wantage convent, however, 'the aweful "war" tension from which we never get away' was being felt. Keeping up with the tremors of the international situation was not easy, since news was restricted to bald summaries given by the Superior at morning conferences, and Ida felt increasingly concerned and isolated. While the Wantage Community was holding its retreat, inevitability asserted itself:

Sunday, September 3rd And a momentous Sunday it is for this morning war was declared... The Retreat went on—more or less quietly—with summaries of the news given us each day. By Friday we knew the worst would happen, and living through that last day was a test of self-control. It was a marvellous retreat—kept at the same high level all through, but one read the trend of events outside in the last day's addresses, when in to the theme of 'Worship' and 'Adoration' was brought that of the necessity of the Cross. It was the contemplative mind coming down to the hard fact of what was happening round us.

Within hours, Australia too was at war.

The Oxford area was a concentration of military camps and aerodromes. On a country drive that was likely to be their last in England, Ida and her companions were suddenly confronted by a private aerodrome converted for war service, packed with bombers and protected by an armed air-force guard. The ominous military hardware stood out bleakly against the rural backdrop, now berried red and black and leaved from saffron to umber, and small village churches in the swing of harvest festival preparations.

The ship she was booked on was cancelled, and then all sea traffic halted: 'the one idea in my mind is to get to you if it is at all possible'. Thankfully, the delay was to last only a month. Her final visit to Wantage was marked, as if to define an era, by the death of Sister Dora, 'the last of those who knew our Mother'. In spirit Ida was already back with CHN, its annual retreat and chapter-meeting: 'I have been following you all through the hours, trying to allow for the difference in time'. The final days were a count-down: 'We have our Embarkation Cards, and our train leaves St Pancras for Tilbury at 1.25 p.m. tomorrow week'. Their ship was painted grey for inconspicuous-ness, carried guns, and steamed over its course 'at record-speed'. On the Feast of St Thomas (21 December) the longed-for moment occurred: 'Our port holes were opened at 6 a.m. and it was with a sense of intense thankfulness & joy that one looked out, & saw our own Australian coast—the first touch of *Home* . . . in spirit we have never been away.'

Her return coincided with the completion of the chapel at Community House—a meditative space washed with wheaten light, 'a city that is at unity in itself', consecrated on 22 May 1940 with the words 'May the God of Peace grant peace eternal to this house. May Christ the Prince of Peace bestow His Peace that passeth understanding, and may the Holy Spirit of Peace speak peace to this House from henceforth for evermore.' The same year saw the endorsement of the new constitution that 'should stand without alteration for many years', and the an-nouncement that the Rule, customary and office were also being revised to make them more appropriate for a Community mature in years and confident in its expectations.

The expansionary spirit had not been dampened by the hectic activity of the pre-war years, or the lack of peace that made the archbishop's words in consecrating the chapel sound so insistent, sonorous and unearthly. In the middle of 1939, Sister Kathleen had visited Alice Springs where she observed 'a most wonderful opportunity for the Sisters... If only we had more Sisters'. Meanwhile, an admirer in outback Narrandera kept urging the sisters to convert her mansion into a hospital, and shortly into the war an invitation arrived for the Community to expand its work into Adelaide. Their gesture of confidence in the future for 1943 was the creation of a fund for building a new Babies' Home; the next year a further two acres at Cheltenham were purchased in anticipation of extending Community House.

However, realities had to be faced, and requests from the Bishop of Goulburn for further commitment to his diocese were temporarily refused because of a shortage of sisters. The kite of expansion could be flown, but for the duration of the war it had to be kept on short strings, and the mood was inevitably sombre. *In Our Midst's* 'A Reflection on the Church and the war' addressed itself to the sensitive question of the relevance of prayer in combating the horrors that had been unleashed:

there is *no other way*. The short cuts all prove failures before long. Many have been tried out. The favourites at present in some quarters are Communism and Fascism, according to taste. A new Social Order is going to make everything in the garden lovely. But will it?

And with Pearl Harbour close at hand, a special meeting of Chapter in December 1941 was told:

our very biggest contribution to the war effort must be our quiet faith—our simple steadfastness. We must prepare ourselves to help other people spiritually as well as materially... I think that must be the special work of the Mother House...to pray for the world... radiating an atmosphere of calm and courage, and of the presence of God.

As, slowly, an Allied victory began to seem within reach, the shape and temper of the post-war world became a preoccupation. The editorial on 'Incarnate Love' reflected that no nation was blameless: 'all have tolerated such evils as unemployment, slum dwellings, malnutrition, insecurity...exalt[ed] nationalism or imperialism'. But a new spirit appeared to be stirring, and class

barriers and national differences might be overcome and social
justice genuinely pursued:

We are not bidden to *like* our enemies, to feel for them an emotional
affection, but we are bidden to love them with the love of the will,
the highest kind of love... Is it too much to hope that they may be
enemies now converted into friends?

In her address to Chapter in 1945, Ida affirmed that the Community too had 'dedicated ourselves anew...to preparing ourselves to play our part in what we hope will be a brave new
world'; but relearning peace-time rhythms was as painful and
invigorating as building from the ashes, and expectations of
quick fulfilment were doomed. The Community and its affairs
were inevitably caught up in the seesawing hopes and disappointments of post-war turmoil. 'There has never been more
sense of frustration and failure', Chapter was told in 1946; 'in
many avenues of our work it has seemed almost impossible to
"get anywhere"'. The widespread feeling that radical alterations
to society were required meant adapting to new methods and an
open-minded preparedness to change.

   Some of the changes were to require a fundamental reordering
of the Community's work.

Actually, the winds of change had set in years before, and the
first of the CHN enterprises to feel their effects was the House
of Mercy. Work there had continued on the lines laid down in
the nineteenth century, except in that famous heart of the
undertaking, the laundry. Despite misgivings in some Council
members as to whether modernization was 'in the best interest
of the girls', machinery had been installed in 1934 and proved
'an unqualified success'. The new equipment enabled girls to be
instructed 'not only in the homely ways of the past, but in the
more modern ways', and there was a gratifying surge in
receipts. (The penitents' moral fibre was not entirely shredded,
however: 'The girls do the actual washing by hand; so they still
receive that valuable training which means so much to their
future'.) With this improvement out of the way, Ida informed
Council of the 'great need for a general reform'; Sister Christina

had retired after 'nearly half a century', in charge, and had been replaced by Sister Bertha who arrived with a decade of experience in gaol and court work and 'modern & up-to-date ideas to cope with the situation of today'.

The urge for improvement had been assisted by a visit in 1937 from the Inspector of Charities, C. L. McVilly, who declared that the Charities Board would not intervene in the affairs of the house if sufficient renovations were made. Though 'the prison like conditions of early days had gone', as McVilly noted, there was room for more to be done— a hefty £6000 worth. *In Our Midst* launched into a spate of propaganda articles to exact donations from that often unreliable flock outside the walls. The editors suppressed the temptation to lament girls who fell by the wayside or disappeared up the primrose path of dalliance, and concentrated on positive outcomes instead:

It has been, or at least we have endeavoured to make it, a literal following of our Lord's command to seek and save the lost sheep. . . no work that has been done in connection with the Mission has a more wonderful history than this, nothing into which has been put more self-sacrifice and hard work.

Examples of astounding rehabilitation were culled from the casebooks. The blacker the unreformed personality, the more satisfactory it was as an example to stimulate potential donors. The occasional old girl was enlisted to recount her time at the reformatory, and 'The House of Mercy Forty Years ago' blithely described a merry-go-round of helpful instruction, hymn singing, sleeping in on Sundays, charades and birthday celebrations, 'a long tramp to Rose Hedge, or to gather heath and wild flowers. . . Whatever happens nothing can take from me the beautiful memories of the good old days at the House of Mercy'. The laundry was mentioned in passing.

By February 1938, after a town-hall meeting and an appeal in the *Argus*, £2500 was in hand, thanks to a spate of bridge parties, meetings and song recitals, usually in South Yarra. McVilly agreed to try to get the Charities Board to raise its contribution to £2500 if the Council provided £5000. The target was quickly reached (indeed, one manifestly successful Old Girl called herself 'Scrooge' and came good with £100), and the new wing—brick to match the old building, and with facilities for domestic training and space for 'indispensable indoor recreation'—was opened in October at a ceremony under the full-sailed oak planted by Sister Christina. Performing the honours, Lady Huntingfield professed herself deeply interested in 'the science of plumbing' and described the sisters' example as 'a life-giving tonic'; the four hundred guests were 'awaited by the House of Mercy girls, in their bright blue uniforms'.

With this effort expeditiously completed, the need to put a rosy gloss on the girls' moral prospects relaxed, and the old preoccupations reasserted themselves. In fact, the dislocations of war aggravated the problem, and the annual reports resume their lugubrious overview, lamenting the hordes of angry 'delinquent' girls, and the 'extremely exacting nature' of the work. 'Bad heredity, or bad environment, or both' were blamed. In the desperate year of 1942, 'forty unruly girls', some under fifteen, produced an 'outstanding' result in the laundry, but their rebelliousness was hard to contain. *In Our Midst* had to admit that, while some girls were rescued, others 'seem to take to themselves a greater energy of evil than before', and the terse entries of the House of Mercy day-books indicate how drastic the problems were, and how uncodified the range of punishments available to the harassed sisters:

4 Feb 1937 Trying day. Girls restless. Devil rampant. Another encounter with Mary on a Matter of Obedience to the Laundry Sisters. Won!
5 Nov 1937 Pearl still in room on hunger strike. Caved in afternoon tea time & came down stairs. Planted lily of the valley outside cloister wall.
23 Nov 1938 Girls naughty. Cows naughty. Major [the dog] naughty.
21 Oct 1941 Both Girls Shorn & put to bed.
21 March 1946 Stella ordered from Dining Room & then decamped. Praise be!!

Even when the task seemed hopeless, the philosophy encouraged normal girlish interests such as renovating the discarded *haute couture* of the smart:

clothes have their place in the self-respect which goes to the making of a good woman...imagine the astonishment of the famous firm if it

were to see the humble 'and Cheltenham' added to the flaunting
'London and Paris' of its dress tag!

In May 1943, a gratuitous disaster compounded the disciplinary
problem when a typhoid epidemic struck, affecting twenty-one
people at Cheltenham, including four sisters, and caused the
deaths of one girl and a postulant. 'The House of Mercy's War
Effort' continued none the less, and energy was turned to
producing camouflage nets—though here, as in most activities,
the chance for moralizing the work was not lost: 'The girls have
to learn by experience that in knitting, as in the weaving of
one's life, mistakes are more easily made than rectified'. Nevertheless, under the guidance of two practised 'netters', they
assembled over fifty nets, fourteen feet square or larger, in seven
months.

The scene seemed set for a continuance of the pattern that
had existed for over half a century, when suddenly the whole
enterprise began to founder. In March 1946, Council was told
that the laundry had been closed because there were too few
girls to operate it. Ida's report suggested that she believed the
recourse was only temporary, but the dearth of girls continued,
and the coppers and troughs were to be permanently silenced.
The Community could salve itself in the knowledge that 'the
main object...had been carried out as successfully as possible.
But times had changed'. The warden regretted cessation of
'the first social service of the Church in Victoria', but he
admitted that it was a drain financially and in the commitment
of sisters. The annual report addressed itself to the sudden and
puzzling change. One explanation for the scarcity of House of
Mercy candidates was the possibility that 'such girls' were now
'in employment and not coming into the hands of the police
under the vagrancy laws'. There was also a philosophical re-
valuation, and instead of making the girls launder for their
supper, emphasis shifted to providing 'facilities...for their general
education and vocational training'.

In her address to Chapter in 1946, Ida discussed the ameliorative approach:

I think we all realise that the day of the old fashioned reformatory has gone, and that newer methods are needed. After much thought, and discussion from every angle, it was decided to transfer the work of the House of Mercy to the Mission House, experimenting there in a very small way with the 'Hostel' idea for the same type of girl.

The disappointing government grant of £8000 meant that the project had to be limited to three or four girls, and nobody mentioned the fact that two years before the Community was re-emphasizing its preference for a two-year term for girls, so that the beneficial effects of the treatment could be prolonged, and that the outcome now pliably accepted would then have been unthinkable. More usually, the Community, like the Church at large, clung tenaciously to patterns of the past, and by the time they had accepted the inevitable the ground they staked out for themselves was lost. Post-war transformation had taken turns that few foresaw.

The demise of the House of Mercy opened the way for a project the Community had been pondering for several years: a retreat house for the diocese. The commodious if somewhat forbidding red-brick building seemed ideal. After the Chief Commissioner of Police had attended the 1945 annual meeting and confirmed the unforeseen decline in juvenile delinquency (that year only eighty girls had been brought before the Children's Court), *In Our Midst* was immediate and unabashed in adapting to the new possibilities: 'New occasions teach new duties, and the Author of all good looks to find, in His servants, a sense of adventure, tempered by a wise caution. How like, and how *unlike*, the work and circumstances of today are to those of the pioneers...' The age of state welfare was discreetly but inexorably dawning.

By the end of 1946, there were no girls at the House of Mercy and two retreats had been held, the building much enhanced by 'Paint and bright chintzes and the installation of electric light in each cubicle'. Retreat House was an instant success, showing a healthy financial potential and used by other denominations apart from the Church of England. ('Very busy day cleaning after Methodists & preparing for Presbyterians. 14 Deaconesses arrived in time for tea.') The trial period over, Council agreed that 'a comprehensive scheme of alteration [should be] prepared', and *In Our Midst* was quick to recognize

Mission House, Spring Street, clear of debt in 1900.

The leafy luxury of St Ives Hospital, East Melbourne, 1918.

'We weave plans for their future careers; but so many pass out of our ken altogether, and all we can do is to hope we have made them more physically fit to face the battle of life': *above* boys at the Mission Hall *c.* 1912; *below* the Children's Home at Brighton, 1948.

that Retreat House was more than an outmoded facility now conveniently converted; it was to be a powerhouse of stability and refreshment in a world of perplexing change:

in spite of our weariness we cannot escape from the certainty that these changes involve a complete *bouleversement* of most of the things which have spelt stability for so many of us, and out of the chaos which surrounds us, we cling ever more firmly, in a world where there is no peace, to the one stable and certain thing, 'the peace of God'—the peace which passeth understanding.

The *bouleversement* of the times descended on the Community's hospitals more slowly but just as decisively. With its new X-ray block and improved facilities ('how we ever managed to exist without a food-room and premature baby room is a mystery'), St George's seemed set for a bright future, and at the end of 1931, Mrs J.G. Latham, president of the Kew auxiliary, hazarded vaguely that 'Great things must happen'. The disappointments were small ones, such as abandoning an experiment in using sheep to mow the lawn; and even these carried compensations: 'we sold the wool clip for 5/-, and the sheep for 1/- one of them was very full of years'.

The sisters maintained the hospital's reputation for sympathetic care and extra touches of fantasy and spirit—especially concentrated in the nursery at Christmas, where special features might include 'a snow and silver effect' masterminded by window-dressers on loan from a city firm: 'The stork, connected by ribbons of silver to an empty cot, brought the Christmas Baby we always love. Not that we really needed more babies'. The understatement in that comment was shown by the fact that 5000 babies were born between 1912 and 1935. So finances were eminently satisfactory; a two-year waiting-list for vacancies in the training school confirmed the hospital's prestige; and patients were even being refused because of lack of accommodation.

This unmistakably indicated the need for a larger hospital, and the momentum was quickened by the Building League formed in March 1933 with Sir John Latham as president, and including influential doctors from the eastern suburbs, and 'an editor of a very important paper'. Even the Charities Board was favourable, while rumours that 'local returned soldiers' planned to build in the area infused a competitive element, further stimulated by the opening of St Andrew's Hospital, the recent extension of St Vincent's, the intended expansion of Bethesda, and as-yet undetailed plans for the Freemasons' in East Melbourne.

Enthusiasm, though, was not easily transformed into currency in times of economic hardship. The government was approached, and Kew Council; there were schemes of loan-raising, and thoughts of converting St George's into a community hospital, thereby attracting public funds. Eventually, with no certainty of the wherewithal, plans were drawn up in mid-1935, and their grandiose proportions brought the number of beds close to one hundred—at a cost of between £40 000 and £50 000. With just £10 000 in hand, garnered through donations and the whopping £2000 proceeds from a fête at the Latham house, Council, which already held a loan of £10 000 from the Royal Bank with Mission House as security, decided that building should proceed. The first block only was projected, including a new theatre, kitchen, laundry and improved beds. The Building League contracted to be responsible for interest payments on the loan, and construction began in July 1936.

Problems were already looming. The reduction of the size of the new building to forty-seven beds may well have rendered the hospital uneconomic before it opened. The third storey was left 'only a shell' because of lack of funds, and £3500 would be required to complete it. Eventually, the sum was raised through debentures and a loan, but meanwhile the nurses' accommodation also needed to be upgraded urgently.

On 3 August 1937, amidst a severe polio epidemic, the new building was opened in a service conducted by Archbishop Head, with compliments from Professor Marshall Allan and the obligatory honours from Lady Latham. *In Our Midst* reported the event with a bugle call of optimism, but behind the scenes a distressing situation had arisen. Ida had decided that a nurse with sounder formal qualifications than Sister Ruth should be in charge of the new wing, and that the latter should go to the United States to study developments in child-care. Sisters Ruth and Cecil, who had managed the hospital and felt closely bound to it, promptly left the Community, never to return, and were joined a fortnight later by Sister Joan who had been in charge of midwifery. Apart from the practical implications, the shock left its mark on the Community for many years in a stubborn resistance to discussing the events. Nearly twenty years later, one sister who joined the Community was temporarily required to change her name because she shared it with one of the defecting sisters. The incident profoundly affected Ida, who must have wondered if her handling of the situation had precipitated its disastrous outcome; yet her own position was restricted by the authorities' increasing demands for professionalism. If, as rumoured, she made several clandestine visits to the Community's house in the Dandenong Ranges to meet one of the defectors and attempt to persuade her to return, that suggests the shock felt by a Superior unused to bewildering assaults on her confidence. Yet in the public arena of Chapter at least she sounds as if she felt completely justified in her determination 'to tackle problems' rather than evade them: the departure of Ruth and Cecil was described as 'really a climax of all that had gone before...many clashes with authority through the years, and difficulties, and threatening to leave'.

St George's sank into a state of chronic debt. The news in May 1938 that it was to get £12 000 from the estate of Miss Hughes, who had made the original gift of Ellerslie, was offset by the burden of substantial staff and wage increases. There was also the lingering problem of extending staff quarters: 'we did not realize the number that would be required, both of nursing and domestic staff'. The Council as well as the Community had underestimated the complexities of running such a hospital; but the brunt fell on the sisters, whose workload was not subject to regulation, and whose equilibrium had to bear the summary departure of their comrades.

Early in 1939, the Health Board wrote requiring better accommodation for all staff, and stipulated a three-month time-limit for alterations to the nurses' quarters. As details unfolded, Council realized that the Board's requirements could be satisfied only by a thirty-room block costing £4000. War-time restrictions prevented a start being made, but even so the hospital's overdraft rose relentlessly, despite several fee increases. In May 1942, the archbishop expressed the hope that St George's would eventually be self-supporting, and added bleakly that 'The general public had to be converted to a state of mind to realise the actual cost of the service it received. The 2 hospitals had been a great anxiety to the Reverend Mother'. A member of Council was blunter: 'Mr Dean asked if the Hospital was run as a business or to assist the middle class, if the former it was quite unsound, when assured it wasn't he suggested an addition to fees'.

'Our One Anxiety', said *In Our Midst*, describing St George's as the victim of 'a seemingly insatiable rise in the cost of maintenance'. Salaries climbed, while buildings were overtaken by galloping obsolescence. For all the fee increases, 'costs have shown a nasty tendency to keep just ahead', and the overdraft loomed perpetually. A £2000 bequest was a palliative rather than a cure, and in a line of metaphor proceeding from the grim to the ominous, there was 'a long road to be traversed before this deserving institution, so capably directed by the Sisters, is free from this strangling incubus of debt'.

The incubus tightened its grip when a 17.5 per cent increase in nurses' salaries meant £1500 a year extra must be found. Again, the only recourse seemed to be an application for a further fee increase, but that was subject to war-time control and long delays. The hospital committee desperately informed Council that the overdraft was stationary for once, because 'the Com. had explored every avenue it could think of to improve it'. The Inspector of Charities, McVilly, who had capacious powers within the welfare system and had witnessed many committees in their death-throes, regularly attended Council meetings, and in March 1943 outlined the alternatives that were open to the Mission: inducing supporters to endow beds; setting aside non-paying beds (thus transforming the hospital into a charitable institution with maintenance support from the government); or emulating the 'very solvent' community hospital at Brighton.

This last suggestion conformed with the government policy of establishing 'a chain of these hospitals to serve all suburbs', and McVilly assured the warden 'there would be no interference with internal control. The Govt would help in providing for buildings & maintenance on poorer beds'. The rest of his remarks, however, indicated that the Council had no choice but to capitulate. If the proposal were not accepted, the government was likely to establish another hospital in the district, and 'St George's would be faced with Govt. opposition', which was rather like pitting David against Goliath without the likelihood of a biblical outcome. The warden, Mother Ida, and the honorary treasurer of St George's were deputed to negotiate with the government.

After six months, no progress had been made in bringing the hospital 'under the Government plan', but the familiar problems continued: shortage of money, shortage of nurses and domestics, shortage of Anglican support when new nursing quarters were needed. By the end of 1945, 60 per cent of receipts were swallowed up by wages, a proportion that had risen 16 per cent in six years. Ida reported that a meeting with McVilly had agreed that St George's was to be recognized as the general hospital for Kew, and to be enlarged eventually to 200-bed capacity. The government would undertake building and maintenance, most probably from the end of 1946, but would not be responsible for existing debts. Meanwhile, monthly losses accumulated intolerably. By March 1946, the situation was judged to be 'chaotic', and meeting the cost of increased maintenance 'utterly impossible'. Wages for domestics had been retrospectively increased; one floor of the hospital was closed, which meant decreasing revenue without the hope of making comparable savings; the overdraft limit was £9000, but the actuality was an £11 000 indebtedness, which rose a further £2000 in the next two months. In May, the gap between income and expenditure exceeded £4500. The reassuring statement at the annual meeting that St George's was experiencing financial difficulty in common with many other hospitals obscured its particular agony.

In May 1947, the Charities Board finally gave permission for the drafting of plans for the enlarged hospital, but by this time the overdraft stood at £16 200, and one more humiliating and fruitless approach for a grant was necessary. The government still had not finalized its plans for conversion into a community hospital, and the annual meeting was told by the archbishop that the situation was 'held up by the slow movement of Govt. authorities, whose intentions were far ahead of performance'.

Mission reports tended to accentuate the brighter touches on this gloomy canvas (the brisk business at St George's; the easing of staff shortages), to inflate the few constricted areas of independence that remained (the empty consolation of being able to consult with their own architects in drawing up plans; the freedom to initiate interviews with sceptical politicians). However, the dismal outcome could not be averted, and the position was worsened by 'the threat of the acquisition of the Mission House' for government offices, since 'St George's overdraft was held as a mortgage on it, & the Bank was becoming restive'.

The impossible became the terminal with the introduction of the forty-hour week, a further increase in nurses' salaries, which quadrupled between 1939 and 1949, and the introduction of the basic wage—humane provisions that partly redressed long-standing injustices, and signalled a major reorientation of the social system. This time, the projected fee increase was wet straw in the flood of change.

May 1948: the Minister of Health and McVilly advised that no financial support would be forthcoming, and that the horrendous overdraft would be absorbed into general funds when building began under government aegis (the bank meanwhile announced decorously that although it would not close a public facility, it did want 'a settled limit for the overdraft'). These two powerful men then became more magnanimous, agreeing to expedite through parliament a bill to remove any incumbrance on the knotty title of St George's, whose future was now dignified as 'a cabinet matter'. As if anticipating a change of regime, McVilly decreed that the hospital should be run 'economically', an injunction that included instructions to the matron to increase the daily bed-average which was running thirteen below capacity. The facilitating bill was delayed by cabinet crisis, however, and the matron was forced to resign when she refused to accept the Board's demands.

Weary of the drawn-out struggle and interminable delays, the Council called a special meeting in March 1949 and framed an ultimatum which was in reality a defiant admission of defeat:

the Hospitals and Charities Commission which had recently replaced the Charities Board as overlord of Victoria's health services was to be informed that St George's would close on 30 June if the government intended to take over (thus ensuring that the Mission would incur no further debts), and the sisters would pull out for the reason—forlorn under the circumstances— that 'theirs was essentially Mission work, & of more benefit to the community'. A second special meeting two months later reported that the government was willing to establish a local committee that might agree to continued management by the sisters. Otherwise, the government would take over lock, stock and barrel, paying 'a fair value'. Of the three alternatives—outright sale, the creation of a government-subsidized institution, or continuance as a church hospital—the last course was understandably but perhaps quixotically favoured by CHN. Realistically viewed, the hope nudged the extremes of futility, given internal problems in the hospital, an overdraft that had soared above £25 000, the government's determination to control the health system, the secularizing tenor of society, and an archbishop who was said to be sceptical about the hospital's chances, and to favour Church participation in homes for the elderly.

The final humiliating factor was the repeated accusation of bad management. McVilly, who must have notched up several careers in attendance at stormy meetings, was 'forced to acknowledge that no hospital could pay its way today', diluting but not dispelling the charge. The archbishop accepted Council's decision advising outright sale, and 'Discussions took place as to whether any stipulation could. . .ensure that it did not get into the hands of the Roman Catholics'. McVilly pointed out placatingly that the Church could retain its influence through subscribers.

The only outstanding matters were the timing of government takeover, and price. The Mission announced that it would not be responsible for debts incurred after 1 July, and justifiably rejected as a basis for compensation the valuation on St George's made in 1942. McVilly, who had probably long been concealing administrative iron behind his public velvet and was perhaps understandably impatient, threatened compulsory acquisition if

the Mission closed the hospital. St George's was formally handed
over to the government on 1 July 1949. In reporting the end,
In Our Midst attempted to soften the blow:

[The archbishop] pointed out that it was quite wrong to regard the
surrender of the Hospital to other management as a failure on the part
of the Mission or the Sisters...

It has now to be recognised that there is no place for hospitals
organised on the lines of St George's. Rising costs and the unwillingness of the authorities to sanction fees commensurate therewith, made
it impossible for a private organisation unsupported by large endowments
or other sources of income to carry on.

This glossed over the fact that legislation provided for church
running of hospitals without boards of management elected by
contributors, and that several continued to flourish under church
aegis. Anglican politics may have been the hidden factor,
leaving church members divided against themselves and without
a united determination to support and save St George's.

In August, the sisters were farewelled by the doctors and
staff, and in November Council accepted the government's
final offer of £154 000 (as against a valuation of £160 000),
much of which was to be put in an endowment account, thus
ending 'a very difficult chapter of the Mission'. For CHN the
emotions were more personal and painful. As Ida said, after ten
years of anxiety over hospital finances, the final curtain had
descended 'with startling suddenness' and the obsequies were
brief. St George's had threatened to bring other Community
foundations down with it:

Our indebtedness had far exceeded the value of the security given, &
it was conceivable that our other Houses as well as the Mission House
would be involved. We were told the Church could not help. Every
effort was made to get government assistance, & to free the property
from the terms of the Trust, but with no success... While the relief
from financial anxiety is great, it is not without grief & regret that we
relinquish such a work.

Despite her reputation for acumen in practical affairs, she expressed a touch of forlorn puzzlement in contemplating the

large paper-value of St George's; 'an anomalous position, to be worth so much, & yet valueless as a security'.

The Community's other involvement in hospital management, St Ives, was also plagued by staff shortages and foundering financially. In her 1947 review of the year to Chapter, Ida found parallels between the two enterprises:

There is rarely a vacant bed in either hospital and patients are appreciative not only of the nursing, but of the visits and ministrations of the sisters. If it were not for this spiritual side of the work, we should almost feel that the difficulties were too great to allow us to carry on. As it is, we can only wait and see and hope for a solution of the Hospitals problem which will ease our burden, and show what our future policy in this connection should be.

Yet that year the Community had reluctantly increased its indebtedness on St Ives to £20 000, purchasing an adjoining property for a 'sorely needed' nurses' home (price £3000). Apart from the substantial overdraft, the cost of maintaining the hospital at the standard expected by its upper-class clientele was an incessant drain on the current account. There was a strong feeling in the Community that they should divest themselves of an over-luxurious facility. Even in mid-depression 1935 devices to ensure that patients were sufficiently cocooned included sound-barriers to quarantine the work areas, telephones in every room, a roof-garden, and decor in 'pleasing half-tones' (*Argus*, 28 August 1935).

Within two years, though the overdraft was static, the hospital's future was in question. A 'spirited discussion' in Chapter resulted in a decision to review St Ives' position in a year. This move was thwarted by a submission from the hospital's auxiliaries to conduct an appeal, and Chapter gave an assurance that the place would continue to function 'provided that no extraordinary circumstances arise, & that the community receives an income of £900 per year'.

With the usual staffing difficulties and oscillations of finance, the hospital continued to survive. When the auxiliaries made a strong injection of funds, the money was applied to renovations rather than to easing the overdraft. Reduced to occasional discussions between Ida, the Sister Superior and the accountant, management looked decidedly perfunctory and episodic. Despite signs faintly rose-tinged, the end was imminent, and this time the action came from within the Community itself. Ida's submission to the denouement sounded contrite and uneasy:

one is abjectly thankful that at the recent chapter the Community expressed its mind so clearly on the subject, and that gives one fuller confidence in making arrangements to relinquish the work and dispose of the property. As you know the hospital has been a great anxiety for many years.

As with St George's, the final throes were complicated and dispiriting. A 'bombshell' exploded when a representative of the purchasing committee of 'City men' asked for an extension of several months of the agreement to pay the Community £35 000 and to assume the overdraft. Two sisters were left at the hospital marking time until the signing on 7 September 1954. Ida wished the new owners well, expressed the remote hope that 'perhaps the Church may have an increased interest in it', and acknowledged the strain suffered by the Sister Superior, Elspeth.

The Sister Superior and one or two others may have been the only members of the Community who seriously regretted the withdrawal from St Ives. One sister who spent eighteen months there in the early 1950s felt that it 'had got to a desperate pass by that stage, by 1951. It just wasn't viable, the way it was being managed...there couldn't be economies on the management level. Again, it was a battle for survival'. Apart from the impossibility of pruning the hospital's lavish expenditure, sisters were isolated from one another, meeting only to say the office, and the effect on community life was destructive. There was no clearly defined spiritual role for them in their work, although the sister in charge 'had a kind of pastoral relationship with patients and their families. They tended to be a certain sort of family... She knew these people'. The fact that the pressures were endured and the sacrifices in community life accepted,

only highlighted how askew St Ives was to CHN's witness
elsewhere:

Whereas we could throw ourselves into battering ourselves to bits into
the other kinds of things, the prayer and the concern for the poor and
the disadvantaged...we found it very difficult to batter ourselves to
bits over people who could have gone somewhere else... In a way it
was all class distinctions. There was the professional staff and then the
patients, and then you went through a swing-door and there was the
domestic staff. You know, you met the cockroaches head on...those
of us who were at the wrong side of the stairs were not allowed to stay
for very long.

The two hospitals run by CHN were probably doomed to pass
into other ownership sooner or later, but the relinquishment of
St George's and the circumstances surrounding that failure precipitated new developments. In July 1949, the month the hospital
was formally handed over, Ida sought Council's permission to
enquire about the purchase of a house suitable for elderly people.
This initiative both conformed with the growing realization
that such institutions were needed, and gave the Mission a
chance of perpetuating the spirit of the Hughes bequest which
had been the genesis of St George's. Some of the proceeds from
the sale of the hospital could be diverted to the new cause.
    Four months later, the Mission purchased a house in the
suburb of Auburn:

Tall trees, flowering trees, shady trees...a house with a personality...
an exquisite vase of hydrangea and strelitzia in the front hall...tiled
bathrooms and tasteful carpets...the dignity of old oak furniture and
tall mirrors, the charm of a beautiful antique drawing room suite
brought from the original Ellerslie.

As a home for elderly women, the house was renamed Ellerslie
after the Hughes mansion which had become the nucleus of St
George's, and the link was reinforced when the chapel from the
Kew hospital was removed and re-erected there.
    The official opening by the archbishop in April 1950 pre-
empted permission from the Hospitals and Charities Commission

for extensive alterations and additions—a bedroom wing, flats, and a chaplain's residence. When confronted by bureaucratic lassitude or unpropitious circumstances, the Mission like its colleagues in the charity stakes had developed a facility to move forwards by moving sideways, or to serve a high end by bringing out the common carrot of monetary reward. Thus the present project was accelerated by offering the builder a bonus if costs did not exceed estimates. Although the government was leisurely in finalizing its obligations in the purchase of St George's, work on Ellerslie progressed, and by July 1953 £79 000 had been spent.

Re-adjustments did not stop there. The government intended to acquire Mission House, and that had sealed the sale of St George's because the title to the Spring St headquarters was held as security for the hospital's overdraft. Of all the changes facing the Community, the loss of its Mission centre established in the days of the foundress was one of the most taxing.

Change, however, was inseparable from the kaleidoscopic range of activities Mission House contained. The depression had multiplied the strain on its resources, with 'cases of real want and starvation', cries of assistance from families 'who received little but bare sustenance', 'girls who could not be dealt with through the Court...none really bad or immoral', as Esther had pointed out, 'but just difficult and troublesome'.

The clientele continued to be 'mostly of the weaker sex', as the condescending cliche put it in the annual reports. The restive but essentially defenceless young female, caught between childhood and adulthood and lacking prospects, provoked some sympathy in her 'urge for a more expansive life', however unfortunate her lapses. In this respect it was felt that 'Too much cannot be said for the influence of the Girls' Club', and two rooms were set aside at Mission House for 'watchful supervision' of offenders on probation. Another diversion for adolescent energy was the establishment of a Girl Guide troop. In March 1939 the 2nd Melbourne Brownies, Guides and Rangers were reported to be in action and appealing for excess clothing, belts, hats, brown shoes and stockings. There may even have been a fuse of radicalism to propel this feminine catching up with the Mission House scouts: 'training in health, first-aid, nature lore, handcraft; but, above all, training in leadership and responsibility and in service of others'.

While attention focussed on the vulnerable female, 'Lads of 11 to 13' who were 'not getting enough food to build them up in these days of economic distress' were not overlooked and were treated to occasional food-filled weekends in the country. *In Our Midst* had to be wary of alienating a readership that was prepared to be challenged but perhaps not to be outraged; but the desperation of the times was met with irrepressible indignation now and then. An anonymous reporter for the paper visited the city's outcasts at Dudley Flats, living in houses cobbled from refuse and debris:

Drunken? Yes. Immoral? Yes. (We asked no questions as to the relationship between the 'Lady of the Manor' and her men.) But surely still fit for something; if we would put the same amount of effort; had and would use as much initiative in reclaiming and making useful these human 'cast-outs' as they have expended in reclaiming and using the rubbish of the tip, what might we not accomplish?

In a justifiable fanfare of rhetoric, 1938's annual report trumpeted:

The chain of service at the Mission House and in the Hall has, as always, been endless. Volumes could be written on the individual cases which have arisen during the year, Mothers, fathers, young women, children—distressed, disturbed, sick, poor, or hungry...all come to the Sisters with their sometimes desperate troubles and problems (involved, often beyond solution). None have gone away uncomforted, unclothed, unfed or unhelped in some way according to their needs.

Despite the exceptional circumstances of the depression, normality was sustained in time-honoured ways. The art of making-do provided emergency supplies: a variegated collection of bathing-suits available for loan for beach picnics; a suitcase of spectacles for a makeshift oculist service. Seminal rituals such as Harvest Festivals and May Fairs were loaded with fund-raising potential, and the serious business of extracting cash was made as enjoyable as could be: 'The Mad Hatter had his tea party close by the refreshment room door and collected the money as his guests came out'. Even annual physical culture displays had their propaganda value, preparing the ground for future solicitations.

Despite a 'year of great national tribulation and anxiety', the 1940 annual report could claim 'these war-burdened months have brought new friends and a deeper consciousness of the high value of the service rendered by the Sisters'. Far from declining, Mission House activity was greater even than before. As headquarters of the Mission, all applications for assistance were dealt with here, and young people admitted to the homes. In 1941, seventy-eight 'problem cases' were temporarily taken in for evaluation. Finding accommodation and employment, supplying household goods, securing medical attention for mothers and families, were not needs that disappeared as Australia moved from peace-time depression to war-time boom.

All these stresses were actually intensified in 'the atmosphere of unrest and excitement occasioned by the war', and the burden fell most on Mission House and the House of Mercy. 'Requirements peculiar to the times' included the need to attend air-raid precaution classes. Black-out provisions were in force at Mission House where the windows were strengthened, first-aid cases assembled ready for urgent dispersal, and clothing was accumulated for possible air-raid victims or evacuated children. Perhaps the most disturbing development was the extreme youthfulness of many of the girls now 'befriended' by the sisters. Whereas in its early years Mission House had generally harboured young women between eighteen and twenty-three, many were now under sixteen, or even under fourteen, 'pitifully young', and often in 'a state of mental anguish'. A sister attended the court daily, often speaking on behalf of the girls, and temporary accommodation had to be provided for fifty to sixty cases a year:

The risk involved and the repellent nature of the work which falls on the Sisters in their contact with some of the cases points to the growing need of decontamination centres such as exist in crowded cities in other parts of the world.

The Mission's sixtieth year was described exhaustedly in the annual report as 'a period of almost insuperable difficulties in some branches'. But with the end of the war, thoughts immediately flew as they had in 1919 to expansion and improvement. 'Several progressive aspirations, latent during the war, have been voiced and eagerness has been shown to give effect to them as soon as conditions are favourable.' In March 1946, Ida informed Council that she wanted the old outmoded Mission House pulled down and replaced by a Mission House and hostel combined, which would 'conserve the energies of the Sisters'. The estimated cost of about £4000 was likely to fall entirely on the Mission, given the government's hardening attitude towards subsidizing charities with a religious overlay. But before the matter was resolved, the government announced plans to compulsorily acquire the whole area, including the Hornbrook School site which still belonged to the Community. In early 1948, several Council members attended a meeting in the Town Hall opposing the scheme, but the government was unswayed and soon confirmed the acquisition, allowing 120 days for compensation claims to be submitted.

The only hope lay in a change of government, but the conservatives elected in 1949 did not reverse the decision. The prospect of losing the Mission's base was anxiously discussed at the annual meeting that year, though some voices counselled philosophic acceptance:

We must all remember that conditions are changing, and a Mission must keep pace with the change; a sentimental attachment to a place or a building was a good thing to have, but it should not be allowed to stand in the way of progress and service to the community.

The search for a new site for Mission headquarters was now a major preoccupation. It had to be admitted that the area near Spring St was transformed, and that many of the Mission's traditional clients had moved elsewhere. For the Community, a new direction was perhaps indicated, but nostalgia for the Mission's historic beat was strong, and the Church was active and owned land in suburbs just a little further to the north.

In August 1952, the suggestion was put that the Mission
should buy property between Brunswick and Fitzroy streets that
was owned by the Brotherhood of St Laurence and seemed
suitable for mission work. St Mary's Mission Church already
stood there, and the Fitzroy area was a poor section of the inner
city, lying within the parish of St Peter's, so there were connec-
tions going back to the first years of deaconess work under the
mother foundress. Council believed that compensation for the
Spring St holdings should equal the cost of a 'similar establishment on a new site with equivalent accommodation', and it
approved the scheme. The warden and Sister Ida began negotiations with the government, and an architect was instructed
to produce estimates for alterations to St Mary's. His original
projection of £40 000 escalated to £54 000, which far exceeded
the government's first offer of a mere £22 000. In November
1955, Council accepted the considerably more generous government offer of £35 000, and the Mission prepared to take over St
Mary's, agreeing to 'make reasonable opportunities for the pastoral
work of St Peter's to continue' through joint use of facilities. In
May 1956, Council and St Peter's Vestry approved the agreement,
and just over a year later the new Mission House was opened in
the presence of 'many clergy in robes...many Sisters & a big
assembly of the friends of the Mission & Members of Council...
a stirring & historical event in the life of the Mission'. Ironically, the Spring St building, occupied for a time by a branch of
the Victorian Police Force after the Community's removal, still
stands.

The move into Fitzroy appears to have been the only one
that was seriously considered, but there were alternatives. For
nearly two years, some of the sisters had worked in the midst of
Camp Pell, the government's appalling temporary housing settlement in Royal Park on the north-western fringe of the city. *In
Our Midst* recounts blood-curdling episodes of mayhem and
near-murder, and one of the sisters involved in the Community's
labours there felt that an opportunity to extend that mission
was lost. She described the bleak physical conditions: former
army barracks with a laundry block at the end of each row of
huts, pathless, and without amenities such as schools and shops.
On Sundays, children were transported by furniture van to the

'The scene might have been taken from a medieval pageant, as the procession of sisters wended its way across the green paddocks, joined by a long queue of white-robed clergy': laying the foundation stone of Community House in 1935.

Sisters in a procession of witness, Kensington (Melbourne), 1958.

nearest church in North Melbourne. She laughed ruefully as she recalled the unpropitious missionary situation: some families 'didn't want a bar of us. . .they'd barricade their doors', believing the sisters were Roman Catholics; 'one of the things we learnt was that we concentrated on people where there *was* a response. It didn't mean that we didn't regularly try and visit everyone, but we *did* concentrate on the areas where there was a response, and some of those people to this day are in touch with us'.

With the help of students from Ridley College at the University of Melbourne, and a short supply of 'young ladies and not so young ladies', she and another sister visited the camp two or three days a week, trying to make contact with families and to keep records of the situation. Holidays, outings, and the business of confirmation and baptism were arranged. The baptism of about seventy-five children one Mothering Sunday, with an entourage of four officiating priests, god-parents, parents, families and friends, with tea and Simnel cake to follow in the bulging church hall, seemed to augur well. To start with, 'we had children by the hundred; then the numbers decreased as the years went on because they moved people out of the camps. . . There was a good response from some children, that's all I can say'.

This sister felt that, in moving to Fitzroy, the Mission may have taken a wrong turn:

I always felt we should have followed our Camp Pell people, out into the housing areas, and worked out there. . . But what we did was we went back on our tracks and back into Fitzroy which we had already left. And the work wasn't there at the time. . . Once the [Housing Commission] flats were built, the work came for a very short while. . .

But different nationalities and religious affiliations of later migrants meant that in the Commission flats too, before long, the Anglican church had only a limited role. 'Our own Australian and British people that we'd been working amongst at the Mission House. . .had gone out into the [new] housing areas. . . where the Church was *hungry* for help.'

Victoria, however, was not the only place to challenge the

sisters' formidable capacity for commitment. At the 1934 annual meeting, a member of the audience had spoken glowingly of the Community's work with children: 'the great essentials. . . a stable foundation & a serene atmosphere, these qualities were so in evidence in the Homes. . . What a child absorbed in childhood would remain thro'out its life. . . what good may not accrue to the whole state as a result of this?' Much of the Community's salvage work had been with children, and for several sisters this work was the core of their practical commitment, satisfying selfless ideals and personal needs alike. Their reputation in the field, and the social situation in which families had to resort to institutional solutions, meant constant pressure to expand the work with children. In 1932, following an offer of the gift of a maternity hospital and children's home, two sisters went to Young, New South Wales, and the diocese of Goulburn enthused about their work with such intensity that it was plain an even wider commitment would be welcome. Council was informed of the voracious 'need of more sisters, as the various branches were continually asking for more help'.

In the mid-1930s, the New South Wales establishments of CHN consisted of St Alban's, Morpeth, former residence of the bishops of Newcastle, set in one hundred acres (forty hectares) and providing accommodation for thirty-eight boys; St Elizabeth's, Mayfield, which housed about thirty girls between the ages of seven and sixteen; St Saviour's, Goulburn, with twenty-two children; and St Christopher's Babies' Home, Lochinvar, a country mansion with 'enchanting gardens', orchards, vegetable and poultry farms, set in an estate of two hundred acres (eighty hectares). The indulgence of the donor of this last establishment extended to providing an annual endowment of £300 and regular gift-bearing visits.

Although the Community was proud of its ability to step into any charitable vacuum where its expertise seemed the answer, the difficulties in staffing and maintaining this far-flung empire were considerable, and a consolidation of effort seemed desirable. As the most peripheral tenancy, Young was abandoned in 1934. The next year, 'the first Home out of Melbourne of which the Community took charge', St Alban's, was handed over to the Church Army. Since the early 1920s, the Community had regretted that it was unable to provide a service for boys to equal its efforts for girls, so this particular relinquishment provoked 'mixed feelings'. The next rationalization was the decision in 1937 to pull out of the Newcastle diocese where CHN had been working for sixteen years; but this was partly compensated for by the bequest that same year of new and larger quarters for St Saviour's Home, Goulburn.

On home ground in Victoria, accommodation, often in the normal course of events 'taxed to the utmost', was even more strained by the depression. A new wing at Brighton had been under consideration since late 1930, when it seemed £5000 for the purpose might be advanced by the state government out of the £100 000 allocated to unemployment relief. But the Committee would have to match the grant and meet subsequent rises in maintenance costs as well. (An ambivalent note—was it pride or resentment?—often attached to mentions of the fact that the government did not contribute to maintenance, although the Mission's institutions were registered with both the Charities Board and the Children's Welfare Department.) An offer by private individuals to raise money for the new wing was also refused, because of the economic uncertainty of the times. Not until January 1934 when the depression had slightly lifted was a decision taken to proceed. The wing was completed in November the next year, at a cost of £1750, almost half of which was contributed by the tireless Business Girls' Auxiliary, and was opened by the archbishop in the Mission's jubilee year in conjunction with a Blossom Fête featuring some of the tiniest inmates topped with petite truncated veils. There were now thirty-four babies at Darling, each one costing little more than 11s per week, *In Our Midst* reported proudly, and sixty-four girls at Brighton, where the attached hostel was said to be more than self-supporting and actually contributed extra money to maintenance funds.

The sisters expressed pride in the development of the children from their often ill-starred beginnings, along with a stoical recognition that they themselves would seldom see the fruits of the vine: 'we see their gradually developing mentality, and we weave plans for their future careers; but so many pass out of our ken altogether, and all we can do is to hope we have made them more physically fit to face the battle of life'. Even modest educational successes were carefully reported—girls who gained intermediate certificates at Melbourne High School (MacRobertson's) or Brighton Technical School. When girls at the hostel, whom the sisters had often nurtured from infancy, were launched on successful careers, such as clerical positions, hairdressing, mothercraft or general nursing, the note of pride became positively maternal. Many of the girls stayed in the hostel, 'the pioneer in Victoria of this form of social service', until marriage. And when an old girl was married in the Chapel of the Holy Innocents, the process of successful nurturing was seen to be finalized, unless the husband proved to belong to the scandalous company of defecting males.

Once the new wing at Brighton had been achieved, attention swivelled to the picturesquely inconvenient Edwardian villa that housed the babies at Darling. In July 1939, Council considered improvements to it, and McVilly committed the Charities Board to cover half the cost—an offer that was later converted to a £324 annual contribution. But Council, perhaps stimulated by the Community's omnivorous instinct for improvement and expansion, had a larger scheme in mind. The war might halt building, but it was powerless to stop plans and anticipations of the post-war celebratory spirit. By May 1943, a new Babies' Home fund held £8000, and an adjoining block of land was bought at the end of the war. Plans were not completed until mid-1947, however, and building was delayed by the government's failure to grant a permit when materials were short and the pressure for post-war buildings intense. A year later, with the existing Babies' Home in poor condition, only essential repairs were being done, and in spite of the warden harrying the authorities the permit arrived at snail's pace eighteen months further down the track.

Council was not so dilatory. In February 1950 the lowest tender of £22 000 for the first block of the new complex was accepted; by May 1951, £8000 in appeal funds had been collected and construction had begun. Within months, the building was opened and tenders had been called for the next section which would require a formidable £55 000. Reverting happily to its soliciting gear, In Our Midst began yet another fund-raising

campaign, and supporters of the Mission stepped on the tread-
mill again: a fête at Brighton that netted £2000; backyard
bazaars, barbecues, street stalls; Australian Teas and Mrs Harold
Holt's 'delightful account of her Coronation Tour'; a concert in
the cavernous Malvern Town Hall. In February 1953, the
Queen Anne perplexities of Yarrayne came tumbling down, and
six months later over £27 000 had been consumed by the new
building.

When it was opened by the governor, Sir Dallas Brooks, in
May 1954 in the presence of over a thousand CHN friends, *In
Our Midst* surged into a high tide of enthusiasm. The Church of
England Home for Little Children was 'a joy to behold', in
fetching pastels and 'glowing golden linoleum'. Cleverly designed
to accommodate its inhabitants, it had child-height wash basins
and a miniature gangway to enable the pint-sized to walk into
the bath; a play centre held modern equipment; there was a
trained kindergartener.

The demand for improved facilities was voracious, especially
in the post-war environment where brave new worlds seemed
possible still. The Mission was hardly in possession of its im-
peccable Home for Little Children, than the Department of
Child Welfare announced that the Brighton Hostel no longer
met its standards. When the government's offer of a rebuilding
grant proved inadequate, Council decided that it could not
afford to provide the accommodation government-sponsored
girls would require, and would cater only for children from its
own Children's Home.

The completion of renovations in late 1957 to the entire
Brighton complex (the hostel became St Faith's) coincided
with the sixtieth anniversary of the Community's involvement
there. A Diamond Jubilee celebration was held on 2 December
by the Warden of the Mission in the presence of thirty-four
sisters, friends and children, and the mood was one of thoughtful
reminiscence. One thousand three hundred and fifty six children
had passed through the Home. *In Our Midst's* reporter made a
reflective tour of the house and inevitably observed the blend of
old and new, the coexistence of the traditional and the progressive: the rose-window in the Chapel of the Holy Innocents
with its hoop of luminous cherubic faces, and the new wire

mattresses and television set; the replacement of 'layers of under-clothes and starched pinafores' by skimpy blue and white gym costumes; the tradition of harvest festivals, and the innovation of 'specialists in psychology' to give advice:

The Victorian, very Victorian, stained glass windows, which were once so popular and then so despised, have come into their own again and seem quite at home as they throw their tinted light on 'Miss 1957', pirouetting in front of the full-length mirror, as she prepares to celebrate the Diamond Jubilee of the Children's Home.

Anniversaries were liable to produce a backward glance permeated with nostalgia and regret, as if the best lay behind; but on this occasion the past was primarily a viewing box for present achievement and a launching platform for future enterprise.

From CHN's point of view as a religious community, the two most significant developments of the post-war years were the absorption of the New Zealand Order of the Good Shepherd, and the move into the mission field in New Guinea.

The origins of OGS, based in Auckland, paralleled those of CHN. The decision to form a community of women, to draw up a rule, appoint a committee to oversee the community's affairs, and to purchase a house, was taken at a meeting in Auckland in September 1894. Mrs Williams, a widow, was appointed Superior as Sister Frances, immediately undertaking city mission work and establishing an embroidery department. The objects of the mission closely followed English example and CHN practice: to visit the poor in the inner city, to assist the clergy in parochial visiting, to minister to the sick and dying, to proselytize among the young, to rescue the fallen, and to visit public institutions in accordance with the chaplain's initiative.

The formative days of OGS seem to have been hemmed in by the thicket of problems and criticisms which cramped CHN. A dispute as to whether the work was essentially parochial or diocesan led to the resignation of the original chaplain. The thorny question of women's work in the Church was critically canvassed in 'the local papers'. The deliberately neutral garb of the workers did not deflect those eager to ferret out Romish sympathies. There was a depressing familiarity in the sectarian querulousness of the complaints.

On 1 May 1900, the mission workers were admitted as novices, and the group took the name Mission of the Good Shepherd. In August 1902, the Bishop of Auckland issued licences to the three sisters, whose work revolved around hospital and prison visiting, management of a children's home, Sunday school teaching, church embroidery, and 'rescuing the fallen and seeing that they were placed where they could be helped to live a better life'. Two years later, the constitution was drawn up and ratified, a procedure that revived the old objections, especially to the taking of vows by women. In reply to critics, the bishop stated adamantly that:

The ministry of women had always been widely used in the Church of Christ, and in the Church of England. Mistakes had been made in the past through want of Episcopal sympathy with the movements; but in this new country they had an opportunity of learning from the mistakes made when the ministry of women was revived in the Church. This sense of Vocation should have opportunities for realization.

Three sisters were professed on 22 December 1905, and the first Chapter meeting took place several days later.

By now, CHN had been in touch with the small group for several years (two members of OGS had visited Melbourne in 1901), and had been asked to advise and assist in its early stages. Still small itself, CHN did not have the resources to branch out into mentorship, but Sister Mary who felt called to Auckland was released, and eventually became Superior. The growth of the Order was faltering and insignificant; by 1928, there were four sisters, one novice, one aspirant. Ten years later, the number of sisters had grown to eight, but the Community's work was constantly threatened by shortage of sisters and the ill health that excessive pressure brought. In 1949, the children's home was taken over by the Church Army; in 1951, another branch of their work was relinquished; and the next year, in a painful process of attrition, the mission house was

sold. It was intended that the Community should live and
consolidate its efforts in the prestigious suburb of Remeura
where a large house had been willed to the Order in 1950 'as a
Rest Home for tired people', terms that might have been designed
for the sisters themselves.

This last development seemed to promise a more stable future,
but the Community was convulsed by the abdication of the
Superior, Mother Margaret, who resigned because of ill health
and joined another community. The group had not experienced
leadership of the calibre of CHN's, and the situation was aggravated by a series of deaths among the sisters and their supporters. A sense of unease and insecurity set in, and even
though a new Superior, Ella Mary, was installed the sisters felt
her to be 'too gentle and too sweet...we didn't think she was
Mother Superior material'. A request for assistance in training
a novice mistress was put to CHN, and two sisters visited
Melbourne in June 1952 with the intention that Sister Emily
should stay for twelve months' experience.

Meanwhile, the home-grown problems remained. After half
a century, some Auckland clergy who 'thought that all women
should be either married or spinsters' were still dogmatically
opposed to religious communities for women. The departure of
Mother Margaret continued to have 'devastating' effects, compounded by the illness and removal of the chaplain. The move
to new premises was also disconcerting: 'it was a very different
kind of existence from the slum area of Grey's Avenue to the
posh area of Remeura'. The house moreover was being renovated
and could not accommodate all members of the Community,
which therefore suffered feelings of fragmentation. They grasped
at a sense that 'we could begin again to live the life of a
Religious Community with added knowledge from the two Sisters
who had been in Australia', but despite several professions, a
growth in the number of associates, and the need for the sisters'
social welfare work, the Order felt disoriented and lacking
direction:

It was probably a subconscious feeling, as nobody mentioned it. But it
had been felt for many years, often buried deep by the demands of
social service, reviving again when there was time to sit and think,
'How?' It was probably something of this feeling that prompted the

Superior to get in touch with a number of other religious communities
and ask them to pray for our guidance.

One sister reflected that 'more than anything else we wanted,
needed advice'.

By 1955, the fiftieth anniversary of the signing of their
constitution, the Superior's health was failing and several of the
sisters fell ill. It had been arranged that future aspirants should
be sent to Australia for their early training, but the entire
Community felt the need for renewal. 'The door seemed to be
closed, except we all agreed we should ask CHN to help us.'
The survival of OGS as an independent entity no longer seemed
possible. The obvious suggestion was that it should merge with
the Christchurch order that now harboured their former Superior,
but the sisters there seemed like 'foreigners', very different in
ethos and customs, and governed by an unusual English lady
who donned layers of clothing to go to bed. The option was
rejected.

The next move was a rather novel one. On the strength of a
bequest that had been made to Sister Emily, three sisters decided
to undertake an inspection tour of Australian communities to
see which might be compatible. A plethora of English ways and
'rice pudding and stodgy food' in Sydney, as against inexplicable
cold and another eccentric Superior in Brisbane, were for one
sister plainly discouraging signs. By contrast, the Melbourne
Community seemed 'so like us', and Ida impressed as 'a darling'.
Although one of the trio hankered after Brisbane, the vote
went to CHN.

The Superior of OGS resigned from office and an urgent
appeal for assistance was sent to Cheltenham. At the end of a
week's visit Ida announced 'I'm going to pack you all up and
take you back to Melbourne with me'. It was decided that the
Community should move across for a two-year trial period, but
the Bishop of Auckland was 'simply furious' and his suspicions
seemed to centre on Ida. 'He wasn't going to have this Australian
female pushing him around. . . He wanted each of us without
collaboration or collusion to write our own personal reason for
wanting to make the move to Australia.' When the sisters
produced convincing testaments, 'he very reluctantly gave his

permission'. The OGS contingent arrived in two groups, in late
1955 and early 1956:

We knew that we were in a static situation in Auckland. . .the only
panic I remember was coming through the Heads to Sydney. . . As we
flew across. . .suddenly I looked down and there was land beneath,
and I thought 'Oh, it's not New Zealand. What *have* I done?. . . We
only brought literally what we could carry.

Two years later, eight sisters from the Order of the Good
Shepherd were received into CHN by the Archbishop of
Melbourne who assured the transplanted New Zealanders that,
although God's ways sometimes seemed obscure, the outcome
was often a masterpiece of hidden motivation. In a return
gesture, CHN took over the house in Remeura as a hostel for
girls in November 1958.

Of all the Community's enterprises, the New Guinea venture
which resulted from a request by the Bishop of Dogura for
assistance in his diocese proved one of the most glamorous and
innovative. As girls, many of the sisters had been romantically
attracted to overseas missionary work, and the Community had
long 'cherished' the hope for such a commitment—unlikely
though it would have seemed in Esther's day. When the opportunity came, CHN took it, and in his article 'New Venture in
Papua' Canon W.G. Thomas lyrically contemplated the implications of the move. Within twelve months, he foresaw, there
would be a sisters' house high on the Dogura Plateau, looking
out over the Wamira Valley to Kaiete where the mission's
founders had landed sixty years before. Now, in the footsteps
of those missionaries came sisters from CHN:

Especially for the women and girls of our Mission area in Papua it
had a special significance. . . The Papuans as a whole have yet much
to learn of the 'dignity of womanhood', and it is part of the mission
of the church to help raise the status of women in the Christian
community.

That sounded idealistic, even subversive; but the realities envisaged by Canon Thomas turned out to be more modest.

Under the sisters' influence, young women would become possible wives for the students of St Aidan's college, and later strengthen their husbands' work in the villages. Actually, the three sisters, Sara, Gracemary and Clare, who pioneered the venture were to find the outcome even more cramped and conventional.

Two of the three were preparing themselves by studies at the Australian Board of Missions' training-centre in Sydney, and gathering outfits and equipment suitable for their destination. Dressed in the especially designed white habit, which 'presented quite a tropical appearance', the three sisters were farewelled by about 350 friends in April 1951, before embarking from Sydney on the 'Malaita' and arriving in New Guinea soon after the catastrophic eruption of Mt Lamington. In their first letters they report they are physically fit and well occupied, looking after several girls who have come in from villages to go to school. The chaplain-general visited late in 1951, and his short account of his visit was accompanied by photographs of Sister Clare standing hieratically in the doorway of the bush community room, while bare-breasted Papuan girls wearing grass skirts like inverted tussocks arrange themselves in the time-honoured style of school forms. When Clare returned on furlough in mid-1953, she amplified on the Dogura sisters' doings. A qualified nurse, she had set up a dispensary at St Aidan's to look after the wives and children of the students. Sister Helen had joined the contingent, and assembled a flourishing Mothers' Union. The number of girls under the sisters' care had risen to thirty, and the sisters were learning the Wedauan language.

This last activity was a pointer to the shocking novelty of their situation—generally unspoken about, but lavishly unfolded by one of the sisters as she describes St Peter's Day, patronal feast of the Cathedral Church, now transformed into 'Festival in New Guinea'. She starts with the setting itself: the Dogura Plateau in its awesomely dramatic position, bordered by sea on three sides, and 'on the fourth by tier upon tier of conical hills. . . reminiscent of some primeval race-memory'. Traditionally a tribal battleground, sorcery, witchcraft, superstition and fear are rife, 'for Satan still lurks in the shadow of the hill'.

The day proceeded predictably enough, if somewhat strangely and intensely, with hordes of villagers arriving laden with every chattel from firewood to sleeping mat to baby, mission boys and girls rushing out to meet relatives, the bartering of village produce for mission supplies, and a procession that circumnavigated the cathedral singing 'Onward Christian Soldiers' with such fervency that the hills seemed to vibrate. Night, that catalyst of the atavistic and the elemental, brings disturbing transformations that signify the unleashing of the old rituals, the inherited instincts. After the feast, dancing begins, 'a wild primitive chant in time with the insistent rhythm of the drums'. The males lead and finally the girls, 'tolerated but not invited', join in:

women were not important in Papua before the white man came, and still have learned but little confidence or self-respect; absorbed into the age-old rite of the tribe...she knows instinctively what is expected of her, and fills her role with grace...a haunting rhythm [that] has power to stir even alien blood...the spirit of old Papua calling to its own. (*In Our Midst*, December 1955)

Highlighting the bizarre, emphasizing the progressive, or con-centrating on the reassuringly domestic, the reports were partly cast to assuage the curiosity of those back home. Behind the scenes, however, the affairs of the outpost were less satisfactory.

In 1954, Ida decided that Flora as assistant superior should visit Dogura 'in order that plans for future development might be discussed'. Flora described 'two wonderful months in one of the most beautiful places I have ever been and amongst some of the most lovable people I have ever met'. The stunning sur-roundings and leisurely approach to life contrasted markedly with her hectic Melbourne round. The climax was Good Friday, its unforgettable 'silence and stillness', the arrival of people from the hills, groups of children pondering the Stations of the Cross, or standing beneath the wooden crucifix that hung from a tree near the playing field.

Yet that may have been a rare moment of peace. There was more going on than the bland official reason for the visit allowed, for despite his avowals about instating the dignity of Papuan womanhood, the bishop appears to have been more interested in his own domestic arrangements, and the sisters were kept busy securing smooth operations on that front:

one of them became a kind of permanent hostess...sort of a something-
nothing, which is a New Guinea slang term. It means just that...
looking after numerous people, and then suddenly nobody at all. One
of them became a sort of boss-cook in the kitchen, and trained a
couple of local girls to do most of the cooking... After about four
years the whole thing seemed to be in shreds... Everybody was up
against the bishop, and the bishop was wailing to the reverend mother.

The upshot of these tropical disturbances was that Ida, who
was too distant to be able to know the full circumstances, recalled the acting work-force and sent replacements, Sisters
Faith and Gloria. Plunged without a specific brief into a situation that was 'a muddle and a mess, without our being very
clear what the muddle and the mess was, except that people
kept coming back wrecks', the newcomers looked around, pondering a creative occupation for themselves, and 'kept hearing
from near and far that what was really needed was some form of
women's education. There wasn't any education in the whole
country...for girls beyond fourth class of the state primary'.
They decided to establish the Holy Name School.
    Apart from their lack of teacher training (and that had never
before deterred the Community from putting its shoulder to the
wheel), there were rough physical conditions to contend with,
isolation, an indignant bishop in the background, who

really just wanted us to sit there and float around looking pious and
keep looking after the housekeeping at Dogura House for him, which
was to feed and bed down all the missionaries who floated through,
plus the bishop. We really felt that if we didn't have something
definite to do, we'd best go home, and he conceded the point with an
ill grace.

They were also the centre of attention, with people in the
forefront and in the offing alertly looking for mistakes. The girls
at the school were well into adolescence, and thus presented a
new version of CHN's old problem of balancing freedom and
control:

the eyes of everybody were on us... It would have been a major
tragedy if anybody had got pregnant, because that would have been

the end of the school...
We tried to run it like an ordinary household, but we had eyes in the
backs of our heads... We were on very thin ice... We all *had* to be
enthusiasts, we had to work like slaves, working up the curriculum
and getting a few lessons ahead... We had to work hard at getting
into the scene, as it were, just picking up the rudiments of the local
culture...trying to feel what it was like to be where they were, and
not running it on too tight a rein.

Sister Faith agreed that from any point of view the school
was a feminist enterprise; but she insisted that it was a co-
operative, creative enterprise in which the CHN sisters developed
and deepened an already existing impetus among the girls, all of
whom were training as teachers: 'The girls came looking to this
school for something for themselves, but [also] something to
take back to their people. It wasn't an idea that we implanted
just fresh; it got built on'. While some of the girls were abject
and without sense of their potential, others from more sophisti-
cated tribes were firm and clear-spoken about their expectations.
The difference was often explained by the calibre of the missionaries who had been in their areas: if they came from one or two
places that had had outstanding women missionaries, they understood that the self-development of women was an important
ingredient in the country's self-realization.

By June 1956, the complex consisted of a house, chapel and
schoolroom built in local style, and a 'European-type dwelling'
adapted as a hostel for thirty-six girls. The older ones undertook
a two-year course with the primary aim of 'teaching girls subjects
which will be of use to them in their later village life', and
helped the sisters look after the chapel, houses, laundry and
garden of the Cathedral Church; sixteen younger girls received
a general education at St Paul's School. *In Our Midst* excitedly
reported the first anniversary of Holy Name School with the
most ecstatic compliments reserved for the emancipatory theme:
'Before, everything was for the boys. Now the girls can get
more education to, and feel that they're equipping themselves
to take their place and part in the new Papua that is emerging.'
('Ae Kapore Bolabola!') By this time, all the girls were educated
under one roof, and the aims were more ambitious, with morn-
ings devoted to 'the Government syllabus' and the more relaxed

afternoons set aside for 'feminine accomplishments' such as housekeeping, sewing and child-care:

A tradition is developing nurtured by the girls as much as by the Sisters. Bolabola is the place for girls who want to learn... Girls write from all over the diocese asking to come, because they want 'more knowledge'; and sometimes they don't only mean knowledge of *things*.

In an atmosphere that the Sister Superior, Faith, described as one of 'constant pioneering', information on curriculum development was often garnered from visiting patrol officers. The government was in the process of establishing a secondary school for girls in Port Moresby, and educational standards were constantly being raised. 'We felt we had to try to keep up or keep abreast or keep ahead if we could.' Numbers had grown rapidly, and would soon reach about one hundred; meanwhile, the age of pupils gradually dropped from seventeen or eighteen to thirteen or fourteen, simplifying the disciplinary problem. Many graduates of the Holy Name School were launched into public careers, and even those who returned to their villages took something of the school's particular impress—aspiring towards positive action, establishing women's clubs, and so on.

In May 1959, *In Our Midst* carried a leading article on the Community's eight years in New Guinea, encapsulated in Prosperine who had stoutly overcome parental opposition to arrive at Bolabola. There is a strong, sometimes cloying flavour to some of the details approved of: the 'European style' dormitory which the sisters would like to build; the basketball and gramophone for amusement; the western garments being made for children so that posture-destroying grass skirts can be replaced by 'cotton skirts and tops'; plaster crib-figures with brown skins. Some of this colonializing description may have been for the benefit of the readership at home; at any rate, the article ends with a far more serious vision of what education might bring about:

At present there are only three courses open to a girl on leaving school: she can train as a nurse at Dogura training hospital, she can train as a teacher, or she can return to her village and perhaps influence conditions of village life. We trust and pray that we are

giving them now something which they will never wholly lose, though
much may be forgotten.

It was hardly full-scale emancipation (not unlike Australia, in
fact), but the school had played its part in this definite reorientation of women's roles by producing nine girls who had
emerged from teacher training in the previous year—a feat
which was expected to establish a pattern.

While the Community was preoccupied with expanding and
adjusting its practical works, a radical shift was taking place in
its inner life. This was determined partly by external pressures,
but partly expressed a momentum of its own.
    Before the 1940s were over, Ida had acknowledged to Chapter
that change in the outward activities of CHN was inevitable:
already, that was manifest in the House of Mercy's shift to
retreat work, and the sale of St George's. In 1948, she suggested
a further inevitability, almost unthinkable till then: the drawing
apart of the Community and the Mission. 'For so many years
the Community and the Mission were one—they were synonymous terms—but that is not true of us now. The Community
has grown into something greater than, and apart from the
Mission.'
    A readjustment of the relationship between the Community's
life and its works was needed. Ida's own vision of the Community's witness had been reinforced by her visit to England
with Sister Flora in 1948, and was symbolized by her determination that Community House should be the hub of CHN's
existence; but in her statement to Chapter in 1949 the readjust-
ment she projected was both affirmative and defensive: 'Our
Life is of the utmost importance—far more important than our
works. With the trend of the times, and the changed attitude
to Social Services, none of [us?] know how long our particular
works will be left in our hands'. The pace of change, painful to
some, was likely to accelerate, and individuals must prepare to
accept the necessary without demur: 'it behoves us to recognise
that a time must come for each of us to step aside when we are
bidden. Changes are not made without reason...we shall not
only submit formally but shall strive to make the will and

wishes of the Superior our own.' Humbly, or at least conscious
of shortcomings and aware of the imminence of change for her
personally, Ida, who had been re-elected for a further five-year
term, accepted 'the mandate to rule' as a manifestation of the
Holy Spirit.

These portents bore down in one direction: the need to make
the Community's common religious life a more compelling
witness. For Ida there was comfort in observing that CHN was
not alone in experiencing the tremors of change. Her recent
stay in England, and the Anglo-Catholic Congress particularly,
had shown her other communities labouring under the same
pressures, since the intrusion of the state came earlier there.
English superiors wrote describing the increasing pernickitiness
of government regulations on their work. The Home Office was
insisting that staff in children's homes should be properly qualified. Even the Central Council of Women's Church Work had
issued a circular calling for sisters working in parishes to undertake
relevant training courses.

In England, one response to this was a growth in the contemplative orders. For CHN, more isolated than its sister communities overseas, and devoted to maintaining 'a balance between
prayer and work', the choice of direction was perhaps more
delicate. Moreover, few of the sisters had that 'knowledge of
life as it is lived in the older convents' which might assist the
progression towards a more introspective mode of community
witness. More deliberate stratagems would have to be employed.
Indeed the advance of the state into the preserves of religious
communities was not simply a shift at the practical level. The
growth of state responsibility was symptomatic of the secularism
of the modern world, requiring a more concerted and aggressive
response from the committed than was needed when the official
belief-system incorporated religious values. 'More than ever is
the need for Christian witness and surely it is the Religious
Orders that must lead the way.' But at least the upsurge of
materialism might 'bring some to desire the opposite', resulting
in increased vocations.

Although the Community's numerical growth had been slow,
it was certainly consolidating into a sizeable force. When its
Diamond Jubilee was celebrated a year late on 19 October

1949, forty-six sisters were present, one of whom, Christina, was 'one of the three foundation members of the Community'. Though she survived the event by only a few months, 'there was a delightful unexpectedness about her. One might be called upon to lament the sufferings of Hosea, of Montrose, or of a chicken produced disconcertingly from the folds of her habit; or again, to chuckle with her over some absurdity, or wonder at the delicacy of a wildflower seen through her microscope'.

Held when 'the lilacs and irises and lilies of the valley [were] just at their best', the huge gathering swelled to 1100, and the procession was a sunburst of luminaries, including the archbishop, the warden, eighty clergy from the diocese and more from elsewhere, the provincial of the Society of the Sacred Mission, priests from the Syrian, Greek and Russian Orthodox churches, associated with the Mission from its inception, sixteen bishops, deaconesses, members of visiting communities, chaplains of CHN houses, and theological students. Sister Ida walked behind her crocodile of nuns. Appropriately, the archbishop's text came 'from the tender Gospel story of the woman with the cruse of spikenard', and he delivered 'an eloquent and scholarly sermon upon the history of the Religious Life and the Ministry of Women within the Church'. The gala ended with afternoon tea under the oak which Sister Christina had planted from a Scottish acorn many years before. Other events were timed to coincide with the occasion: the re-election of Ida, the installation of Sister Flora as Assistant Superior, publication of the biography of the foundress, and the second conference of superiors of Australian communities.

'We must arise betimes too, and meet God early': this extract from a seventeenth-century sermon by John Donne appeared in *In our Midst* at the start of the 1950s. 'Early Will I Seek Thee';

Now if we looke for this early mercy from God, we must rise betimes too, and meet God early. God hath promised to give *Matutinam stellam*, the Morning-star; but they must be up betimes in the morning, that will take the Morning-star. He himselfe who is it, hath told us who is this Morning star; *I Jesus am the bright and Morning starre*. God will give us Jesus; Him, and all his, all his teares, all his blood, all his merits; But to whom and upon what conditions? That is expressed there, *Vincenti dabo*, *To him that overcommeth I will give the Morning-star*.

The Community's endeavour had to be to bring its outer and inner life together so that the two flowered from the one stock or core. Needs still outstripped available human resources. In 1954, a priests associate group was formed, not to raise money but to celebrate the eucharist, publicize CHN's work in parishes, and 'pray for the Community & for an increase in vocations which was most important & necessary'. Despite the new emphasis on the Community's life of witness, the old instinct to expand into new work still had to be met: New Guinea, New Zealand, a proposal (ultimately refused) by the Department of Mental Hygiene that the sisters should run a hospital—government funded—for mentally retarded girls.

The twenty-fifth anniversary of Esther's death was commemorated in September 1956, and amidst a litany of remembrances came the plea 'that there may be such increase in number as Thou knowest to be needful'. The Community, Ida informed Chapter, was its 'largest to date, 50 professed with the N.Z. Sisters & 1 Noviciate all told'. To accommodate this substantial complement, Council agreed to transfer a generous block of land from Retreat House to Community House where a new kitchen and a refectory to seat seventy to eighty were planned. These commodious facilities were completed in 1957.

In 1958, Council paid tribute to Ida who was to retire later that year. 'Her sound judgment, unfailing courtesy & loving sympathy have marked her period of office as a time of planned development resulting in a widening of the various activities of the Mission.' At the start of 1960 her successor, Sister Flora, could report that with one recent profession and five more imminent, the Community was in a state of vibrant growth. But the 'planned development' had been partly in reaction to irresistible and devastating change, and the Community was about to find itself overtaken by an entirely unpredictable happening. In July that year, the vivacious Flora was diagnosed as having terminal leukemia, and in early November she died.

She was at centre stage for so short a time that she seems a victim of destiny, more a spectre than a presence. Eroded by illness and responsibility, she had little chance to leave her imprint on the Community, yet had she lived her personality seemed to promise a new style of Superior. Her warmth was infectious, her sense of humour irreverent, her religious outlook unmarked by sanctimonious pieties or adherence to rank. These qualities show most vividly in the letters she wrote from England in 1948 when she accompanied Ida in the routine peregrination around the English communities.

The duo arrived in March 1948 to an England still suffering the aftermath of war. The area around St Paul's was devastated, and the whole of London was scarred, while the damage to the fabric of the city was matched by a grim but disheartened fortitude in Londoners themselves:

It just makes one cold to see it... No wonder the people on the whole seem very weary & depressed & many of them very pessimistic— sure of another war very soon. Others say that no country is able to go to war *yet*, but of course everyone is frightened of Russia.

Dependent on food parcels for a touch of luxury, and severely rationed, the population resorted to its famous facility for queuing ('Everyone just falls into a queue & awaits their turn'). In democratic solidarity, ration books and identity cards were issued to the itinerants.

After a brief, unimpressed look-in at the Convent of the Presentation, Highgate, they headed for Wantage, Flora 'literally knocking at the knees' in fear that she might 'disgrace C.H.N.' 'Well', said the mother general, meeting them at the railway station, 'we've managed a funeral for you'—thus fulfilling the first part of the promise that a profession, a clothing, and a burial would be put on for their visitors to observe. In fact they had exceeded their commitment by providing a double funeral, thanks to the recent expiry of 'two old ladies of 89', while the sight of 'eight very old Sisters' wheeling the coffins into the chapel suggested that there was some risk the occasion might accidentally be overdone.

Adjusting to a Community whose on-the-spot numbers oscillated between sixty and ninety sisters, many of them old, blind and deaf, required alertness. Even saying the office was a major challenge ('Trying to find one's place is simply *dreadful*...at least 10 books...all back to front from ours'). The softness and speed of the singing, rationing of baths to once a week, meals eaten standing, were all additional trials. 'Only two sisters ever

sit & they are both very old & look as if they had had strokes.'
The bulk of the day seemed to be spent in chapel, and the pace
accelerated as the days went by, so that even keeping awake
was a labour, exaggerated by anxiety about not being alert
enough to fulfil such allotted duties as early morning watch in
chapel. Once one started to cope with its demanding routine,
however, there was the stimulus of observing all aspects of the
Community's life: from the novitiate with its 'brilliant young
things', to St Joseph's the girls' reformatory (now dubbed an
approved school in line with government policy), St Thomas's
convent, the Wantage branch house, a small contemplative
group which occupied the Bishop's Palace at Cudderston, the
school at Abingdon.

In April, a stay at the Community of the Epiphany at Truro
made Wantage seem easy and home-like. Most of the sisters
were 'at least seventy', and Flora was immediately struck by the
'great distinction... between the sheep & the goats', which
even required a separate residence for the 'second order of nuns'
who were not permitted to say all the offices, and were obliged
to do much of the heavy work in the superior house. Somewhat
guiltily, Flora admitted that she preferred the lower order. Even
meals had a bizarrely ritual effect, as of tempting fate, since the
oldest sisters acted as waitresses, 'many lame, several deaf &
one almost blind', and not all these stalwarts managed to
transport soup to the table without disaster. But Truro was
formidable in a variety of ways, down to its pinched spring
weather. The facilities run by the Community could not compare
with CHN's, St Michael's Home being 'a most dreadfully
depressing place' where the girls worked nineteenth-century
style in an antiquated laundry with equipment that seemed
designed to make their labours harder. Both the Second Order
House and the Children's Home were 'very cheerless & particularly the [latter] which is positively dreadful... I have never
been in a more depressing place'. The Australian visitors were
impressed, however, by the attempts to provide a free and
natural atmosphere for the inhabitants, a policy that extended
to the girls' reformatory, in defiance of the bleak physical
conditions.

'I am quite convinced ours is the nicest Community I have

seen.' Flora's verdict applied even more wholeheartedly after
the visit to a community more rigid still than Truro: St
Margaret's Convent, East Grinstead. She found herself alienated
and saddened by its extremities: 'So much that is done is so
unnecessary & disloyal to our branch of the Church'. At least
the convent at Highgate, despite its persistently bowing novices,
was distinguished by a co-operative atmosphere and the sisters'
dedication, while the Community of the Holy Name at Malvern
Link was exemplary in its loving support between sisters and
compassionate care for unmarried mothers and their children.
Highgate, however, had 'only *one* young novice' in training; it
was a symptom of changes which would later afflict her own
community.

Wantage still retained pre-eminence in her affections, and
the return there in June for the last part of the mother general's
tripartite promise, the clothing of a postulant, confirmed her
feelings of acceptance: 'I could hardly believe it possible in such
a huge community that there could be such a homely, friendly
atmosphere'. The community retreat at St Thomas's was the
crowning experience, the singing gave the impression that all
the many voices had blended into one, and the organ was the
very instrument played by Esther before her departure for
Australia: 'I felt very near indeed to her in spirit, although I
never had the joy of knowing her in this life'. When the
Australians left for London, every member of the Community
clustered warmly at the front door to farewell them.

'Flora by name, Flora by nature': after her death this saying
became the phrase with which to explain the ephemeral in her,
and at the same time to accept its loss. The final issues of *In
Our Midst*, May 1961, soberly recorded the loss and its unforeseen
aftermath:

The end came at six o'clock on the morning of November 6 when, at
the Queen Victoria Hospital, the fourth Mother Superior of C.H.N.
passed quietly and peacefully into the nearer Presence of the Lord
whom she had loved and served so faithfully... On November 30 the
Sisters assembled in chapel to elect their new Mother—Sister Faith
was duly elected—the fifth Mother Superior of C.H.N.

6

THIS STATE OF EVERLASTING OVER-EXPOSURE

It nearly killed people. And it nearly killed me... The local community who supported the Children's Home or the Mission House, or whatever it was, would immediately fly to the Bishop, and there would be top-level pressures brought to bear, and you could be made to feel completely amoral, if not immoral, for ever venturing to think that the Sisters have to be protected from this state of everlasting over-exposure.

Sister Faith

Faith gave her first address to Chapter in September 1961 in the shadow of Flora's death. Her emphasis was on the individual and collective challenge to the Community:

when she in whom we had placed our whole trust and confidence as our earthly leader was being withdrawn from us into the nearer presence of God, our future seemed uncertain, even precarious... It has been for each one and for the Community as a whole, a fresh launching out into the deep, into waters perilous and unknown, committing ourselves in blind faith and steadfast hope to the unfailing charity of God.

For Faith personally, the challenge was multiplied to almost overwhelming proportions. She was in her mid-thirties, almost saucily young to be a mother superior, and had been professed for a mere eight years at the time of her election. Since 1955, moreover, she had been in the New Guinea outpost. Not only were many of the Community unfamiliar with her, she was unfamiliar with them and many of their works, an ignorance most difficult in her dealings with the Mission where managerial skill and financial shrewdness were required.

These disadvantages were enough to disqualify her in her own mind; the gravest impediment, though, was a complete temperamental disinclination for the task. Her New Guinea companions remembered that they had virtually to push her onto the plane to return to Melbourne when the dying Flora recalled her to a seemingly inescapable fate. She was naturally retiring, sometimes distant, introverted and intellectual rather than extroverted and pragmatic, drawn to the mystical and contemplative quarters of the religious life, rather than to its more outgoing manifestations.

This catalogue of disqualifications, however, was outweighed by a largeness, intensity and grief in gauging the world's temper, a sense of the Community as a microcosm in tense and intimate relation to the macrocosm; and such an awareness was evident in her first address to Chapter. It was not only CHN's private affairs, but the world at large that confronted them: 'a day of crisis for the human spirit', requiring 'supernatural faith and courage'.

The sense of crisis had penetrated to the heart of the Community where internal matters, such as difficulties in revising the constitution (only the second major revision in eighty years), bred 'an unsettled and hypercritical attitude of mind and a certain weariness of spirit'. Amendments to this intractable document had been accepted at last, and revision of the Rule might follow. The painful reluctance of the Community to alter its structures was an ongoing trial during Faith's term.

Some of her recommendations therefore called for a redirection towards inwardness, a more sacrifical intensity. She suggested that, while corporate fasting was not to be insisted upon, such acts 'could be a spiritual weapon used for spiritual ends'. Mortification, prayer and self-denial; the death of self; to be so keenly aware of the pulses of good may entail an equal sensitivity to the strength of evil, and Faith's spiritual thinking was marked by vivid consciousness of this. 'We have to get rid of the "old man", and as our Lord spoke to his disciples of the evil spirit, "This kind cometh not out but by prayer and fasting" . . . There are many devils that can be driven out only by prayer and mortification.'

Her injunctions to reaffirm and deepen essential commitment
were partly temperamental, and partly stimulated by knowing
that the state was poised to take over 'the social services
pioneered by the Church'. Co-operation with other agencies,
not duplication, was to be aimed at. The Community was
advised to be willing to assume responsibilities not catered for
by government instrumentalities, and to be ready to reconsider
its approach, particularly in the institutional care of children,
long the sisters' most sentimentally appealing role, and now an
area of rapid change. Contraction of the Community's far-flung
efforts, and concentration on 'Community life', were part of the
acceptance of change.

The mantle of Mother Superior was a heavy but inspiriting
one.

In the letter Sister Flora sent us from hospital last year she wrote that
her years as Mother had been the happiest of her whole life. Many of
us must have wondered at her saying that, having seen her so often
strained and over-burdened, and yet I can now understand the truth
of it. At the time of my election it seemed, humanly speaking, a
hopeless situation. I had neither natural qualities nor experience to
bring to the office... I have been aware, constantly, of your prayers
and your loyalty and that they have been given always in spite of my
obvious failings.

This inaugural address had a note of personal and prophetic
pain that distinguished it from previous addresses to Chapter.
Faith's preferred reading included some of the Christian mystics,
and she had absorbed from them the imagery of paradox where
darkness is radiant and emptiness teems.

The theme of deepening the Community's spiritual life was
readdressed the next year, and developed into a critique of the
tendency whereby, in the face of advancing secularization,
many fall back on 'natural goodness and natural virtues'. For
religious, the life to which they are summoned, 'a life of astonishing simplicity, of almost, by the world's standards, scandalous
unreason', was the reverse of the prevailing pattern and could
not 'be lived in the power of natural virtues'. The temptation
towards mediocrity must be resisted, and required a total and

united response eschewing over-reliance on individuals, on the personal, and on the yardstick of natural goodness favoured by society. So the comforting and sustaining community of other people, while a manifestation of God's intentions in terms of necessary 'human help and support', should not distract from 'our dependence on God; rather it should be part of our love for and dependence on him, and move us to a more wholehearted abandonment to his will... We need to bring ourselves back continually to what we know is the ideal'. Failure to realize and adhere to this led to 'individualism and pride' and untroubled acceptance of 'a petty round of self-pleasing, disguised as necessity to our own eyes'.

The pressures on the Community and its uncertain future could not be ignored. To start with, there was the failure of suitable candidates to offer themselves as novices. Most of the many approaches came from those who were unconsciously taking refuge from the tribulations of secular life, and did not offer convincing evidence of vocation. The shrinkage might be interpreted as God's will, but it might alternatively point to the Community's own failure to offer a compelling example. The gulf between these seemingly incompatible possibilities, along with the Superior's references to her health and inadequacy, suggested a fundamental unease.

In whatever way the decline of the novitiate was interpreted, it could only be an ominous indicator of the future, even though at present, with sixty-three professed sisters, the Community was as large as it had ever been. Portents of change hung over the work, too. While traditional institutions were still needed—as witness the recent opening of St Anne's, a hostel for working girls attached to St Saviour's Children's Home at Goulburn—their replacement or transformation seemed inevitable. Social workers had been appointed to the two children's homes, and technical skills were increasingly expected of those working in the welfare field, so professionalization seemed obligatory. Two sisters were soon to participate in child-care training programmes run by the Social Welfare Department. At the same time, another reorientation had taken place, as emphasis swivelled from the nurture of the individual

child to attempts at sustaining the family as a unit, with consequent difficulties for the sisters who were also bound to the
timetable of the religious life.

The challenges extended to the still-burgeoning New Guinea
field, where the Australian administration's forceful approach to
education required incessant and onerous adjustment of work
places and curriculum. Although one of the sisters at Holy
Name School was a primary teacher, a lack of trained teachers
in the Community increased reliance on secular staff—with a
corresponding dilution of influence. Even the possibility of an
indigenous Papuan religious order looked harder to attain, since
'such a life would cut so gravely across background and tradition,
much more deeply for women than for men, that there is need
for much prayer and thought before definite plans can emerge'.
The establishment of a school for girls had aroused the suspicions
of Papuan men; the founding of a religious community for
women would quite possibly be taken as a more massive affront.
And even the most optimistic prognosis was governed by the
proviso that 'we cannot count on having unlimited time before
us in Papua'.

The need to preserve the essence of Community life, while
embracing changing techniques and attitudes in a technocratic,
materialist and escapist world, involved painful, unavoidable
conflict. Adaptation could mean unconsciously acceding to alien
values. The challenge was to gain the benefits of sociological
advance without being undermined or deflected:

We should take careful note of the conclusions of social and scientific
research, make use of such improved techniques as are available to us,
but we should take even more care that we do not become infected by
the humanist spirit that inspires much of the welfare work done in the
world today. I say 'infected' quite deliberately, and the choice of word
does not imply a derogatory attitude towards those whose contribution
to the welfare of mankind lies in this particular field. But let us be
quite clear that for the religious this spirit is an infection of the world
that can destroy the whole fabric of her life in Christ...a vehicle
for self-satisfaction so cunningly devised by our adversary as to go
unrecognized.

To act within while living without the world required a much more delicate balance than in the days when the provision of charity was accepted as the natural expression of Christian activism by a society that saw a strictly limited role for government in countering social distress, and was content to let the burden fall on whatever selfless shoulders there were.

In 1964, visiting England, Faith was encouraged 'to find the same ideas [as those she held for CHN] operating in a most dynamic, and I believe, fruitful way, in the life of other, more experienced communities'. Faith was in her fourth year of office and, unlike her predecessors on the trail who moved about with attentive CHN minders, she travelled to England alone:

I felt I wanted to be *free*, because if you've got another sister there's a certain obligation to see if she's OK, and if she's managing. I wanted to be completely free to give myself to each community I went to. . . I was going to experience life in another setting, so I wanted to be free to experience it.

Ida had planned her visits largely in an imitative spirit, to compare working methods but primarily to garner spiritual borrowings from the source for a Community that in many ways was still an English model with an Australian tinge. Faith's format was analytic; she wished to appraise how the English communities were adjusting to the vastly changed situation in which they operated, an analysis that might enable CHN to manage problems looming in the future, and confront them before they did damage.

I mostly went to the sort of mixed-type communities like our own. . . I had a specific programme for myself: to visit certain communities just to see how they lived, and to go to several other places to see how they worked, and two communities to see how they tackled the changes in child-care but stayed institutional. . . I'd planned it carefully months ahead. I'd picked up the way things were moving in some of these communities, and thought *that* would be interesting to see, because that's what we're heading for. . . The signs were there. One had to just deal with it, but I suppose I was positive in the sense of looking at how other people have coped with it.

This summary of her intentions may represent a private commitment made at the time, rather than a publicly declared programme, for her tapes back to Melbourne record many of the same preoccupations, reactions, interests, as the letters of Ida and Flora. She was, after all, writing to the same diverse audience, many of whom might focus on the tribal differences between communities, as expressed in their office, daily routine and clothing. Yet, despite her more intellectualized approach, or perhaps because of its constraints, her comments are more guarded than Ida's rich motherly intimacies and Flora's appealing girlish confidences. Her personal reticence comes through, and even though she was adroit in producing sharp vignettes of monastic foibles, one is reminded of her reluctant small talk, partly unconfident and partly abstracted.

The first stop was Wantage, 'an obvious must' for any visitor from CHN, and in ferment at 'the prospect of twenty-seven Mothers coming into retreat... quite an impressive collection of starch and serge'. Wantage, she observed, had provided the model for 'all our formularies and customs', a general philosophical approach to the religious life, and a formula for daily routines. By comparison with the detached metropolitan politeness Ida and Flora had often experienced, the Wantage sisters were avid for information about CHN, especially the work in New Guinea; but Faith found that conversation on home matters often sparked off a Catherine-wheel of confessions about 'all sorts of hair-raising and soul-shattering things that have happened during the course of the last hundred years... as there are fewer of us we have, perhaps, fewer saints but also fewer skeletons'.

Described in her tapes, life at Wantage seemed straightforward and normal, with a few amiable eccentricities. Privately, she felt that 'a lot of things seemed quite mad... I think they were probably just stuffy English ways, that seemed incredibly stuffy to an Australian'. It is hard to imagine Ida with her rock-bed of adherence to English practices, voicing such a heresy. Some of the other communities were similarly frozen into postures that no longer seemed relevant, either commonsensibly or philosophically. Even the sister-community of CHN Malvern Link was 'at that time very formal'; at conferences held twice daily sisters asked permission for the rest of the day's activities: 'to an Australian, that was a big joke...mind you, at the time we'd have to ask permission to use the telephone, and we did'. The Community of the Epiphany at Truro, which had had no novitiate since Flora's day, was 'an archaic survival... I went for about five or six days, and wished I'd made it two'. And the remaining Clewer sisters were rattling around in a huge palace at St George's Windsor—a situation that projected a possible scenario for CHN's future: 'they'd got twenty years ahead of us, to the point where they were going to diminish, and they had to get out of this old mansion and think about life out there'. Unpalatable though they were, certain portents had to be taken seriously.

But there were brighter and fresher signs: Whitby, a new community in Yorkshire, was unhampered by 'the sort of conventual rules of nineteenth century'; and the Community of the Sisters of the Church, 'terribly, terribly proper in my youth', was 'beginning to open up a little bit', making innovations in child-care which CHN might well match, while further interest attached to 'how the sisters managed their life in a community and managed to live with children in flats'. The Kennington sisters in turn wanted to learn more about Australian adoption procedures, an opening for reciprocity.

As she moved from community to community, Faith encountered two major areas of change. New social attitudes were being accommodated, particularly in child-care. She observed the London County Council's work in this field, and felt that its family-group cottages were the model to adopt. She was also impressed by a Hertfordshire children's home run by the Methodists along similar lines. CHN's children's homes might not be heavily institutional, but large groups necessarily meant the loss of the personal touch, and:

the consensus of opinion would appear to be that the Methodists do quite the best work in England in this line, with Dr Barnardo's coming along in the fore too, but that some of the anglican work is still rather old-fashioned. I'm afraid that's just us, isn't it? It seems to be so with the Anglican Church the world over.

One had to avoid becoming hidebound and arthritic.

The other major area of change was in the simplification of the office. The monastic diurnal was being used increasingly, 'an English translation of the Benedictine rite, much simpler than the one we are accustomed to, and which purports to be the primitive use, shorn of its later accretions'. English and American Anglican communities, Orthodox, Roman and Lutheran groups had all adopted it, in what 'seems to be regarded as part of the movement for unity'.

Faith saw in these practical and ideological shifts relevance for CHN. There was also comfort, especially for a community that existed in relative isolation, in evidence that 'all communities have the same problems and face the same difficulties. We do, of course, know this intellectually, but it makes quite a difference to actually hear the superiors speak about them'. She used her observations as a means of encouraging more flexible attitudes in those members of her own Community who confronted the possibility of change as if it were a spectre from the underworld. The problem was not entirely an internal one, either, for it was clear that the Anglican hierarchy in England was more receptive to experimentation than its Australian counterpart:

I gather from what one hears around the house that some sisters are very much for [liturgical experiment], and some are very much against new innovations. Others are all for sitting on the fence and seeing what comes out of all the experiments before doing anything here. That, of course, is rather our attitude at home, isn't it, that we will wait and see which way the Australian Church jumps, if it ever does jump. Here the Communities seem to have no difficulty in getting permission from their Visitors to do all sorts of things if they want to.

The most personally significant stop was at the Sisters of the Love of God, Fairacres, the community she had been attracted to when she first felt called to the religious life, and the place where she was to experience a serious breakdown six years later. She arrived there 'tired of living out of a suitcase, tired of saying other people's Offices, tired of keeping other people's customs, and what else? Oh, just with trying to be intelligent!' Tired, she might have added, of answering queries on every matter from silence to seating in refectory, from food to footwear.

Suffering from a raging cold, she was put to bed and doctored with a quota of milk and whisky, delivered by a novice with the trepidation of one who believed she bore something incendiary rather than medicinal. Faith felt that the depth of their solicitude must indicate she looked quite frightful, but couldn't tell because there were no mirrors.

The attraction towards this community was confirmed by experience:

I felt very much at home there, more so, I think, than in any other convent I have been in. Their life is very simple and one had an impression of a very vital and vigorous spirituality and sense of direction in all they did, and the quiet of the House was just balm to the soul after all the running round I have been doing. In fact, if it hadn't been for the time there I don't think I could have faced the next month.

The community was also in a healthy state numerically, with eight novices and two postulants (two more arrived while she was there)—perhaps an early indicator of the trend which over the years would bring a renewed increase to the contemplative communities. In the calm confidence of Fairacres there was both a personal sign for Faith, and something she perceived as an intimation for CHN:

You may remember my saying before I came away that though I mightn't come back with any new ideas, I *might* come with some old ones confirmed. One of my old ones that I've had for a long time is a wish that we as a Community could give more time to prayer. You may not agree, and I can imagine many of you holding up your hands in horror and saying, How should we find the time? But we do, in fact, find time for what we want to do, don't we?...and who is there to pray, especially in the Church in Australia?... It's been very noticeable that the most vigorous and vital of the English communities are those which *do* give more time to prayer... It seems to me to be a crying need in an age like ours, where everything is breaking up and disintegrating, that there should be as much as possible of this unifying power abroad in the world.

Meanwhile, her own community was attempting to cope with change in its practical commitments. By the mid-1960s, sisters were participating in child-care, probation and religious education courses. CHN had relied on the multifariousness of its activities, reacting to needs as they arose, in the belief that a wholehearted response compensated for lack of specialized training. But the age of the professional had arrived: 'It is not acceptable these days to be jack-of-all-trades and master of none'. For many of the older sisters a new life as a professional was not possible.

For the Community as a whole, the devaluation of its currency of hard work and learning-by-experience was demeaning, and stirred anew its lingering suspicion of the educated who might also be the over-educated. The response varied between an almost voracious preparedness to ascend the ladder of professionalism, to a fall-back on the old values of compassion and humility:

if people have to have a social worker's degree or a psychiatrist's degree, then I'm out, because I don't happen to have any of it; but if I *care* and I go on caring no matter what they do—You have to try and let God use you, and not think you've got all the answers.

In some sisters, the inflexibility that often gathers round old age was exacerbated by the habits of old-style conventual existence. There was also an irony in the fact that their vocation had demanded they relinquish the very ambitions—the successful getting-on—the world now required of them. Some of these sisters must also reflect that, when they grew up, higher education and professional training were privileges rather than rights, and that they had not been born into privilege. This can produce a wry amusement at the pretensions of the certificated at conferences and seminars, and even at the enthusiasm with which some sisters have determined to qualify themselves so that they can operate on equal terms with other professionals. There are practical problems in any case, when numbers are falling, in maintaining the work-force while others take extended time for study. Rather bitterly, it was observed that the Community's effort to professionalize itself has been partly self-defeating because some of the sisters who were given special dispensations for study have subsequently left.

Despite the demand for ticketed respectability, the old instinct to move in where need showed itself survived. Educational work at Winlaton, an institution for juvenile female offenders, was extended. There was increasing co-operation with the Brotherhood of St Laurence in the inner suburbs; and when the Community's work at Altona was felt to be sufficiently established to hand over to lay people, a replacement was found in 'an intensive programme of pastoral visiting in Airport West'. Concern to meet and match the outside world was demonstrated in increased participation in conferences and seminars on theological and welfare matters, closer interaction with seculars, the undertaking of hospital chaplaincies (dating back to 1949, when a start was made at the Queen Victoria Hospital), the continued court work and an extension of the work among unmarried mothers. An ecumenical group-therapy programme, sponsored by Roman Catholic and CHN sisters, was operating at Fairlea Women's Prison, while Mission House was gearing itself for 'future ecumenical action' in the labyrinth of high-rise flats being constructed in Fitzroy.

As an entity, however, the Community was most strongly attached to its work among children. Its original clientele had been the women and children who lived near the first Mission House, and for many years sisters, whether maternal or not, were liable to find themselves thrust into the demanding environment of the various babies' and children's homes. But institutional child-care was being revolutionized, and if CHN were to continue its involvement, change was obligatory. At Brighton, the main house was converted into flats and St Faith's became a family unit, reflecting the new philosophy that workers should provide 'something nearer to a normal family life for the children'. Despite the seriously disturbed nature of the children concerned, the move was felt to be beneficial, and gave several of the sisters an especially intimate mission in caring for a small group of children.

On the other hand, the Babies' Home at Darling had increasingly become 'a clearing house for wards of the Social Welfare Department', and the government body was a more appropriate manager of short-term care. Chapter was warned to expect 'radical change'. By 1967 the home was being used as a temporary refuge for unmarried mothers and deserted wives and their children, and negotiations for its sale were in train. Launched on the expectation of unchallenged continuance in the field, the Community's most modern home for children had been operating for only thirteen years. Once the sale was accomplished, 'new work in an area of need at present untouched', rather than a reorientation of work with small children, was favoured, given that CHN's activities were limited by numerical constraints. Amidst all the pain and disintegration of relinquishment, the prompt recognition of defeat was at least a courageous way of ending that long chapter.

The Community's work with children had not been without difficulties and deficiencies, many of which were determined by outside forces. For one thing, there were so many children who needed care, and the prevailing disciplinary attitudes were often oppressive. Some of the attitudes, however, were the Community's own. 'There was a fairly tight discipline, but there was an understanding. The kids accepted it and the sisters accepted them, and they could go just so far...things had to be dealt with in a disciplinary way because that was the known and accepted way.'

The sisters themselves reported some of the more idiosyncratic and avoidable blemishes: adherence to authoritarian strictures and bleak institutional formulae for no good reason; occasions when the sisters applied the vow of poverty more rigorously to their charges than to themselves; the retention of unhappy and unsuitable people in child-care; unreal expectations, such as the maintaining of silence at some meal times, and an overdose of church attendance; the subterfuge of photographing children in their Sunday-best before returning them to their less charming everyday clothes. Of course, variants of many of these foibles were the ruling mode in plenty of suburban homes.

The rarity of abuses, not the fact that they happened, is perhaps the most convincing testimony to the selflessness of those sisters who were prepared to devote their lives to the care of children whose futures they could in no way determine, and who might suddenly be whisked from their hands. Probably no

one in the Community regretted the demise of the large institutions, but when the Community's role at Brighton shrank to
insignificance, the outcome was devastating for some—especially
perhaps for those for whom giving up the expectation of children
had been one of the most painful consequences of joining the
Community.

The big question mark was how would the sisters live then, because
we'd got used to generations of living cheek by jowl with children...
People never enjoy giving up territory, do they? And there's always a
certain sentimental attachment to what you can *see* with children's
work... There were certain people who found that very difficult to
accept for themselves, and because they were who they were and what
they were, it was difficult to see the Community moving out there, or
that there could be any changed role for them with children.

Yet sometimes transformation rather than relinquishment
was what change meant. Retreat House had become used to a
bursting engagement book; but then, as other conference centres
were established, it could revert to its original purpose as a
place for those who required a haven of contemplative quiet.
The sisters relinquished their work at the hostel in North
Adelaide in order to take over the Retreat House which already
existed at Belair in the Adelaide Hills. At Goulburn, facilities
were improved to cater for a smaller number of children, though
the home was plagued by illness and frequent changes of staff.
In Auckland, the situation was stable, and the New Guinea
scene was flourishing, with academic successes for pupils of
Holy Name School both in public exams and at the University
of Papua New Guinea, while as a direct offshoot of the school
influence, the indigenous Community of the Visitation at
Hetune was growing with 'signs of the authentic religious spirit'.
Whatever the Community made of it, change was the most
persistent feature of its life, even though that life had been
founded on immutabilities of belief.

On all side the principles that we have grown up with are called in
question, and not only by irresponsible elements in society. Philos-
ophers and artists, economists and theologians, are all seeking new
definitions, reaching out after what seem at first fresh sources of

inspiration, for a faith that speaks to the present condition of men...
But when we ponder the ideas and formulae of what is called the new
theology, we seem chiefly to be juggling with words and interpret-
ations; there is little genuinely original thought revealing fresh aspects
of reality... Even what may seem at first sight new and revolutionary,
the marriage between theology and science...is not foreign to primitive christian thought, to the theology of St Paul or the mysticism of
St John. It would seem that the seeds which flower today are those
that germinated two thousand years ago.

Acceptance of change did not mean abandonment of discipline,
for 'those who hold discipline in contempt...are slaves in
revolt'. Indeed, the shift the Community was attempting, from
collective to personal responsibility, required a personal discipline
more soundly based than ever. Law and discipline, though
currently discredited, were essential to human progress.

By the mid-1960s, CHN was seriously reconsidering many of
those customs and methods of government which had reigned
inviolate since Esther's day. A change of vows was projected
(despite a few sisters' misgivings that lack of finality meant a
withholding of absolute commitment), and a consequent extension of the training period in the juniorate. The Community's
time-honoured fixities no longer seemed inevitable. In 1965,
modifications were made 'in an endeavour to bring the spirit of
the community to fulfilment in contemporary terms'—an adjustment that produced disquiet and disorientation in some,
and almost certainly firmed the grounds for a reactionary motion
in a few. The initial changes involved simplification to the
habit, which was still in the voluminous style Esther had worn,
and in the recitation of the office. The next year, the 'first
elective chapter for profession according to the new constitutional
method' was held. Faith observed that the revised provisions
and the altered relationships between individuals which followed
had the effect of deregulating Chapter into 'an arena or a rather
crude form of debating society'. This would certainly not have
done in earlier days, when any grievances dissolved into more
or less compliant obedience before they were dragged forth for
formal scrutiny.

Two years later, a radical revision of the customary to recognize individual rather than collective responsibility was prepared

for presentation to Chapter. A general 'necessity to overhaul our Customs' and to initiate 'ordered experiment' was admitted. The temperate and impersonal language of the assessment obscured the disruptive nature of the alteration, and the disturbances for individuals—especially perhaps for the Superior, who had to calm communal disquiet as well as salvage her own sensibility.

The attempt to reformulate relationships in the Community produced such tensions that a restitution of the old ways might almost have seemed justified. In 1967, the Superior felt constrained to include in her annual address admonitions concerning the proper modes of interaction between the Superior and the Community at large. Complaints of authoritarianism might actually disguise an unwillingness on the critic's part to give herself fully to her vocation. On the other hand, the Superior was required to encourage in the individuals within her domain 'full opportunity for growth in responsibility and determination'.

Maintaining a balance was delicate, painful and costly. Two professed sisters had that year been released from their vows. The compassionate tone of Faith's commentary on their departure differed markedly from the fierce summaries Ida made of 'warped' qualities which had resulted in an earlier defection, and from the barely suppressed anger of Flora's announcement of a similar event. The circumstances that surrounded the sisters' departure meant 'a time of considerable heart-searching for us all... Again, there is no need for panic, or even disquiet'. The tally of such departures was mounting, and Faith admitted in retrospect, with a ruefulness that discounted the distress, that such announcements 'became quite part of the scene'.

Nowadays we tend to treat them a little more rationally, but they're still painful. If you've lived on very close terms with somebody for ten, fifteen, twenty years, and then they make that sort of break it goes fairly deep personally... My overriding feeling would be that, if we were talking about failures, it was we who had failed the person. We hadn't somehow supported them or provided what they needed for a reasonably full and satisfactory kind of life... When people really get to a point of desperation, then everything folds up...everything might come tumbling down in a great hurry.

These breaks reverberated beyond the fate of individuals, into the collectivity, causing 'a great deal of confusion and hurt and *fear*. After all, we were getting smaller'. The reactions of other sisters ranged through incomprehension, anger, sadness and acceptance, often depending on age. One older sister was convinced that the relinquished vocations had always been flawed, while her younger colleague accepted the departures as a challenge to reaffirm her own commitment. Fury that devoted sisters had been driven out by the Community's demand for conformity contrasted with anger at the disappearance of one sister who had been allowed large privileges and was seemingly being groomed for a key position. The reaction, usually not condemnatory, was naturally strong when the one who left was a particular friend. One sister who was herself in a state of turmoil saw the process as part of an upheaval in the world at large, and substantial reasons for what has occurred may be located not so much in failures of the Community or individuals as in a general devaluation of spiritual meaning, the crisis in authority, the erosion of personal certainties.

With the culmination of trends which had been developing since the late 1940s, the next few years saw the Community's virtual withdrawal from its traditional activities.

The year 1969 was deemed of 'particular challenge and decision for the Community... The whole value of our life as christians and religious is called into question today...we have felt the increasing strain, at times an intolerable strain'. Apart from outside pressure, internal difficulties of change impinged; there were revisions to the archaic customary which had become an urn for the small dry bones of an unusable etiquette; a similar reworking of the constitution where unrealistic notions of authority were enshrined; the decision to rewrite the rule in more accessible and acceptable language; the attempt to strengthen horizontal bonds between members of the Community, in place of the traditional hierarchical structures. All these delicate reworkings of the fabric added to the strain. 'How difficult it is for some of us to give up our authoritarian attitudes, to relax our rigid codes and structures. Some of us don't feel safe without them, and habit dies hard.' Necessary though they were, forms needed to be liberating. Permanence and rigidity were no longer options, for change was 'just the one thing that has come to stay'.

Meanwhile outside the walls the Community was experiencing a 'growing sense of uneasiness...about the quantity and quality of the work we have undertaken'. The blow that struck closest to the heart was the decision to restructure the Mission to the Streets and Lanes in the wake of a social worker's review of its operations. Within a year, an executive director of the Mission had been appointed, and the decision to sell Mission House and to consolidate with the activities of St Mark's, Fitzroy, had been made. Soon new Mission projects were staffed solely by seculars.

In its counsels, the Community might acknowledge the wisdom of withdrawing from many traditional areas of work, 'in order to develop a more effective community life, work and witness over a smaller area', but the symbolic importance of being unintentionally, yet as if by design, squeezed out of control of the Mission House and its activities was immense. One of the sisters who was centrally involved felt it to be, although perhaps inevitable, needlessly hurtful, even 'cruel'. Personal tensions made a difficult situation harder still. A stiffness that suggested resentment on the part of the sisters who were used to being in charge of the Mission House was not assisted by the well-meaning but sometimes clumsy approach of the new director. The sister in charge of mission services, who had been appointed to relieve the Superior of the dual burden of administering the Community and managing the Mission, felt that her position did not develop the degree of independence that it warranted. Perhaps a more fundamental error had been made in not answering an appeal to undertake mission work in Broadmeadows, where the kind of family that had traditionally come to Mission House had moved.

The changes produced a Mission that was professionally adept and knew exactly where its money went; but as with the scent of a commercial rather than home-grown flower, some intangible had evaporated. The Community may have been a little slapdash with Mission finance at times, but 'the work got done and the people who needed help got helped, and in some ways it was a much more *sensitive* organization because we were very *close* to it all. Now it's organized. You can account for what happened to every *cent*, but some life is ebbing away while you put your case and get it accepted'.

CHN's retrenchment went on. The withdrawal covered a wide front: the branch houses at Goulburn and Auckland which had involved the Community from 1933 and 1958 respectively; some chaplaincies; the Department of Extension and Evangelism at the Mission House; work in adoption. The last was one of those changes which were welcomed rather than regretted. CHN had been involved in adoption for most of its history, much of the activity being conducted with an informality that the sisters themselves knew contained some not-so-hidden risks. The balance between happy and miserable outcomes was always fragile; *In Our Midst* printed disapproving stories of would-be parents who arrived demanding surrogate offspring as like them as possible; and the burden of arranging satisfactory adoptions was therefore easy to discard although most of the ruptures were exceedingly painful. One sister, who was fated to be on the spot for several finalizations, briefly described the stress of one break:

we were leaving Goulburn altogether, and of course that was a traumatic time for the three of us who were left in Goulburn, because the sisters had been in the diocese for over thirty years and the diocese didn't want to let us go. And the children of course, children in a children's home found that [it] was difficult for them.

Upheavals of that kind were humanly disruptive and required a strong effort of will to ensure that the threads were wound off without permanent damage to the spindle. In the face of an understandable temptation to panic, Faith exhorted the Community not to see all this as a calamity; and yet the intensity of the retreat suggested an unbearable attrition.

The only luminous spot in this gloomy prospect was New Guinea, where a first profession had taken place at the Community of the Visitation at Hetune, and Holy Name School continued to flourish. Even here, the Community's tenure was uncertain: 'there is a unanimous opinion that we should continue

this work at present. Certainly, there is no one else currently
prepared to press the claims of women's education in the
diocese... the time. for withdrawal from the school does not yet
seem to have come'. But eventual withdrawal seemed inevitable;
only the timing was uncertain, and independence for Papua
New Guinea and consequent political disruption were likely to
precipitate the final decision.

The Community had long responded to calls for assistance in
work they did so well, yet the definite territoriality about the
way in which properties had accrued reflects, perhaps, a yearning
for security. The desire for consolidation and a protective barrier
was particularly evident in the accumulation of parcels of land
around Community House, to give, in Ida's words, 'ample space
for quiet and seclusion'. It was a design that some older sisters
had set their hearts on, and was made possible by the sale of
market gardens which surrounded the estate. With the purchase
of another four acres in 1945, the Cheltenham property consisted
of twelve acres and was deemed to allow 'ample space for future
needs', but purchases continued until the late 1960s. Perhaps
the Community sensed that their fate was firmly concentrated
on the mother house and that their wide territory outside was
doomed to diminution.

When the Community left the institutions, the moves were
not merely severance with places and practical functions. They
meant relinquishing a spiritual investment and the endowment
of holiness. Every house that the sisters took up was a house of
God, and the sacred nature of the occupation went below the
stones, bricks and mortar to the earth beneath. Buildings and
landscapes too were imbued with symbolic force. The letter
Sister Elizabeth wrote the Community from the Holy Land, in
1935 during her visit to Wantage to train as novice mistress,
is a testament to the powerful attachment aroused by sacred
places:

One is shown the reputed footprint of our Lord on the rock which
breaks through the stone pavement. It is most fascinating to see how
the rock breaks through at nearly all the holy places, so rugged and
stable amid much that is tawdry and changing... Beneath the convent [of the Sisters of Sion] recent excavations have revealed part of

the *original* Via Dolorosa, the very stones over which our Lord must have passed on the way to the Judgment Hall. . . I have stones and flowers and mementos of nearly all the Holy Places.

After the spirit, stone, its seeming opposite, offered the next gradation of permanence, and its symbolic force extended to the human element, for the sisters were 'living stones' in the rubble of uncharged matter. The Community had always emphasized the outflowing of spiritual power from its buildings, from the laying of foundation stones to the deconsecration of chapels. Secular structures were opened with pride; the places of worship were consecrated with praise. Every nook and cranny, almost, was included in a ritual of sanctification. When Community House was dedicated in 1936, the *Age* reported that 'Every room was entered and dedicated'; at Ellerslie, the archbishop undertook a tour of blessings in which only the bathrooms were denied consecratory mention.

Wherever CHN went, from the distorted honeycomb of inner Melbourne to the rippled escarpments of Dogura, one of the first acts was the creation of an oratory or a chapel. Disposed with ceremonial correctness and housewifely late-Victorian stiffness, the altars were the heart, the head and the eye. Special sentiment attached to the Mission House, partly because it represented the Community's first work, partly because of its connection with the foundress. The nostalgia evoked by this institution was captured in *In Our Midst*'s inimitable style in 'The Door Progresses' (November 1957) which traced the Mission House through its various incarnations from Little Lonsdale St to Fitzroy. During Ida's office, Community House became the spiritual hub, the 'Mother House', and Chapter was bidden: 'To us who live in the Mother House now is given the privilege of making the tradition for the future'. Compellingly or repellingly, its force has gathered: one sister would like to see the place sold up ('I hate the atmosphere. I feel as if I want to destroy it. . . There's no room for me to express myself spiritually'), another finds its psychic power so overwhelming that 'it always cuts me up into little bits; I'm sort of fragmented here'.

Throughout the Community's history attention had been lavished on description of its dwellings, especially the interiors.

Images of departure were preserved with loving determination. Old St John's School in Latrobe St was photographed amidst its own rubble with a surviving arch time-defyingly inscribed 'This is the house of the Lord'. In the early 1980s, when three sisters moved into a tamely suburban dwelling near Community House to attempt the enclosed life, the place was named the 'House of Christ the King'. As far as possible in a world dedicated to obsolescence, the Community tried to carry with it some of its most cherished effects, even when they were not elegant or beautiful. Icons given by the Syrian Orthodox Church, who had held their services in the first Mission Hall, and embroideries such as the six by four banner stitched by the sisters in their crannies of spare time in 1906, were easily put in the saddle-bag, but more substantial items demanded determined feats of translation. The claustrophobic wood-lined Chapel of St Laurence had been transported from St George's to the new Ellerslie; and a memorial window from the chapel at Brighton accompanied Sister Margaret Anne to Box Hill Hospital where she had become chaplain. Windows were moved from Spring St, to Fitzroy St, to Napier St, where the low ceiling could barely accommodate them. But such rites of transfer were not always possible. When the Children's Home at Brighton finally came to be sold, the Chapel of the Holy Innocents was lost in its totality, despite last-ditch attempts to save the stained-glass windows with their bud-like infants and seraphim. Such departures severed life on several levels, and when they came in multiples the dislocation was hard to bear.

The Community's plight was exacerbated by a destructive tendency in some of its members to resist co-operation with and to resent direction from the certificated people who now controlled the social welfare scene. Yet one of its most worthwhile new involvements, the Brighton Family Centre, was directed by seculars and employed a sister who had launched herself with verve and determination into the challenge of the professionals. The Community was urged to avoid 'ignorant criticism' and to listen to qualified people whether they were Christian or not: 'life will not become any easier and we certainly cannot live it in isolation'. Recognizing that 'much of the work we once did can now be better done by others' could still be offset by the awareness that 'we have something unique to offer, in co-operation with members of other professions'. The difficulties of adjustment, particularly for older members of the Community who had long expected supremacy in their domain, were formidable, and the usual problems of retirement were given a biting edge by the realization that the close-down was abrupt, communal and comprehensive.

At the same time, the internal trends that threatened the very existence of the Community were confirmed: the shrinking of the novitiate, the desertion of some sisters, the increased attractiveness of the contemplative life, ageing, death. To build strength from within when the materials were failing or unavailable required superhuman dedication. The novitiate, which had dwindled from a peak of about a dozen in the early 1960s, was further weakened when some of the younger sisters withdrew. In 1972, it shrank to one; two years later, with the profession of that contender, it ended, and 'only one serious new-style aspirant' had materialized. Admitting that the collapse of the novitiate was generally welcomed 'because we don't really quite know what we want to train postulants for' was essentially defeatist, and disillusion surfaced further in the irony of Faith's comment in 1975 that of several aspirants 'one...may even arrive'.

If the world had moved on, CHN, while affirming its core of commitment, must move on as well or vanish like any other antediluvian species—but that at times seemed the hardest of all things to explain:

We'd been changing the novitiate training programme...since the early sixties, but the sisters' attitudes hadn't changed very much, except among the younger ones... What they were discussing in the novitiate and what the sisters out there expected were sometimes quite dissimilar... We used to have discussions about how the religious life was changing and adapting, and what our expectations of the novitiate ought to be, but it didn't seem to make any difference for about twenty years... It really did break when there wasn't a novitiate...there was a cut-off point, and we just had to leave it alone, except the poor souls who agonized over what was going on.

In 1973, three more sisters were released from the Community, making a tally of seven such departures in the previous six years. Some of those who left were not recent arrivals but sisters who had been with CHN for their most fruitful years. Rejection was matched by withdrawal. Contemplative living was hardly a choice, almost a necessity, but its appeal grew in natural reaction to the state of a world consumed by materialism, afflicted by catastrophe, and poised for annihilation. As well, there was the removal of those responsibilities which had tied the Community so meaningfully to the active life. In 1974, two sisters requested to live 'in greater silence and enclosure', after attempting the contemplative life within the Community's daily round. The next year, a group of five had chosen 'a more silent and enclosed life in our midst'. Responsibility for aged and chronically ill sisters accrued; death became an ever-present reality. In 1972, Ida, Superior for over twenty-three years and one of the last embodiments of the old stability, died after years of tragic incapacity. The next three years saw the deaths of eight more sisters.

External and internal factors seemed to be undermining CHN from each side, as changes undertaken in an attempt to build up inner strength proved debilitating instead. The Community was felt to be in 'daily danger of losing our vision of God' and succumbing to 'a failure of nerve'. The principle of authority, central to the Community's mode, competed with the principle of self-determination. Faith felt constrained to reiterate the view that personal responsibility had a corollary in the need for greater internal discipline. Even the Community's commitment to the concept of religious poverty was undergoing a sea-change: 'we still behave as though we are socially privileged people. We expect special consideration and shrink from sharing the common lot of poor people'.

Panic at numerical decline and withdrawal from much active work was aggravated by a failure to grasp that these two factors were interrelated. The answer lay in a return to 'our primary commitment', rediscovering the truth that a religious order was not 'a community of action' like the army (an old metaphor of Esther's), but 'a community of being', 'a microcosm of the whole body of Christ':

the old understanding of obedience was based on...the superior giving the orders and the sisters giving an exact detailed obedience.

This has been the model on which religious communities have in good part functioned at least for the last two centuries. I don't think we need here go into the matter of whether it was right for them to function so much on those lines under the circumstances of those times with their pressing, unmet social needs and their social structures, but we do have to ask ourselves if it is right for us today.

For the Superior, still caught willy-nilly on the pinnacle, the feelings of bewilderment and futility in some of her sisters, impatience for renewal in others, represented a painful personal challenge—particularly when the diversity of vocations, once welcomed for the rich possibilities it promised, now threatened to fragment the Community further:

It's difficult for any one of us to see it whole. One sister sees us as called to prayer and active ministry, another as called in future to a more interior prayer, to more silence; yet another to a form of community life in which all these vocations can be fulfilled in the richness of diversity. Which one is right? I do not know the answer. Our Warden frequently tells me that nowadays nobody, including leaders in national and academic life, the professions, business and industry, can see very far ahead, can plan for the future. Everything is provisional and passing.

But to admit that CHN was beset by the transience and relativity bedevilling the world at large was embracing a further dimension of suffering.

In the words of one of Faith's favoured spiritual mentors, Teilhard de Chardin, 'Suffering holds hidden within it, in extreme intensity, the ascensional force of the world'; but that resurrection is hard to endure, and even harder perhaps to communicate. Each year the positive approach seemed less attainable, and a tone of personal impotence and desolation forced itself into Faith's addresses. Retrospectively, she explained this by saying with deceptive lightness that she had 'run out of steam'; at the time, her meditations on suffering had a deeper tone. Their force went beyond the weariness of long years in office, to try to reach towards whatever invisible processes were straining to manifest themselves within the Community:

Our early Sisters knew something about fear, doubt, humiliations.

Humiliations are part of the heritage into which we have entered, and the corporate humiliation of confusion and uncertainty we are experiencing should lead us to a deeper faith and confidence in the One who has called us... Battered from without and from within by our doubts, fears, prejudices, we must find our internal centre of gravity in the indwelling Christ.

Extreme though the sense of turmoil and dereliction was in these addresses, the Community was experienced in contemplation of the significance of suffering, collective and individual. Esther's 'Notes on the Religious Life' are bleak and axiomatic on the subject: 'All suffering becomes fruitful if borne as a cross, not in the spirit of a prig, but as a humble follower along the Via Dolorosa'. In her address to Chapter in 1946, Ida made one of her periodic comments on suffering in its more domestic form: 'Sometimes it seems as though we have more than an ordinary amount of sickness, and it may be that is part of the vocation of the Community'. She was proffering an explanation in metaphoric terms of what the Community's mission might mean. In the years ahead as CHN began to withdraw from active involvements, one of the hardest duties of the Superior was to convince disappointed outsiders that 'the sisters have got to be protected from this state of everlasting over-exposure', since they, like ordinary mortals, fell ill. The incidence of physical and psychological illness has in fact been dauntingly high—offset, admittedly, by the astonishing longevity of some valiants.

When the sisters ruminated on their own illnesses and those of their colleagues, they usually offered a multi-faceted explanation whose emphasis varied according to the individual's place on the Community's spiritual spectrum. The first component mentioned, especially by those who categorized themselves as Martha-types, was pressure of work: rising at five as a novice, for example, to light the coppers in the House of Mercy laundry, or singlehandedly assisting forty children out of bed and through breakfast without 'any training or help'. Some older sisters contrasted the regimen of their youth with the softer expectations of a later lot: 'in our day you went until you dropped, and when you stopped you usually stopped for a long

Walking with the governor's wife, wimple slightly askew: Sister Christina and Lady Huntingfield at the opening of the House of Mercy extensions in 1938.

'She put her in her mother's place, the mother she'd never had': Esther, the Mother Foundress, and Sister Bertha on board ship bound for England in 1927.

The nursery at St George's Hospital, at Christmas 1938.

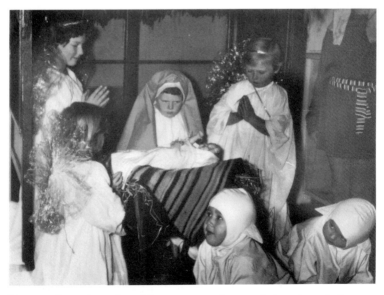

Nativity play with a solemn Mary, winsome sheep and pleased angels, late 1940s.

time...it was almost a physical impossibility'. The individual's drive to keep extending the limits of her endurance was matched by the system's determination to extract the maximum—partly out of necessity, partly because the more rigorous the discipline, in some people's eyes, the better. 'Some people just by nature place tremendous burdens upon themselves by the work they undertake, quite apart from what's put upon *them*.' One sister emphasized the system's failure to enable a reasonable outcome: 'I think probably in days gone by there was too much hard physical work. I think it was unbalanced... Unbalanced work and play, if you like, work and leisure'.

A second way of explaining the prevalence of illness was to recall the highly stressed situations some of the Community's work involved, and the pressure this put on vulnerable personalities. The most emotionally draining jobs were probably supervision at the House of Mercy, with its pitifully young but highly resistant 'fallen women', and the court work associated with the Mission House, which usually involved confronting the multiple tragedies of families who hovered on the rim of survival. The pressure was worsened by the Community's reluctance to provide specialized training, and by the failure of experienced sisters to pass on insights to their successors. Combined with the rigor of religious observances, the demands often seemed overwhelming.

A third part of the explanation related not so much to the system's demands for superhuman strength, but the arbitrariness with which individuals were placed here or there on the Community chessboard. Some sisters were summarily pulled out of situations in which they were established and creative, with unsettling results all round. One sister, who has an advanced Pied Piper's touch with children, was removed from one of the children's homes and forbidden to return lest her reappearance interfere with adjustment: 'I used to find my nails digging into the palms of my hands, and I got an ulcer. I didn't mind being moved, but I *did* mind not going back to the children...they thought I didn't care that much.' Novices and sisters might also be allotted work entirely unsuited to them. This was especially liable to happen at the children's homes where sisters were sent under the assumption that they were naturally maternal, and

that if they weren't, their souls would benefit by the forcing
process. The results were sometimes comprehensively disastrous.
One sister spent seven years at the Babies' Home struggling to
manage the children and crying herself to sleep nightly. Her
statement on the way she sees this damaging period of her life
encapsulated the philosophic meaning the Community found in
illness once it cast aside the code of self-suppression:

I think most people have in some way crises, maybe not what you'd
call an actual nervous breakdown... We've learned to verbalize how
we feel and what we've been going through... I think personally that
you just can't help other people unless you've been through a healing
process yourself, and once you start on a healing process it never
stops... It's no wonder we had a lot of breakdowns and people
leaving...when you come into this life there's no escapes, you're
faced up with yourself and you have to go through some kind of
breakdown situation because that's part of it, and you either clam up
and shut it out and pretend it hasn't happened, or you move into the
healing and become what in fact you're meant to be, more a whole
person.

Another sister put a slightly different orientation on her account,
shifting the emphasis from the psychological to the metaphysical:
'it's the long-term healing of our inward needs...a healing of
all the areas that haven't been given to God'.

The core of the sisters' explanation of the significance of
illness is that it is an inescapable part of spiritual formation;
that illness has both a chastening and an edifying function; that
suffering is a purifying process that simultaneously proves the
individual's worthlessness and her capacity for improvement:
'For he maketh sore, and bindeth up: he woundeth, and his
hands make whole'. Body and soul are a unity. Illness is a
metaphor for the unregenerated condition of the soul, and a
paradigm for our human existence which is both physical travail
and spiritual journey. Illness often sparks off a vocation, and is
the crowning test of a sister's life. One of the sisters considered
the years of painful mental decline endured by one of her
colleagues, and commented: 'To me, it was just God's progress
through her, something she had to pass through in order to
become the person she had to be'. In this schema, humiliation

must be final and complete. Illness is integral to the problem of suffering, and entwined with the function of prayer as both submission and supplication. The problem of suffering is the volcanic core of the Christian mystery, and on the human level, it enables penetration of and assistance with the sufferings of others. One of the sisters who engages herself physically and mentally with the particular suffering of humanity, especially in a concern with South Africa to which she was drawn when she first considered joining the religious life, said with thorny humility: 'I feel I've got a particular vocation to sharing in, or being very aware and holding for the suffering of the world, and I guess some of the things that I've *been* through have enabled me to understand some of what suffering is about'. She might have been talking of the Community's collective vocation.

Human suffering, the sum total of suffering poured out at each moment over the whole earth, is like an immeasurable ocean. But what makes up this immensity? Is it blackness; emptiness; barren wastes? No, indeed: it is potential *energy*... The whole point is to set this force free by making it conscious of what it signifies and of what it is capable (Teilhard de Chardin), *Humanity in Progress.*

At the end of 1976, the Community withdrew from the Holy Name School at Dogura. The school had aroused passionate loyalties in those sisters who taught there; they had also frankly enjoyed an environment where they could operate creatively and independently outside the constraints of more established institutions, especially perhaps without the powerful and ponderous formalism of the mother house:

we were away from the Community House, the influence of that. We were independent, we were forced to be. We had to make our own decisions, and yet live the religious life in a small community... The only job you had a choice in was New Guinea. That was regarded as a vocation within a vocation.

There was also the pleasure of acting firmly for the overlooked young women of the country:

we did fight for those girls. There's no doubt about that. And we took great pride in what our girls did, what they could achieve. They weren't popular with the boys for getting where they got. So it's the same old story. They had to be encouraged, and it was a great thing when they got somewhere.

The achievement seems to have been a lasting emancipation: 'I have been told that a lot of the women leaders in the country today, if not most of them, are people from the Holy Name School'.

Although the decision to withdraw produced disagreements about when and how, there was consensus among the sisters working in the school that the Community's association should end: 'I felt it was *appropriate* for us to be leaving when we did. From a personal point of view, I was sorry to be leaving the country... But I felt it was *right*'. The move came 'when indigenization was fairly strong, and to be honest I felt it was right it should be indigenized'. But the sisters emphasize that they were not forced out by the government. As with many other CHN enterprises, the time for change had come. Some of the sisters who were working at the school had been there for ten years or more and were tired; 'the job' had been 'done'.

The forces of nationalism also affected the Community's other sphere of influence in New Guinea, the small Community of the Visitation which had been 'nourished' and 'mothered' by Sister Faith. Although this group was partly a growth from the Holy Name School, the intention had always been that it 'should not be a replica of CHN...it should be a Papuan Community'—a daring proposition in a culture where marriage was, even more than in Australia, 'very much the cultural norm'. As with the school, the experience with the new Community was an inspiriting one:

I was struck by the wonderful simplicity of it. They had a lot to teach us... They're a deeply spiritual people... I think it was always in their minds that, when they were able to, the sisters would look after themselves and we'd withdraw, but be around in the background to offer whatever support was needed.

Inevitably affected by the impetus for independence, the Papuan community showed signs of restiveness and was advised to

appoint its own guardian, while a CHN sister remained, in sometimes uncomfortable circumstances, as adviser.

With the withdrawal from Dogura, and the relinquishment of
control over the Community of the Visitation, the Community's
only practical involvement which maintained its tenor was
Ellerslie. An initial feeling that the changed relationship with
the Mission to the Streets and Lanes was beneficial, turned to
dismay at developments there, a feeling that it was becoming 'a
purely humanist organization', a disappointment hardly eased
by the admission that CHN was not equipped for the modern
managerial role.

From 1976 until her resignation in early 1981, the Superior's
addresses were terse, uncomforting, even despairing. She feared
the obliteration of 'our first call', and saw signs of 'bitterness of
spirit or at least resentment' at the external and internal
demands, a tendency to blame others for faults of one's own,
whereas the Christian ought to transform challenge and disruption
into creative opportunity. The touch of personal and prophetic
pain that had been noticeable in her first address to Chapter
had become a thread of self-doubt and dislocation:

I speak as one who through self-will and stubbornness has had more
than one experience of personal disintegration. . . As I look back on
my own first call, and remember the clarity with which I visualized my
goal and my own part in the passion and intercession of Christ, I see
how often and how far I have wandered out of the way.

A deepening experience of 'the mysteries of God' entailed a
more drastic and disturbing encounter with 'the mystery of
evil'. 'I think we have been experiencing that during the last
two or three years.' Awareness of evil and 'the tendency of
created things to crumble into dust. . . the pain of being plunged
into that multiplicity which swirls about one and slips through
one's fingers' have become pervasive. 'For we wrestle not against
flesh and blood, but against principalities, against powers, against
the rulers of the darkness of this world, against spiritual wicked-
ness in high places' (Ephesians 6: 12).

In 1979, Faith spent seven months away from the Community, and found some comfort in observing that English
communities were making their way through upheavals that

paralleled their own. On her return she praised a 'real growth in acceptance' in the Community, despite 'several areas of conflict' that continued. In her last address as Superior in September 1980, she began by quoting Julian of Norwich—'Our love and our trust must be alike large'—and looked forward to 'a kind of second spring of our community', a growth in 'the practical lessons of corporateness', and an appreciation of 'the riches of our diversity'.

7

LESS AN HONOUR THAN A BURDEN

The office of Superior is less an honor than a burden for it has been said: 'Those who govern will be rigorously judged'.

Sister Esther

In her 'Notes on the Religious life' Mother Esther reflected on the office of Mother Superior; it was both an injunction to apprentices joining the Community, and an interior monologue in which she meditated on the difficulties and tribulations of the role.

Much of her emphasis is on its involuntary, onerous nature:

The office is not self sought, it is constitutional and not exercised by the will & usurpation of its possessor. On the contrary it is a hardship forced on one, not sought—an office created for the common welfare and advantage of the Community... She deserves the pity of all, weak woman as she may be... She must not expect to have a good time... in fact she must expect crucifixion sooner or later... No one who has tried it, wants to rule. It is so much easier to obey... Her duties are often depressing & saddening to the Spirit and the life makes great demands on the whole nature.

Apart from a burdensome spiritual authority, her formidable responsibilities included the administration of discipline, the maintenance of the Rule, the regulation of the Community's economy, visitation of its branches and institutions, and the supervising of novices. In return, the members of the Community

offered absolute obedience, on the understanding that the authority vested in the Superior emanated from God. Given that
divine source, submission was not 'blind obedience', and yet
loyalty was expected to be so comprehensive that no adverse
opinion of the Superior could be communicated to any outsider.
'This is difficult for it may be the case that many of the Sisters
are really superior in every way to her who is their head!'

The Community's prayer 'For the Mother' gave a vignette of
the needed virtues and strengths:

Give her clearness of perception, firmness of purpose, readiness of
resource, unfailing love and acceptance in the eyes of all; fill her with
faith and trust in Thy Presence and strength; make her patient,
cheerful and gentle to those who oppose; meek and humble-minded;
and grant that she may find her place among those who follow the
Lamb whithersoever He goeth.

The reality was more problematic and required the juggling of
paradoxes. The tension experienced by every sister in mediating
between the real and the ideal, mundane possibility and spiritual
aspiration, was multiplied for the Superior into a labyrinth of
potential inner conflict. She was required to possess qualities
which in ordinary life were often at war with one another. A
high degree of spirituality needed to be accompanied by practicality and forcefulness in managing the affairs of the Community
internally and externally. Humility had to be matched by the
exercise of authority. Yielding before God, the Superior had
often to be adamant before the world. Most communities would
not have been established but for the determination of an
uncompromising, even cranky personality, and a measure of
charisma made for successful leadership both within and without
the Community, but the spiritual hazards were considerable.

The terms of office provided their own conundrums. The
office was elective, but once elected the Superior became supreme
with no limit, until recently in CHN's case, on her tenure. The
qualities that made her a suitable candidate for the distinction
were susceptible to untimely alteration, and the charisma of
office could be taken over as a personal possession. The vow of
obedience freely donated to her could clear the way for tyranny,

while the firmness of purpose required to sustain the Community could become wilfulness and imperiousness, and the historical opponents of sisterhoods had not hesitated to play up the actual or supposed excess of several powerful English Superiors. At the level of personal survival, the responsibilities of office made things harder. The Superior exemplified 'the hidden life', yet experienced a life of unremitting exposure. She was in the bosom of the Community, yet her position entailed an often gruelling isolation. Although she possessed unquestioned authority, she could be manipulated by her sisters, largely because her pre-eminence made so many dependent on her. As the head of the Community, she needed qualities conventionally masculine, and indeed gained her own power and independence on condition that most women continued to be subservient; but although she exercised a man-like command, she was still subservient to the all-male hierarchy of the Church of England, so that despite her manly toughness, a high degree of womanliness was expected of her—even though, in a further paradox, she along with all women who chose the religious life had violated a central tenet of femininity by breaking the sacred bonds of family obligation. She was thus expected to be both submissive and masterful, dutifully conventional and circumspectly unorthodox, a subtle blend of contrarieties; the lamb but also the eagle.

The founder of a community is the creator of its temporal stability, its particular ethos, and its communicable tradition. In those communities which survived, the foundress was the one in whom the community's past, present and future were timelessly entwined: the source of its authority and the centre of its mystical being. Because of her position as the generator, her human qualities, though lovingly referred to, had to be subsumed in mythology.

As recounted in the authorized biography by Sister Elizabeth, the story of Mother Esther is fairy-tale-like—as strange, and as inevitable, so that fortuitous events seem to be moulded by fate towards their inevitable outcome, securing her legitimation as the foundress.

Born on 26 May 1858 at Sutton, near Stalham, Norfolk, Emma Caroline was the eldest child of Thomas and Sarah

Silcock. With her younger sister, she was educated at 'The Ladies' School', Dedham, Sussex, an establishment run by her aunts. She attended chapel with her maternal grandfather, George Barber, whose own father had left the Church of England to become a Baptist, but she disliked the austerities of Baptist practices. Leaving school at seventeen, she went to Brussels for two years to advance her skills in music and French, and came under the influence of a Jesuit, placing herself under instruction in the Roman Catholic faith. Knowledge of church history, however, gained through having taken the Cambridge Local Examination, had made her aware of the Church of England's claim to true Catholicism, an awareness deepened by contact with her mother's cousins and a close companion, Alison Dale, all of whom were influenced by the Oxford Movement. Her own authority was thus secured by having scrutinized alternative practices before selecting the authentic way.

Emma, as she was still known, was confirmed into the Church of England on the evening of St George's Day, 1877, at St Mary's, Bryanston Square, and she subsequently stayed with Alison Dale 'at the Mother Houses of many of those Sisterhoods which had been called into being by the Holy Spirit as the essential Catholicism of the Church reasserted itself'. On one of these visits, she demonstrated her forthright rigour by refusing the aristocratic distinction between choir and lay sisters many English communities still observed. To the question, 'When are you coming to us?', she replied 'Never! Or not until you give up your lay Sisters'. She could thus be seen to anticipate a democratic CHN tradition that sharply distinguished the antipodean community from most of its English precursors.

The offer of a post in Constantinople to teach the daughters of Turkish nobles was rejected on the prompting of her spiritual adviser because the terms forbade her Christianizing her pupils. She then taught at St Mary's school, Wantage, and asked to be received as a novice in the local Community of St Mary the Virgin with its commitment to the mixed religious life, both practical and contemplative, receiving the habit as Novice Esther Emma on 18 October 1884. She was said to confront difficulties with the recklessly unaccommodating response taken from her namesake's book in the Old Testament: 'If I perish, I perish'. Showing an instinct for mission and rescue work, she spent the early part of her novitiate in London at St Anne's Mission House and St James's Home, Fulham, before returning to Wantage as organist and assistant to the choir mistress.

Her diminutive stature, fine features and reputedly delicate constitution made it doubtful that she would be able to continue at Wantage, but her departure was precipitated by a fall from an organ stool. After a stay in an Oxford hospital, six months in plaster left her with a permanent scar and caused such deterioration in her condition that she was advised to spend twelve months in a warmer climate to avoid the risk of a tubercular back. South Africa was suggested, but Esther sailed for Australia where she had relatives. An early introduction to Mrs Darlot, treasurer of the Mission to the Streets and Lanes, and a meeting with Canon Handfield, aroused her desire to 'help for a time this poor and struggling Mission' before returning to Wantage. On 5 September 1888, at the age of thirty, she took up residence at Mission House.

The biographer's tone and emphasis hint at the existence of a pattern in which the divine will is manifested through apparently chance circumstances and vicissitudes: the considered but unerring movement towards Anglicanism's true faith; the rejection of an exotic job in infidel Constantinople; the preference for the kind of work which would exactly suit her mission in Australia; the emergence of truth through suffering brought about by the bizarre unexpectedness of her fall at Wantage; the choice of Australia and the first contacts at Melbourne: apparently fortuitous happenings which brought her to a speedy fulfilment of her vocation. Missing from the account is the information that her father was an irresponsible ne'er-do-well who deserted the family when Esther was four and repaired to Australia for sixteen years, after which he returned and a son who became the indulged pet of his reconciled parents was born. Similarly, no mention is made of her mother's status as housekeeper at the ladies' college run by the family, or of the bequest that enabled her to study in Brussels—a result of her grandfather having disinherited his son. Nor do we learn that

Esther's chosen course was not fully approved by her family. (On the other hand, family instability itself may have helped to absolve her from the conventional filial round.)

As created by Sister Elizabeth's biography, the mother foundress remains untainted by foible and frailty. She becomes a communicable myth, the mother of the mothers, of the lineage of the Virgin Mary. In addition to her super-womanly characteristics, a masculine strength and endurance are attributed to her. She was seen to be both mother and father of the Community: 'behind it all, though very well supported by the other good Sisters, I see that wonderful little woman, so wise, so knowledgable, so courageous, so masterful and yet so kind'. To her 'lies the credit very largely of making the catholic aspect of our Church's life and worship understood and accepted in Victoria, and the practice of the Religious Life for women a recognised and valued element in the life of the Church in Australia'.

To the mother's task of being 'custodian of the spirit of the home, setting the standard of conduct and watchful that nothing lowers its tone', was added 'her warrior spirit'. She would fearlessly intervene in street fights in the Mission House environs. Businessmen who were associated with CHN's work submitted testimonials to her manly grasp of the Community's business affairs; 'she was a great administrator'. Her conscientious appearances at meetings of the Mission Council are reported in the minutes as if a superior being had descended to the ordinary human plane. Rapier wit is mentioned. Asked for an insight into her character, a Wantage sister described her as 'somewhat of a pickle'. At the same time, her feminine frailty, exemplified in diminutive stature and encapsulated in the term 'little mother', made her masculine powers even more astonishing. Now, more aware sisters find the determination of early reporters to detect the qualities of both a good man and a true woman rather comical.

In the Community's earlier phases, Esther was almost synonymous with its spiritual vitality. For many years, Chapter observed a minute's silence in memory of the foundress and her work. Anniversaries of seminal events in her life have been carefully marked. Reverence for her way of doing things extended to preserving even her domestic arrangements. A sister recalls that, as an over-enthusiastic novice, she was left alone at Mission House one Saturday afternoon and decided to reorganize the furniture, fixed like a diorama from the days of the mother foundress. When this piece of unbidden initiative was discovered, the old lay-out was promptly restored.

After her death, the emotion attaching to her symbolic status probably intensified. Community House is her living memorial where the object of gathering all the sisters as a united force, not feasible in her lifetime, was made possible. For many years, her example was the singular force that overshadowed the achievements of other members of CHN and explained much of its resistance to change. Photographs of her, pale-faced, with prominent eyes, firm mouth and an expression of uncompromising certainty, are displayed at several places in Community House. Anecdotes revealing how exceptional she was used to be relayed in a spirit of uncritical admiration, while visits to England gained sentimental piquancy from encountering those who had known her before she left for Australia. For years, she generated something of a cult figure's magical awe—a seeming paradox given that transcendence of personality was one of the Community's ideals.

The need to preserve the foundress as an icon has diminished over time. Almost no one now living remembers her personally, and the stories that attach to her have lost the vivacity of contact. The process has been confirmed by the changed situation in which the Community finds itself, where Esther's assumptions, though their core of spiritual meaning remains, can no longer be translated into the practical sphere with the same sense of unerring direction and certitude. These days some of the sisters feel that Sister Elizabeth's biography wanders a little too earnestly in the shadowy chamber of piety and leaves much unsaid on the human level. Certainly, the Mother Esther created in the past had the hieratic unsmiling anonymity of a medieval Gothic carving of a saint.

By contrast, what emerges in one series of her letters is a remarkable grit and tenacity. In their feminist assumptions, and slightly querulous singlemindedness, the Esther one meets here is a true child of the English sisterhoods. The letters were written to Blanche Patterson, the eldest daughter of Anglican parents forcibly opposed to her taking vows, and the saga was to extend over a decade before the aspirant was safely ensconced in the bosom of CHN.

The first surviving letter, of 4 October 1912, showed Esther's forthright—indeed, steely—opposition to the parental constrictions that hemmed young women in:

In almost 3 weeks we are to open the Hospital [St George's] and I now go there nearly every other day to see after things... I got a letter from your mother. It was very decided, and I think parents have no right to say their daughters are to do this or that after they are of age, provided there are no real duties calling them to sacrifice themselves to their family.

However it will only be for a time. If they see you are decided, they will yield in time. One of the Sister's father was very angry with her. She simply said she was coming here & he vowed all sorts of vengeance but she came, and now he is rather proud of her I think & is quite reconciled.

Esther deferred to some expectations that daughters would behave in a properly filial way, but she was vigorously against supine submission and shrewdly understood the pattern whereby opposition gave way to acceptance, then was supplanted by quiet pleasure in the unusualness of a choice which ceased to be disreputable and became distinguished. In Blanche's case, a predisposition to tuberculosis compounded the parents' disapproval, but Esther's astuteness made her understand how the obduracy of one party could simply strengthen the determination of the other. Translated to the committee arena, this patience in allowing human nature to work its way to a conclusion she herself desired could be a formidable weapon.

Several months later, she expanded her advice to Blanche:

It seems wise to leave home for a week or so. It seems to me that your parents are going the very way to make you hate being at home... It seems difficult to advise, but if I may do so I would suggest you go away from them for a time... You have only one life to lead, and cannot be expected to take the same view of it as your parents, whom I presume would cordially sanction your marriage & removal a hundred miles or more.

Esther's own experience of diverging from family expectations, and the dispersal of her family, had perhaps heightened an independence of spirit augmented again by her contact with the redoubtable Wantage sisters. Throughout the episode, she was carefully practical. She foresaw a need for temporary employment, given that postulants required money and clothes. Again, 'You would have to pass our doctor', she writes: 'This ought to satisfy your people. I have had diptheria 3 times so I know something about it'. But her emphasis fell on the young woman's rights, and her duty to herself: 'It may seem to encourage undutifulness but I do believe that no parents have the right to prevent a daughter following her own vocation in life. It is your life, not theirs, & you will have to account for it'.

Ten months later, the matter was still unresolved, and Esther devised a further stratagem extending shrewdness into cunning: 'You seem to be in a hole—This is a way out—*come to S. Georges as a Probationer* & I will see after a time if I can get you into the Melb—to be trained for us!... Tell your people you have accepted position as pro in a Melb. Private Hospital'. If this device, which bordered on misrepresentation, proved unworkable, she advised Blanche simply to come to CHN and begin her novitiate, secure in the knowledge that 'you will then have tried to please your parents'. It did not work. Health problems intervened, as tuberculosis developed in lungs and spine, and Blanche returned reluctantly to her family. But her ambivalent status, caught between the pressure of domesticity and the call to religion, resulted in unhappiness and unease. In July 1915, Esther wrote again:

Your letter made me quite sad. It is almost always the way when a girl goes away from home & begins a new life in a different sphere. She never can really enter into the family life again! Any more than if she was married...if we take up the Cross to follow we must expect all sorts of opposition and obstacles... Good night my little Novice. Keep up your heart. All is well. There will be a Kin ready for you.

The protracted affair dragged on. Two years later, Blanche's uncertain position, neither in the Community nor out of it, was creating problems beyond those of her own well-being. Writing from northern New South Wales, Esther indicated that the

Community's image might be prejudiced by the appearance in habit of one who was not quite a nun. Perhaps because public acceptance of the Community was still tenuous, her anxiety reflects the need to avoid any hint of irregularity. The foundress advised Blanche that she might wear the CHN habit at Mission House and on visits to the doctor, but not elsewhere:

It is not because I cannot trust you—but it will furnish a precedent which might do the Community a lot of harm... We are praying that you may come back, but we do not yet know if it is God's choice, and you will have to have a long Noviciate I fear.

Blanche's health continued problematic. Esther attempted to comfort her by indicating that they shared a physical weakness:

sent away for the good of our poor bodies, which St. Francis used to call—'his Ass'— If only we had head & wings how nice it would be! But then perhaps someone might knock out some feathers... somehow I feel that if I had not come away I should have died this winter.

By April 1918, she had decided that the long-drawn uncertainty was mutually damaging:

I now have come to the conclusion that you had better break from us! I'm afraid when your year is up you know you will not be able to do the work required. And it will only make you worse to prolong the agony... You may think me cruel! I am sure I do not mean to be... It is a cross, for you are ill through no fault of your own... But as you say wearing a habit sometimes & a regular dress sometimes wont do! It will harm the Cmty and keep your wound open every time you have to get out of it again... God does not want our work, He wants our wills—and it may be He wants you to lie aside for a time.

Blanche marked Esther's 1918 letters '(Special ones) the year I went away ill & *did not come back* till 1922'. Throughout that year Esther maintained a comforting correspondence, focussing on small details of Community life—white violets for the altar, the thirty-fifth anniversary of her postulancy at Wantage, the profession of Sister Winifred, Sister Christina's stay at Montrose—but the recurrent theme was the seeming impossibility

An arrangement of children on the verandah of the Children's Home at Goulburn before the trek to church, 1915.

Dressed in the especially designed white habit which 'presented quite a tropical appearance': Sisters Sara, Gracemary and Clare with the Mother Superior shortly before leaving for New Guinea in 1951.

'I was struck by the wonderful simplicity of it. They had a lot to teach us . . . they're a deeply spiritual people': the Community of the Visitation in New Guinea, 1971.

that Blanche's sense of vocation could be satisfied. The painful
irresolution reminded Esther of her own past tribulations: 'As
you say—"why did you come here?"—I felt the same when I
had to leave the Community in England and yet God had other
work for me to do [on] the other side of the world. I have been
at it for 31 years now! So cheer up'.

In October 1922, the long wait was over and Esther was able
to advise Blanche on the realities of community life as a fully
accredited novice:

I am so glad dear that you are coming back... A great many things
may come to shake a Novice. You will probably see Sisters inconsistent—Sisters you may not approve of—Perhaps these 5 years have not
only taught you to have patience with yourself—but they may also
have shown you that others have to do the same with themselves. No
Sister is perfect—but she should be trying all the time to be perfect...
I hope you will come up on Wednesday & we will seek mundane
things in the shape of serge & print.

Blanche was professed two years later at the age of thirty-four
and was with the Community until her death in 1979, con-
founding the portents of her early illness by living until she was
in her ninetieth year.

Esther had followed through the realization of Blanche's vocation with patience, compassion, humour and vigour. A much
later insight into her personality is given in a diary written by
Sister Bertha when she and the mother foundress visited England
in 1927. Esther was within four years of her death, and making
what was likely to be her last visit to the homeland she still
cherished. Here again, one sees not the full figure, but glimpses,
unexpected angles, as the mirror is tilted. Instead of the usual
relationship of humble admiration and unquestioning subservi-
ence of the younger sister towards her superior, Bertha is capable
of cheeky self-description ('N.B. from henceforth the person
calling herself the "off step", (whatever that Austral [?] title
may mean), will be designated by all *comme il faut* Christians as
"*the other* one"'), and capable of irreverent observation too.
Esther's way of coping with shipboard life is shown as comically
obsessive. She continually packs and unpacks; 'she finds that

she has a habit in her cabin for every mood of weather & gets annoyed 'cause she cannot wear them all at once'. The ritual of hauling out the cabin trunk and reviewing its contents induced Bertha to remark impatiently 'Wish I had the owner here. I'd put her in it & heave it overboard'. There is much relentless embroidering of caps: 'I have finished 4 caps so am going to read for the rest of the time. The Mother is ashamed of me. She knits'. Continual activity, as a justification of time, bred by the Protestant ethic and matured in the daunting routine of CHN, was perhaps an inescapable need.

In some respects, Bertha pictures Esther as a child who needs to be manipulated for her own good. She must have outlets for her energy (Bertha escapes by rising early); on the other hand, her tiredness must be cossetted without admitting that it exists; Bertha organizes a restorative glass of muscat and a biscuit, commenting that she pulls the strings 'but musn't let the Mother know'. At Port Said she absconds while Esther 'had a sleep & the Second Officer took charge of her'. Eventually, the routine stabilizes and her companion can relievedly report, 'The Mother herself again. At last I feel I needn't go to sleep every moment'.

Esther's unworldliness, at odds with her experience of the life of Melbourne's slums, comes over as a reticence that approaches ineptitude ('so dreadfully shy & quiet at the table') and a rectitude that produces the occasional comic confusion. Offered rump steak at dinner, Esther responds with prolonged, incomprehensible silence, before retorting: ' "If you talk any more dirty talk to me I will leave you"!! The poor Captn couldnt convince her that the rump was the aristocratic part of the beast in the eating line'. In England, the pair settle into a flat in Southwold Mansions where the caretaker's amazement at their materialization suggests that they 'might be Red Indians'. The plethora of mirrors invites irreligious vanity and displeases Esther; however, as Bertha saucily observes, 'it wouldn't do to smash them for her as it would bring bad luck'.

Despite an initial 'not very cordial' contact with the sisters at St Anne's Mission, on working ground the relentless search for activity that characterized shipboard life is abandoned, and Esther's commanding competence reasserts itself. A permit to visit Holloway ('a huge structure & the Melbourne gaol was fashioned much after it') is secured; visits are made to 'Night rescue homes', the Radcliffe Settlement, the Church Army headquarters, the East London Maternity Hospital, the Children's Court. Some charitable hideouts such as the Salvation Army's shelter in Stepney existed on a razor's edge of sufficiency, and raised the question of the fate of those who could not afford even the moderate charges. Bertha laconically recorded that 'the officer in charge could not say'. Comparisons with their own methods and facilities were inevitable. At Barking the Girls' Home provided for fourteen hundred girls and babies and had an imposing hospital—largely the gift of Australians—with trained nurses in charge; but the CHN pair found its appliances antiquated, and felt that something was lacking in the spirit of the place. At Stamford priory, a Wantage branch, the hostel for unmarried mothers with its 'outside asbestos house' for the babies was deemed vastly inferior to CHN's homes. As usual, that major instrument of reform, the laundry, was closely observed and assessed, often to Cheltenham's advantage.

Visits to the sisterhoods stimulated waspish comment on their rituals, practices and personalities. The Sisters of Bethany, Lloyd Square, went in for genuflecting so much that 'wicked Mother' was prompted to consider 'a certain proverb about familiarity'. Her critical spirit was further aggravated by being denied access to the Superior by 'her guardian Angel, i.e. a cross-looking Sister'. Indifference to the visitors was repeated on a call to the St Elisabeth of Hungary Sisters at Earl's Court who were housed in an unprepossessing terrace with unkempt garden: 'a very rude Sister came to the door after a long wait & said the Mother was away! Ahem!!!'. At the other end of the scale of courtesy, the welcome was effusive, 'very cordial, almost affectionate' at St Lucy's, a branch house of St John the Baptist, Clewer. Meanwhile, the archaism of various communities was observed. A Clewer branch house at Leamington was fenced in by 'obsolete Rules'; another order had brought its already rigorous Rule to such a pitch that no novice would present herself for subjection to its pristine severities. Even at Wantage, the elaborateness of some of the ceremonies was deemed excessive. Yet Wantage had greeted its former novice with an emotional 'Welcome home', and at Malvern Link the English Community of the Holy Name provided a pleasant interlude: inspection of the printing room, the gift of an authentic recipe for medlar jelly, and a chance for Esther to describe the activities of their sister-CHN in Melbourne. Thoughts of home were never far away.

Strictly tourist activities provided a respite from the serious business of observing with ornithological dedication the range of Anglo-Catholic practices. There were visits to Hampton Court, the Chelsea Flower Show, Kew Gardens, and the rest; Esther found the Royal Academy exhibition 'greatly deteriorated since her day', while Bertha attended a tea-party in Birmingham 'to meet various ancient relatives...gay old sparks agile as monkeys with all their 80 odd years'. But the heart of the enterprise was in making contacts with the sisterhoods, and visiting institutions whose activities paralleled those of CHN. Here the visitors could begin to measure what their own Community had achieved, and what might lie before it still.

None of these glimpses in the mirror shows the ascetic, steadfast spirituality at the heart of Esther's mission. Something of that can be seen in her *Notes on the Religious Life*, written in 1914 and long retained as one of the Community's Mosaic tablets, her three meditations on *The Life of Entire Dedication under the Religious Life*, and her 'clothing' meditation.

Although the *Notes* strain to escape the limits of nineteenth-century formulae and a narrowly channelled education, their emphasis is understandably often fixed on practicalities: the attainment of 'sanctified common sense', the rule of 'method and order, not vague & undefined emotions', advice which will order the Community, strengthen its superiors, and sustain its members. These quarter-hour lessons, short exhortations not submitted for debate or subjected to criticism, are pitched to individuals exceptional in the sincerity of their hearts rather than the subtlety of their minds. The lack of originality, avoidance of the esoteric, and historical simplification may be partly explained by their being tailored for novices of varying backgrounds and abilities. Esther was also operating in accordance with the precept, 'Not to acquire new ideas but to burn in old truths'.

Employing a sometimes savage array of verbs (the self is to be 'torn out—broken—corrected'), and couched in the iron plates of moral theology, negatives are much emphasized: for 'we are liable to the same temptations that are found with worldly people', without the dispensations allowed to more commonplace lives. An all-inclusive catalogue of mortifications is presented: the senses, the tongue ('your most unruly member'), sleep 'and the longing to dream', the imagination; 'above all mortify your will'. The most cheerless reminder is that 'constant joy in life is another name for constant temptation and danger'. Despite this excursus into the drastic, palliatives are offered: a tight concept of authority is qualified by the humility such a teaching office entails; realism and idealism are balanced; judgmentalism is tempered with compassion. Concerned with protecting the Community's public image and private sanity, much of Esther's advice is far more practical than first appears. The need for an 'invaluable touch of humour' and a clamp on 'all fussiness' are underlined, and a sardonic understanding of human weakness surfaces: 'If there is one thing that is really a difficult thing for the average woman to do is to declare herself a sinner'.

However stern with oneself, one must grow beyond any 'hard and forbidding' nature. Another spectre was the possibility of becoming 'a sort of Uriah Heep Sister. . .punctilious about self denial, & yet [with] no poorness of spirit'. Although there are touches of nineteenth-century prudery, and the paranoiacally fearful attitudes that went with it, Esther's advice to novices is chiefly concerned with the establishment of mature selfhood, avoiding absurd extremes of discipline and spurning both self-torture and self-approval. 'Selfishly absorbed introspection or morbid scrupulosity' is debarred, as is that self-contemplation which is 'the devil's parody of self-examination'. Personality control has as its end the transfiguration of 'unutterable self surrender. . . Perhaps the most merciful. . . Sister is She who is Emptiest'.

Essentially, Esther's writings centred upon the spiritual order, 'the world within', commanded by 'the inner voice' and existing in 'the hidden life' which flourishes in 'the abyss of the Love of God': 'there are many pictures, many peoples, and many countries may be in the world within'. Metaphoric apprehension of this distant interior landscape divides into the benign (gardens, gold, water, lake, veil, mantle, girdle, bird) whose central image is the family, and the threatening (fire, abyss, poison, battle, weed, worm) whose pivotal form is the army. When she moves into this realm, her language is transformed and becomes rapturous—never more so than in the clothing meditation which is the verbal counterpart of her photograph at profession: timeless, ageless, incandescent, like the rock-crystal cup from Mycenae:

The history of Esther is pecul[i]arly applicable to the Religious Life... Your Spouse was crowned with thorns & you surely would not seek for roses... But if it be the oil of myrrh which will be offered to you, the sharpness of the myrrh will be rendered endurable to you by the oil of Love... Six months with sweet perfumes. On the day of your espousals you must not only be purified with oil of myrrh, but you must also offer to the King sweet perfumes... You must not only renounce sensual pleasure, you should be able to present the sweet spices of mortification... Remember the words of Mordecai to Esther...could a seraph desire a more sublime vocation.

The combination of human and superhuman qualities, the interweaving of vulnerability and indomitable strength, is evident in Sister Elizabeth's account of Esther's final years. After the trip to England, her amazing energies seemed to flag—a falling away whose poignancy was accentuated by the loneliness that was part of her increasing deafness. The disability, which had sometimes occasioned playful exasperation at her expense, now became a tragic element in her decline, but it was also symbolic of a spiritual state of withdrawal and detachment. In a strange way, it may even have helped to sustain her extraordinary resilience. *In Our Midst* reports that she had surged into a Mission Hall assembly for some robust playing of her hardworked harmonium, or had joined the small boys in their gym class. Within a few days of her death, she attended the annual meeting to present her assessment of the Mission's response to the severity of the depression: not surprisingly, she decides it is inadequate and must do more. For as her biographer gathers the last days together, it is not on 'a sense of achievement and victory' that she rests, but on the awareness of the mother foundress that, compared to the need, the achievement was small.

Esther's work had gained widespread and admiring recognition. At its close, however, as throughout her labours, that was not enough. She was seen to be mentally preparing for the relinquishment of earthly matters in realization of the essential spirituality of her call. The 'added tenderness' of her final days was interpreted as foreshadowing the ordained end:

In proportion as that which she had wrought for God and His people was recognized, so there grew in her a sense of detachment and a strange diffidence about the part which she had played. Perhaps it was simply that her warrior spirit did not know what to do with success; that it produced in her questionings which were never present in the time of battle. Perhaps as the last stages of her pilgrimage led upwards, she saw that she could lay down her work only in the spirit of that other visionary who cried, 'so much to do. So little done'... perhaps we shall see that this absence of a sense of eclat was part of that stripping of earthly things which was to prepare her for her last great call.

On 2 September 1931, she quietly left the chapel during the saying of the office and was found outside in a state of collapse. She lingered for several days, cared for by the sisters, two nurses from St Ives, and a doctor friend who paid her the tribute that 'She was given to this generation to keep men's faith in goodness alight'. Sister Alice, who was to succeed her as Superior, and Sister Christina, the survivor from the trio of Little Lonsdale St days, were recalled from Newcastle, and a chain of intercession was organized in chapel and in Esther's room. She died on 11 September and was buried in Cheltenham cemetery in her Wantage habit with the wimple, veil, cross and girdle of CHN. 'A sky lark hovered above us and sang sweetly during the burial service', according to Sister Louisa. Perhaps as a necessary confirmation of the foundress's personal legend, death was said to be accompanied by an impression of youthfulness, beauty and serenity, as if the debilitation of years had been stripped away and youthful vigour and freshness restored.

On 14 September, Holy Cross Day, Requiem Mass was said by her request at Mission House, a setting familiar to the poor among whom her work had been concentrated. The archbishop, several bishops and many priests were present; 'prominent knights, doctors and government officials mingled freely with the poor folk of the neighbourhood'.

When Esther's decline became seemingly irreversible during 1931, Sister Alice was recalled from St Christopher's, Lochinvar, and became Acting Superior. After the foundress's death, she was elected Superior at the age of sixty-four on the understanding that she would rule for just a single term. Although she had been in charge of several branch houses since her ordination as a deaconess in July 1900, she does not seem to have had a strong image in the Community—an impression reinforced by photographs in which she stands correctly, even self-effacingly, always in full regalia, fine-featured and fine-boned, gentle and unassuming like a paper flower. She seems to have been a choice for the interim only, singled out because—except for Sister Christina—she was the longest professed member of the Community, and thus provided a link with the past.

The temporary elevation of this low-key figure near the age of normal retirement indicated that the Community had failed to think seriously about an appropriate successor to Esther, perhaps because that would have seemed tantamount to turning the superstitious awe that she aroused against her. When Alice retired after the three years she had stipulated for herself, the official accolades understandably strained to muster achievements which could be attributed to her. The two mentioned—the decision to send Sister Elizabeth to England to train as novice mistress, and the impetus to create a mother house—were not due to her initiative alone. However, her eulogized tact and kindness probably made her an ideal bridging figure who allowed the Community's sense of dislocation to disperse before it gathered its forces for another thrust into the future. Despite her seeming frailty, she survived to die at the age of eighty-eight in 1955. Her successor was a Superior in the classic mould.

Ida Ann Voumard was born in South Australia on 14 November 1886, the eldest of the five children of Louis Voumard, French—

Swiss in nationality, Huguenot by religion, and a watchmaker and jeweller by profession, and Rose Voumard who was Roman Catholic. As a compromise between the differing religious affiliations of the parents, the children were reared in the Anglican church. Later, the family established in Victoria, first at Yea and then at Shepparton, where Ida was educated and came under the influence of the local vicar, Dr Law, and another devout Tractarian, Percy Hume.

When she entered the Community to test her vocation in 1909 at the age of twenty-three, her younger sister had died. Ida was left as the only girl in the family, and her father bitterly opposed her decision, cutting her off from personal contact for many years. As a qualified teacher, she taught at St John's School in Latrobe St, and in 1916 was appointed Superior of the Children's Home at Brighton, a post she held for eighteen years. In that role, she exhibited managerial and innovative capacity, inaugurating the Children's Home auxiliaries, holding the first Community retreats, and overseeing the building of the Chapel of the Holy Innocents, which was consecrated in 1929. From her position there, she was elected Superior in 1934 at the age of forty-eight, continuing in office until 1958 when she resigned. Extracted from an entry in the 'Book of the Dead', these bald details provide only a skeletal image of the unswerving leader who steered her Community through twenty-four expansionary years. All reports suggest that Ida was a woman of exceptional force, who continued Esther's tradition of fervent partiality for the Community and a willingness to embrace practical challenges. By comparison with the plain yarn of the written sources, the verbal reminiscences are complex, coloured by the fact that they come from sisters, relatively young when they encountered her, whose initial awe was likely to be transmuted by time into critical awareness of her failings.

She was essentially a nineteenth-century woman imbued with conventional attitudes to social questions and compliant acceptance of ecclesiastical authority. 'A very disciplined person and a woman of her age', one sister assessed, without specifying her natural milieu, and went on to slot her into CHN's chain of authority, 'greatly blessed in our mothers, because each one has been a woman of her age'. Matriarchal rather than maternal, a

lover of ecclesiastical splendour, she enjoyed being the centre
of attention, although hearty Australian disapproval of hierarchical excesses in some English communities broke through.
She stood squarely in the authoritarian tradition, attracting
comments like '[I was] absolutely in awe of her...a figurehead
in the Community' and 'a very warm affectionate person, but
very very forceful'. She seems to have been impressive rather
than charismatic, but one sister detected a compelling radiance:
'she seemed to be shining and whenever I think of Sister Ida I
think of that sort of glow she had'. Lacking a creative and
questioning intellect, possessed of some foresight but little penetration of deep-seated change, she was shrewd rather than
perceptive, a consolidator and expansionist whose didacticism
and unsubtlety melded into an appropriate mode for the Community of the 1930s and 1940s. Complementary qualities that
lighten this severe picture can be gathered from letters from her
two English trips, where her interest in people expresses itself in
vivid, even gossipy accounts of their appearance and behaviour.
She has a 'feminine' interest in clothes ('We enjoy seeing the
frocks at dinner—all the lovely furs have come out now') and
enjoys the breathless immediacy of the moment: 'trees bursting
weeks early', 'a delicious *pancake* (& lemon)' as a sweetener in
post-war Britain's overwhelmingly monotonous diet, coming
away 'laden with bananas & frangipani' from a convent in
Colombo. An appealing emotionalism shows in reports of stirring
church services, while her consciousness of rank is offset by a
sense of humour and an eye for the grotesque.

Freed from the mythology that attached to the foundress, Ida
can be viewed on a more human level, but she nevertheless
attracts a secondary legend, strongly based circumstantially, in
the pervasive belief that she was 'a great builder' and 'a very
astute business woman', who 'put this Community on its feet
financially' and had 'a brain like a man, which in those days
was a very big compliment'. Although reference to her effect on
the Community's spiritual life is made, the emphasis is usually
on her astuteness in the arena of practical affairs. This concentration on her abilities as an administrator is sometimes offered
as compensation for her inadequacies as a mentor and may be
exaggerated. She was undeniably a woman of force and efficiency,

but many developments during her term office came from un-foreseen requests for CHN involvement, while the creation of Community House was a long-term intention, already underway when she was elected. Her power to see things through, rather than creative instinct, was probably the source of belief in her capacities as an innovator. Moreover, one of her pet projects, the desire to reproduce many English community practices, was resisted. Strengthened during her second trip overseas, the scheme was prosecuted through cheerful but arch sermonising:

You have heard me stress 'silence' over & over, & in spite of my terrific failure in that direction you'll hear me preaching it again when we return... I wish some of us could learn to *love* silence, & respect silence rules—it would make all the difference to the atmosphere of the House, and give each one of us a chance to be more recollected. But I must not preach any more till I come home!!

Balking against this blatant persuasion was 'a bunch of very strong women...this Community's always had a will of its own...if she made us vote for something and they didn't want it, they just didn't do it... She tried to introduce silence to a group of women who...wanted some, but not that'.

Another trait that aroused a more stressed reaction was the tendency to foster favourites, preferences that one sister described as approximating to 'crushes'. This all too human foible was a particular temptation for Superiors, who were isolated from intimate contacts and often tacitly expected to indicate a line of succession. An added trap was the possibility of endowing fancied individuals with particular spirituality, detecting a piercingly authentic vocation that gave divine validation to essentially idiosyncratic choices. In Ida's case, the discrimination was seemingly aggravated by a disconcerting tendency to drop those whom she had singled out. Several sisters basked tem-porarily in the spotlight, but for at least a decade the star that outshone all others was Flora: 'She became blind, she couldn't see anybody else...She relied so much on Flora that Flora to her was the *only* choice'. This fixation may have been Ida's way of compensating for her difficulty in establishing relationships. She admitted that her inability to respond to animals and children was a personal deficiency. '[She was] the sort of person who didn't really know *how* to communicate her feelings. Although she had a very deep love, she was not able to convey that fact to other people, and they didn't recognize...[that] in fact really she was trying to express love'.

Even Ida's most diplomatic supporters admit that she had 'a hard streak' and never admitted to making mistakes. Her policy of forbidding sisters to return to their long-term work-places, justified on the grounds that a reappearance was bad for both the removed sister and her successor, was dismissed as 'all tommy rot when it's...boiled down', a practice especially damaging to children who had 'their security...cut from under their feet': 'She hurt a lot of people, and she realized that in her last years, but she didn't realize it while she was doing it...I felt sorry for her, but if you kill a thing in a person it dies'.

Some explanations of her authoritarianism involve admiration for her tough leadership and fearlessness when confronted with difficult decisions; she was 'really strong, could really do hard things. Totally authoritarian, but that's what religious orders were like'. A belief that mother superiors ought to be dictatorial for their own good and collective stability also survives. Moreover, Ida had inherited a difficult situation, although she may have blown up the problems to establish the legitimacy of her actions: '[She said] the foundress had let a lot of things go, because she was old and she hadn't held a tight rein...things had got too lax, therefore she had a pretty hard task because she wanted to bring things back into line'. The job was taxing, and strength was needed to subdue obstreperous sisters. More personal explanations embrace inheritance of a bossy streak from her obdurate father, and an instinct to protect the delicate Flora in advance by taking the odium of harsh decisions. Perhaps, because she was hard on herself and had to contend with serious physical disabilities (a chronic kidney complaint, angina and increasing deafness), her expectations of others were equally rigorous. Her own defence is capable of more than one interpretation; 'it's the only way I can do anything'.

Whatever the cause, the charisma of office and the charisma of person became entangled in Ida's last years at the top, to the detriment of stable, impartial authority. Her behaviour was marked by a grimness that can be interpreted as a determined, perhaps desperate attempt to retain power; she became 'very, very aggressive' and 'dogmatic' as her hold weakened. Even those who do not admit a degree of arbitrariness say that she should have retired earlier. Some believe that in this pathetic attempt to shore up her declining advantage she gave too much power to the chaplain, allowing him automatic right to attend Chapter when he was usually admitted only by permission. On the other hand, he may have taken advantage of her eroded position to abrogate rights to himself in a style that was readily available to the priesthood. Certainly, the two fell out, and Flora was left to deal with the troublesome cleric. Claims that this arbitrary behaviour stemmed from the ravages of old age are undermined by Ida's own statement to a special Community conference called in 1947 partly to air grievances about her performance:

Many sisters have said they have come sometimes to tell me things, but have not been able to, because I rebuffed them. I don't love them enough, and they can't come freely to me...if it is true that there is a fear of me right through the Community, it is very wrong of you to keep me where I am...whenever the time comes for me to lay down this office, I shall do it thankfully. My only grief will be that the mistakes I have made will necessarily be part of the burden of my successors.

By the mid-1950s, the feeling that Ida should go was so strong that an unprecedented attempt was made to remove her from office in 1954. In an act of defiance, the Community selected Sister Frances, a woman of Ida's age, as its alternative candidate. When the election was inconclusive, Chapter voted again and Ida was dutifully reinstalled, but the humiliating implications of the tussle were unmistakable, and Ida's contention that she wouldn't have minded a more youthful challenge was unconvincing, given that her heir apparent would not have stood against her. She stayed at the helm for another term. One of her last achievements was to mastermind the absorption of the Order of the Good Shepherd, a move accomplished with a reassertion of the old vigour. Her post-retirement years were marked by disappointment, sorrow and incapacity. Poor health prevented her from joining the group working at Remeura, Auckland, or following a long-standing desire to experience the contemplative life. She saw her successor die after a tragically short term and became increasingly enfeebled, physically and mentally. She could not entirely reverse the feelings aroused by her peremptoriness, but one sister, who felt that Ida's human understanding did not include appreciation of her own quirks, felt reconciled by contact with Ida during the years of weakness 'because I saw quite a different side of her'. The thwarted capacity for love and humility had become dominant.

After Ida's departure, the old authoritarian pattern could never re-establish itself, for reasons that were both personal and objective. Flora was rock crystal to Ida's basalt, and although few on-the-spot observers detected shifts, the monolithic structures that had sustained the religious life for so long were shifting inexorably on their foundations. The nexus between the individual and the times could be detected by an astute observer:

[Flora had] been brought up in an autocratic school, and I suppose by today's standards she'd be left standing and gaping, because people simply wouldn't have asked her things. They would already have done them. But she wasn't the disciplinarian or the authoritarian figure that Sister Ida was. She'd grown up in a different way...so almost unconsciously things just changed and geared themselves differently, and people adapted themselves...without thinking very much. It wasn't a major change, but it was already moving.

The vignette of Flora's life in 'The Book of the Dead' is permeated with sorrowful foreboding, as if key events in her life were premonitions of sudden, early death. Elspeth Flora Dean was born on 10 October 1914 at Newport, Victoria, to English parents who were faithful supporters of the Anglican Mission. She was educated at Ivanhoe Girls' Grammar School, coming under the influence of its headmistress, and attended St Peter's with her family, 'a church which she always loved for the beauty of its ritual & the depth of its sacramental teaching'. In November 1937, she was admitted as a CHN postulant and clothed six months later. Nicknamed Martha by her mother, she wrote that she 'wanted to help poor people and I thought the best way to do it was as a Sister in this Community'. Her novitiate was interrupted in 1939 by a breakdown in health, caused by separation from her mother and 'contact with some of the sordid tragedies' of mission work. She was professed on St Aidan's Day 1940 with sisters Marian and Gracemary, in the first profession to take place in Community House chapel. Periods at the Children's Home, Brighton, Mission House and St George's were followed by assuming her first major responsibility as sister in charge of Retreat House. After accompanying Ida to England in 1948, she was appointed Assistant Superior the next year. Destined for the supreme office, she anticipated a 'petrifying' responsibility and suffered another breakdown that resulted in her 'being relieved of office on Christmas Eve [1950?] and given to her people for some weeks'. In 1953, after acting as bursar and secretary at the mother house, she was reappointed to her previous office, 'regaining [the Community's] confidence by the way in which she handled difficult situations'.

Following Ida's resignation, she was elected Superior on 7 February 1958 and installed ten days later, an outcome invested with inevitability: 'coming events had cast their shadows before and she was not unprepared. The sudden shower of tears which followed the Chaplain General's announcement of the election gave way to quiet joy as the Mother-Elect looked round the Sisters...with a mothering smile, saying to Sister Ida "I have got a large family, haven't I?"'

Whereas Esther was the creator who embodied enterprise and vision, and Ida was the builder whose term was characterized by control and consolidation, Community mythology ascribes to Flora the persona of reconciler, who offered love and vulnerability. Mention of Flora's name almost invariably produces the one response: she was a beautiful person, a tribute applied to her personality and extended to her physical beauty. In photographs, the face has an open, reassuring beauty rather than a challenging, awesome beauty, sunniness not ethereality. Her fineness evokes the jonquil and almond blossom, early morning, spring, not the more complex flowers, darker moods of day or more ambiguous seasons. The beauty was not merely physical, the harmonious features, the oval face, joyous smile, elegant figure; for a quality of personality, imprinted on her image, radiated a warmth that flowed to embrace the whole world and each person simultaneously. The adjectives and phrases she attracts are hyperbolic: 'very loving, very concerned, and very considerate for everybody, tireless', 'saintly...outstanding...she had *everything*', 'the most magnetic personality ...dynamic and full of vitality...a tremendous sympathy, empathy. People just fell on their faces'.

Her name completed the effect: 'Flora by name, Flora by nature', or 'like a beautiful flower'. Her appetite for 'love incarnate' was felt to be extraordinary, unwittingly detracting from the more modest capacities of her sisters. With 'that ability to give herself to the last degree', she provided 'a glimpse of what God's love is like'. Everyone loved her and she loved everyone, adored animals, would leave her bed at night to follow the call of a distressed animal. God gave Flora to the Community to heal the wounds that had been opened by Ida: 'it was the chaplain who said to me "Our next Mother Superior has to be full of the love of people and love of God"...and this is what she was'.

Gentler and more accommodating, she paved the way for Faith, under whom the authoritarian mould was painfully broken. Although the bridging time was tragically short and the precise nature of the shift indefinable, she represented a change from martinet Superior to healing mother. Infinitely accessible and limitlessly elusive, the outpouring of love celebrated by the sisters is Flora's uniqueness, the particular aura that must attach to a Superior to explain the historical succession in both human and divine terms.

Closer questioning complicates the initial response. Most sisters who knew her agree that she was probably not an ideal choice, for reasons that range from the mildly compassionate to the trenchantly critical. A tenacious belief that a Superior should dispense driving leadership and be firm, even a little ruthless, clings: 'She was too sweet... You've got to be tough in those positions. You've got to learn to say "no" and stick to it'. The feeling that she lacked the necessary resilience extends to speculation on the self-destructive potential of too much kindness:

I think her position would have killed her, just the same as too, in a metaphoric way, it killed Sister Faith, because they were both too gentle. . . a Mother Superior needs just a streak of hardness. . . At the time, people were *absolutely* devoted to her. . . to an excessive extent. . . She was the person that when you were talking to her. . . you were the only person in the world, even if she had twenty others lined up waiting outside.

Although startlingly attractive, 'she didn't seem the motherly type'; 'she never came across to me as a very strong person. Always someone who in some ways I felt I had to protect, not someone in a mother role'. These comments show an unspoken expectation of unconventional maternal strength. The contrast between frailty and a demanding position produced one explosion of anger against the superhuman response expected: 'This is where I get angry, because why should she need any more physical strength than you or I or any other sister. . . It's the expectations of the Community on that person'.

She was felt to be too easily influenced and chary of making decisions: 'She ruled by her heart and you really need a bit of head too. I think the Community suffered under her. . . because she was *so* beautiful in every way that outside people were attracted to her, and she spent, an *enormous* amount of time outside the Community with people'. Her fondness for animals is sometimes attributed to a sentimentality that diminished deep concern for people. The expectations aroused by her lavish and demonstrative nature may have made her outgoingness a little overblown, a little automatic: 'she had the gift of making you feel that you at that moment were the only person in the world, but you *also* knew at the same time, at *exactly* the same time, that she made every other person feel that way too'.

Details of professional training or work experience before she entered the Community are not given. She was not intellectual and did not encourage sisters to gain further qualifications. She came from a secure, even wealthy background and wore a stylish habit that distinguished her from her plainer colleagues. One observer saw beyond the graceful, winning exterior and offered the startling opinion that she 'found responsibility very difficult. I think personally that she didn't really give any of that [impression] to other people... I think probably repressed anger was part of her personal problem'.

Over all these demurs is the sense that 'the job was too big for her', a distinction thrust upon her by Ida, an unchosen fate that she disliked, even feared: 'She took on that role, as a daughter, to help [Ida], drive her everywhere, look after her, and I think Flora found that the burden was *unbearable*... I don't think she probably ever wanted to be mother. She would have been far happier looking after the dogs and cats'.

A degree of displeasure may have attached to her as heir apparent, and her position may have been further compromised by her predecessor's expectation that she would be able to manipulate behind the scene: '[Flora] said to me one day "I'm tired of being pushed and pushed into these positions"... She used to come out and say "Who's the Superior of this Community?"'

Yet there is a belief that this fine-grained bloom 'would never have been the person she was if it hadn't been for Sister Ida'. That Ida selected a type opposite to herself suggests a longing for the softer qualities. A mundane explanation to the narrative is that she surveyed the field and found a dearth of leadership material. However, the patient grooming had discouraged the flowering of others and set up expectations that could not be thwarted. A more ambitious interpretation accepts the human element, but treats the earth-bound actors as enablers of God's will: '[Ida] probably saw in [Flora] things that she didn't have herself, and I suppose it's part of life, that life is circular, and the gifts of one are necessary at a particular time, but having given those gifts, then some new gifts are required'.

Flora's tenure was heartbreakingly short. Addressing Chapter in October 1960, she discussed her impending death from leukaemia, which had been diagnosed that July:

I cannot but know how devastating it was for you all when the verdict was given... I have been wondrously upheld and will never be able to express the appreciation of all that has been done for me. After being, as it were, given very few days to live, God has willed that there should be a return to a measure of health, and surely these weeks or months—whatever they may be—must be for some good purpose of His own, maybe for further preparation for the future... We have been brought sharply to face the fact of inevitable changes, and the Community must be as strong as possible to face the future, whatever it may hold.

No matter how brave the words, the prospect of the death of a relatively young Superior so soon after her election to office was a shattering corporate experience that must have stirred uneasiness about whether the Community was unreasonably hard on its Superiors, especially when a nature like Flora's, accommodating as the pelican, had been subjected to sapping confrontationist politics, such as the protracted tussle with the chaplain-general. However, in some ways Flora's illness was a bonding experience, a 'St Martin's summer', that drew the Community into sorrowful unanimity to face the crisis. Her illness was so far advanced that she was expected to die at any moment, but she lasted for several months, staying at Community House except for blood transfusions. Finally, aware of her desperately weakened state, she apologetically asked to be allowed 'to go back to hospital a day earlier [than was planned] or I don't think I shall get there'. She died at the Queen Victoria Hospital on 6 November 1960.

Sister Faith was elected Superior at the end of the month in which Flora died. Only ten years professed at her election, and without years of apprenticeship as Assistant Superior or in other key positions, she had come to the Community in a highly individualistic manner, an insight that is available from her own description of her life. Self-declaredly a born rebel, she came from an erratically Presbyterian family (her mother was a church-goer, while her civil engineer father was indifferent) and spent most of her school days at Fintona Girls' School as a boarder. She 'decided that God was going to be my target', calling herself an atheist, although she admitted later that agnosticism was a more accurate description of her philosophical state.

In the early 1940s, she went to the University of Melbourne

to do a science degree and joined the communist-dominated Labour Club as an expression of her socialist convictions. The student body had been depleted by the war and, after a year of study during which many of her friends joined the forces, she left, determined to do 'a real war job'. After several failed efforts at persuading the authorities of her usefulness to the war effort, she was employed as a laboratory assistant, moving between various munitions factories to examine equipment. It was a time of mental confusion; a radically different side of life presented itself, but she felt that there were no common reference points between herself and the factory girls. At the age of nineteen, she returned to the university to do a Social Studies Diploma, still rebellious, bent on setting 'the world to rights', determined to avoid binding commitments to any particular philosophical system. At that time, social studies students were required to fossick through a voluminous valise that contained intellectual fragments ranging from psychology to comparative religion. An assignment in the latter area brought her 'very unwillingly' and, given her dogged agnosticism, with a sense of foolishness to 'a sort of intellectual conviction' of the existence of God that was linked with unabsorbed and unaccepted childhood experiences, not specifically religious, rather a generalized but unmistakable awareness of harmony and order in the universe. A corollary of this realization was the necessity to act on its consequences. She 'made straight for Rome', but she was alienated by the rigidity of the Roman Catholic Church in the 1940s, a watertight concept of authority that reached its apotheosis in the pope, and by 'a sort of mystification rather than a mystery...elements of magic'.

Having rejected the obfuscating Roman solution, she found herself the potential spiritual spoil of two other Christian groups, both 'very competitive...everyone was trying to get hold of this likely Christian', a keen bevy at St Peter's who tried to snare her for their fellowship, and earnest contenders at Queen's College at the university, where she found Sunday evening gatherings dull to suffocation. At St Peter's, where the ceremonial was impressive rather than inordinate, she had her 'first religious experience of the presence of God...awe which is very unusual for me...humility which is quite uncharacteristic of me...love'. The total sensation was an 'all or nothing' experience that connoted acceptance of 'a complete claim on my life by God'. Determined to make up her own mind, keeping her counsel, she resisted pressure to align with any faction, but kept going to St Peter's. After coming under the aegis of Father Walter Green, parish priest at St James, East St Kilda, and CHN's chaplain-general, she finally decided to join the Church of England. A man both wise and cunning in his understanding of human nature, he put her in a confirmation class of unruly small boys and 'middle-aged to elderly pious ladies', a mix 'guaranteed to put anyone off'.

At the same time she made her first visit to Retreat House and the chapel where her 'most vivid experience was of the cacophony'. To the musically sensitive—and Faith was an accomplished pianist and singer—the singing in chapel, with Mother Ida intoning loudly, always on a different note from the rest of the company, was more gruelling than inspiring. Other practices were 'to a bumptious youngster looking in...archaic and off-putting'. Nevertheless, the contact blossomed involuntarily into 'a sort of homecoming', and further visits convinced her that the religious life was intended for her. Strongly attracted to the regimen of prayer, she considered joining a contemplative community and gave herself two years to decide, while she continued work as a psychiatric social worker at Royal Park, daily confronted by 'so much suffering that there was no way, humanly speaking, of alleviating'. The self-imposed testing time contracted to eighteen months, and her decision was sealed by conversation with Father Stephen Bedale, the formidably tall director of the Society of the Sacred Mission, who noncommitally heard her unburden herself with reasons that favoured the contemplative life, capping the one-sided interview with a disconcerting question: 'And what's wrong with these sisters?' The possibilities seemed bluntly narrowed to a single way. Ida was 'rather surprised' at her approach, while her mother was 'furious...livid' because the enterprise looked distastefully 'Romish'. However, she was mollified by a visit to the Superior whose consternation equalled her own, suggesting that the headstrong candidate was not expected to last the distance and would solve both their problems.

The postulant herself anticipated lasting only a week and, the week passed, thought that each emolument of time would produce the injunction to depart. She felt minutely scrutinized and under suspicion, largely because of her anomalous 'half-educated' condition. The dual uncertainty as to her reaction to the system and the system's reaction to her amounted to 'a precarious kind of existence'. Her six months' postulancy were spent in the barn-like kitchen of Retreat House, where she learned 'to skate' through the culinary motions, though not how to cook, surviving because of a 'spiritual substratum of which one was barely conscious because of exhaustion'. The day after she was clothed, she was sent to Brighton where the normal complement of two sisters, with little outside help, was responsible for the physical and emotional care of forty children in the home and twenty girls in the hostel. At the mercy of these 'incredible statistics' and illness among the inmates, she concluded that all were 'battering against the system' but, although discipline was unavoidably tight, the atmosphere was warm and accepting. When she was professed in 1951, she felt that she had 'arrived' and 'a new sort of race' was underway.

After stints at St Ives and Mission House, she was sent to New Guinea at the beginning of 1955, becoming a founder of the Holy Name School, in defiance of the bishop who simply wanted 'a few white veils floating round Dogura' thoroughly impregnated with 'the aroma of holiness'. When Flora's fatal illness was registered, Faith was recalled to Community House to act as conventual Superior. On her return, she observed an elusive but significant alteration in the Superior's role and in Community behaviour:

we thought we hadn't changed, we had unconsciously. . . in what we were willing to do and say. . . People thought they were going on exactly as they had in Ida's day and before. . . everything was very small and very exact when I came into the Community. . . It would not have surprised me if the orders had come out to measure how much bread went on to the table for breakfast. . . exactly so many cubic centimetres per head. . . People were, by today's standards, not exactly lavish, but life wasn't quite so tight and constricted.

Most sisters in the Community who knew Flora and Faith agree that, as Superiors, they represented a break with the past. In Flora's case, the radical nature of the shift lay in the abrupt termination of her life, rather than in possessing a personality that would implement dramatic change. As she described herself in her invaluably lucid and objective account of her life, Faith was 'a comparative newcomer', professed only ten years, and largely an unknown quantity; 'one didn't exist until one had been around for twenty years'. She was thirty-seven, decidedly green for a Superior, and had spent the previous years in the isolation of New Guinea. She was unfamiliar with the management of the Mission, so the lightning elevation 'didn't appear to me a practical option...it kind of fell upon me suddenly... [it was] just as bad for the Community as it was for me... [I] just let the machinery roll on and hoped at the back of my mind that I would disappear at the end of three years'.

However, her 'abysmal' ignorance of her empire 'had the advantage of sometimes allowing me to say why, and for a lot of things there wasn't really a very good reason'. In tackling outmoded customs and stale attitudes that were sanctified to ossification by habit and time, she was aware of a larger dimension: '[It was] a very difficult time partly because of that attitude of ours that we were set and fixed now for another twenty or thirty years, and then we *weren't*, but also life was changing so much generally in the world, standards, structures in the Church and in society'.

Others in the Community were seemingly less surprised than Faith by the turn of events. Sisters who had worked with her felt that the progression was natural, if not inevitable. One fellow novice had long felt that Faith might prove to be the most exceptional of those outstanding women who had governed CHN. More pragmatically, the indefatigable Ida was purported to have carried on a strenuous lobbying campaign for Faith from her couch at Ellerslie. Nor did the pile-up of negative circumstantial factors allow for her formidable personal qualities. The complexities of establishing her religion and vocation promised a leader in whom the deepest currents of spirituality were surging. Although she claimed to be only 'half educated', she was an exceedingly complex woman of disturbing intellectual

subtlety and percepience, familiar with and responsive to the
Church's lustrous mystical heritage. Once again, the Community
seemed to have found the right person to guide it. Esther and
Ida were natural expansionists, cut from a nineteenth-century
template, reacting with vigour and decisiveness, speedily stepping
into the breach, possessing sharp rather than vacillating minds,
all attributes essential to guiding the Community through its
formative and expansionary years. Faith's fate was to preside for
a long and tortured period of internal and external change.

The quality that fitted her most strikingly for guardianship of
the Community at this critical time was an almost delphic
ability to project events, a gift often grievously painful for its
owner: 'other people were not anticipating. . . I can often see
that something's blowing up long before other people notice it'.
This foresight was accompanied by an ability to understand the
conundrums of people's reactions to change—the mixture of
fear and excitement, openness to change on the conscious level
while an inner resistance still operates, sudden backtracking
into the safety of the known, the subjectivity underlying seemingly objective responses. The situation was complicated by the
fact that the Superior's role was still fixed in expectations of a
directional maternal presence who was expected to make 'all
the decisions'.

Faith's personality made her incomprehensible to some and
set up a current of unease in others. She is widely described as
shy, an epithet that suggests a simple nature, discomforted in
ordinary social situations, but uncomplicated shyness seems an
inadequate description. Certainly, her relationships outside the
Community were limited, partly from choice, partly because
her nature deflected casual intimacies. She lacked Ida's compelling authority and Flora's halo of appealing sweetness. She
had no small talk and did not suffer fools gladly, a quality
shared by all CHN Superiors. Even on home ground, this
incapacity with trivialities produced awkwardness. One self-
avowedly shy sister recalls being called aside by Faith to discuss any worries, and the rushing silences that swirled around
them when neither found a way to overcome their reticence.
'Disturbing' is the pointed though imponderable adjective used
by those who were not her particular confidantes, while a few

found her 'secretive', a description that prompts questions without hinting at answers. The only example of secretiveness offered is that, with a 'complex' about her tendency to stoutness, she obscured when and what she ate, or whether she ate at all. She avoided talking about her own problems and perhaps could not afford that luxury. One sister, who observed that all communities experienced a problem with secrecy, felt that complexity 'at the top' compounded this problem and left some individuals with little alternative but detaching themselves from the stresses.

Suggestions of an unfathomable depth of personality tease out a skein of hyperbolic, even fulsome phrases. She was 'a spiritual mother', 'a woman before her time', 'a woman of vision and she could see things that other people couldn't see', 'the absolute gem of the Community', 'a woman apart', 'such a mysterious person...an incredible unassuming person'. She 'could only interact on a deep level or not at all'. 'Although she was mother she had this separate life of her own.' 'One can know a person so well and not know them at all, and Faith very rarely talked about herself, her feelings, her aspirations, longings.' Her extreme sensitivity and aloofness rebounded on both her and the Community: 'I always felt that [these qualities] hurt her... The difficulties were there, but [the Community] didn't quite link them with Sister Faith'.

While most emphasis is placed on her more sombre and enigmatic traits, and exaggerated by the fact that most of these reflections were made in the emotional turmoil that followed her sudden, premature death in August 1985, a minority celebrate a diverse nature that included gaiety and talents in the areas of housewifery and culture. She was 'a wonderful storyteller' and had a ready sense of humour. Despite the culinary incompetence that characterized her novitiate, at St Ives she proved to be a 'wizard' cook, whose specialities were home-made chocolates and ice-cream. She had a fine voice and was an accomplished pianist, a skill mostly reserved for times when she stayed alone in the Community's house at Mornington. In New Guinea, the constraints seemed to drop away and the spirit of joyous independence reasserted itself, along with an endemic sense of fun that had to be carefully monitored at home.

Although Faith and Flora were dramatically different person-alities, parallels are drawn between the two: 'Both she and Sister Flora identified too closely. They didn't have the ability to cut themselves off and it destroyed them'. Neither had robust health. A severe breakdown in Faith's late teens has been suggested. Within three years of her election, she had developed a severe ulcer, and later suffered from asthma and arthritis. The illness that most affected her was a catastrophic breakdown in England in 1970 while she was staying with the Sisters of the Love of God at Fairacres. The collapse lasted at least six months and reduced her to despairing helplessness. A gratuitous element was the tactless handling of the crisis by some members of the host Community, who 'in *front* of her...literally tore her into shreds'. After several weeks in hospital, a recuperative period was spent at Burford Priory in the Cotswolds with an enclosed Benedictine community. Wrapped in the melancholy splendours of late autumn, the Elizabethan house with its mullioned windows, terraces, herb-beds, walks lined with topiary and wood giving on to a river, and the serene atmosphere was a refuge: but when she returned to Australia:

she came back looking like a scarecrow. I can remember one night. It was a festival; it could have been Christmas Eve, because I remember it was dark. It was always the custom for the Mother to go out and wave the Sisters from the other houses off after a midnight mass, and I remember going out that night, coming out of chapel, and she'd just done that, and she looked so half-dead I remember just gathering her in my arms and she *clung* to me like a child...she gave up *herself* and I'm sure God never asks anyone to do that.

Her quality as a 'born' or 'natural' contemplative lies at the heart of the enigma of her personal destiny. Furthermore, in a dreadful irony, the faculties that made her the right Superior for the time also intensified her personal difficulties, and at times compromised her relationship with others. Writing from England in 1964, she referred playfully to a tendency to over-reach herself that had landed her in the Fairacres infirmary: 'It isn't, Sister Rachel, that I object to cultivating docility towards you, just that when one is at home one can't help being aware of the fact that one could so easily become pampered and so I always try to go the extra mile that proves to be the extra one too much'. Although personal experience of suffering enabled her to ease the agony of other individuals and the Community, this lavish willingness to assume intolerable burdens attracted the criticism that 'She wasn't sensible about herself. That was one of the irritating traits which I think probably we all found... She'd just do it and have to struggle'. It rebounded on her in other ways 'because she was so understanding people almost ate her up'. Attentive sympathy contrasted glaringly with the extension to others of the demands she made on herself:

She had a very acute sense of judgment...[and] a martyr's spirit... She had no sense of timing or judgment [of] when she had enough or when another person had had enough . . . She didn't have the capacity to know when someone had got to the end of their limits... It wasn't just her fault, because she had been *isolated* by virtue of her position.

As well, her knowledge of human nature was 'limited, because she's only got us'.

Her intellectual complexity was another double-edged quality, necessary to guide the Community through internal tumult and external challenge, but prone to result in the kind of inaction into which Hamlet argued himself: 'she left the deciding to other people', or 'it was hard to get her to say yes or no'. This tendency towards indecision was aggravated by the need to negotiate between the factions of the Community, which included some fearsomely hide-bound individuals: 'It would have been an extremely difficult time for anybody to be in office because [it] was a time of very radical change'. The impossibility of satisfying all viewpoints may have made her, by default, side with the conservative element, sacrificing her personal views, establishing another putative justification for her feelings of inadequacy and prolonging the process of change. A mitigating factor was the liability of authority to dissolve under the load of strident and competing demands: 'She was powerless in some respects. In some respects they're all powerless'.

By the mid-1970s, the strain was crushing. Faith's isolation was magnified by her reluctance to 'either seek or get a lot of support for herself'. Her raw sensibility increased her suffering and her inwardness. Her omnivorously empathetic nature meant that 'everyone went to her with their problems'. She never showed anger, and perhaps there was anger. In 1975, a motion was put to Chapter to limit the Superior's term of office, an impersonal recommendation with unmistakable personal intention. Consideration was given to withdrawing the motion, but it went ahead. The motion was rejected, and Faith was re-elected. Her reaction to the incident may have been ambivalent. Conscious of weariness, she may have feared continuing in the onerous role, and yet a personal void would have been created. She was only in her early fifties, and the past offered no precedent to suggest a part as elder stateswoman, or a stance of dignified abstraction from power. Esther had died in office, Alice had modestly filled the breach, Ida capitulated in her seventies, Flora had been snatched away. Apart from the lack of a defined attitude for abdicated Superiors, Faith may already have been experiencing that sense of having lost her personal identity that was to dog her. Retirement would have confronted her with the task of rediscovering an identity long held in suspension.

In the event she made her own decision, announcing her resignation at the beginning of 1980. This time the Community allowed her to go, aware of her massive achievement in slowly delivering the Community's power of witness 'right into the twentieth century', and holding it together despite the anguish. She looked back at the 'terrible business' of dismantling the Community's enterprises:

It was often a painful experience, but it was a joyful one too...a sort of growing one... I personally didn't ever experience that fear of the future, but I was very aware of other people's fear... They were really wanting...somebody to show them how to go, where to go, what to do, how to do it, and you see I don't think life's like that any more.

Sister Elizabeth Gwen became Superior in 1981 in what was probably the most genuinely democratic election that the Community had ever conducted. Over the years Faith had placed contenders for the post in positions of responsibility, and

a sister whom she had favoured in a way uncomfortably reminiscent of Ida's partiality had left the Community. Elizabeth
Gwen had fulfilled important roles in her career at CHN,
including ten years as novice mistress, and three years as Assistant
Superior:

I wouldn't say that I expected to be [Superior]. . . I didn't want to
enter into a lot of talk about it. . . but several sisters said to me 'Oh,
you know it's quite on the cards that you might get into the hot seat',
and so I didn't pretend that I didn't know that it might happen. I
didn't *want* it.

Much of her experience before coming to the Community
suggested that she had leadership potential; and yet she preferred
practical duties such as the bustle of Mission House to the
imponderable obligations that attached to roles of spiritual
guardianship. Mission work was 'such a contrast and a relief
after the responsibility of the novices for so long that I really
threw myself into it and thoroughly enjoyed it. . . when I finally
carved out a sort of pattern for myself up there, I really loved it.
It was nothing very spectacular'.

Mother superiors, like prime ministers, are subject to the law
of comparisons. Succeeding Faith, on whom many sisters had
become emotionally reliant and about whom the Community
had developed a guilt complex, was a challenge that was
heightened by Faith's awesome spiritual authority and her comparative youth at retirement (her successor was actually slightly
older than her). By contrast, Elizabeth Gwen admitted to shyness
and lack of confidence, qualms that are evident in her self-
effacing conversational style when asked about herself. Apart
from Faith's personal legacy, the inheritance was complicated
by more impersonal considerations, for Faith had set the Community on a course that had strengthened the attraction of
enclosure and had muted the Community's activist image within
the Church.

A tall, large-framed woman, Elizabeth Gwen is the only
child of English parents, 'Australian-born, but otherwise you'd
say I'm English'; but she seems quintessentially Australian in
her mannerisms, vigorous approach and a conversational style

liberally peppered with colloquialisms. Her mother came to
Australia in her late teens, while her commercial photographer
father was sent to a warmer climate for the vague but ubiquitous
'health reasons'. After a period of obscure adventurousness in
Canada, he moved to Melbourne and was taken into partnership
with his father-in-law, becoming manager of the business after
the latter's death. Elizabeth Gwen was educated at Lowther
Hall, an Anglican girls' school in Essendon, where she was sent
because her father, who liked to show the world that he was
doing well, defeated her mother's preference for the state system.

Her progress to CHN, like many such progresses, has an air
of inevitability about it. Her father was a staunch Anglican and
her mother, originally Wesleyan, in deference to masculine
dominance, was confirmed when she married. The Anglican
commitment was underlined by the woman principal of Lowther
Hall, who 'had a very great influence on my life...[although]
she never spoke specifically that I can remember of the religious
life'. However, this compelling feminine example was absorbed,
and Elizabeth Gwen later discovered that her teacher had belonged to the Society of the Sacred Advent in Brisbane.

Elizabeth Gwen's father died when she was eleven: 'I didn't
realize what a blow it was until years later actually, because you
tried to protect your mother instinctively'. She had been close
to her father and found communication with her mother difficult
until many years after her father's death. Her mother, in return,
found her secretive, and family relationships were further complicated by her mother's remarriage three years after her father's
death, an event more disturbing for the silence that surrounded
it than for the fact that it happened. Tragically, she was to be
widowed a second time before Elizabeth Gwen joined the
Community. The nexus of grief and the failure to express it
fully must have powerfully affected the young daughter. The
year after her father's death, Elizabeth Gwen decided that she
wanted to be confirmed, a decision postponed first because of
her youth, and then because of temporary lack of interest. The
school principal prepared the girls for confirmation: 'I also went
to some of the classes at the local church, but it was the ones at
school that really affected me, and I can remember...thinking
vaguely... "When I grow up... I really think I ought to do

something for God" '. The instinct was amorphous, not a missionary call, not the wish to be a nurse or a teacher, the three branches of service that commonly drew women to the Community.

After leaving school at the intermediate level, she spent a year at that dedicated manufactory of female office workers, Stott's Business College, largely because she still lacked specific direction and her mother favoured the business course. Subsequently, she worked as secretary in a motor and finance company during the war, a stable but humdrum position that sparked a feeling of dissatisfaction: 'the thought kept coming to me then, I've got to do something *more* with my life than just this'. Except for a brief period of rebellion that did not focus on intellectual dissatisfaction, her involvement with the Church was continuous, especially with the then extremely vigorous Girls' Friendly Society. This association resulted in her participation in a twelve months' Professional Youth Leadership Course that had been introduced immediately after the war by the Social Studies Department at the University of Melbourne. At the beginning of 1947, she became assistant organizer of the GFS for the Melbourne diocese, and soon after attended the second world conference of Christian Youth in Oslo, an idealistic ecumenical gathering that included theologians and clergy who later became prominent in the World Council of Churches.

The six-month trip included time in England, sightseeing and contacting relatives, and stimulated—apart from a fortuitous fondness for cheese, the only food in Norway not severely rationed—a continuing enthusiasm for the ecumenical movement. Aware that the course of her life was changing, and reluctant to return to unstimulating office work, she was astounded to find herself replying to a question from an English companion ' "Oh, I think I might be joining a religious community" and I thought "What have I said?" Well, it had been floating around in my mind before I went overseas'. Several unconnected threads of experience seemed to be lacing into an unmistakable pattern. Occasional contacts with CHN had been made, and a tour of Community House instigated by that clever proselytizer, Sister Elizabeth, was decisive: 'when I walked into that chapel... I thought "this is home for me", and I went

back home and I thought "Ohh, ohh, no, God... I want to
serve you, but I don't want the religious life. I might have to
wear black stockings and I couldn't bear that"'.

Marriage still seemed the natural outcome, and 'the thought
of me knuckling down' was uncharacteristic. She had had brief
contact with the Sisters of the Church and 'somehow I *knew*
that if God *did* want me to go to a religious community, it
wouldn't be to them. I knew it would be to CHN...something
of the spirit of the Community can be seen in its members'.
CHN had a certain stubborn Australianness and classlessness.
While in England, she had been particularly unimpressed by
the division of choir and lay sisters at Truro, the 'prim and
proper' atmosphere, the spirit of eternal vigilance typified by
the sister in the ablutions block who appeared to be timing the
showers. She 'finally arrived on the doorstep [of CHN] towards
the end of 1950' at the age of twenty-seven. Moving into the new
environment was not as disruptive as she anticipated. A con-
tributing factor was the camaraderie of the novitiate: 'Constance
Mary [the novice mistress] would go solemnly through the
customary...*bathing* must *be* in a *costume* consistent with
modesty and with women companions only...we'd have a good
giggle...we just didn't let it get *into* us'. A complicating element was the reaction of her mother, who found the decision
dismaying and interpeted lack of natural intimacy in the fact
that she had been informed by letter: 'I didn't have the facility
...to talk to her really about it...one of the things I regretted
later'. For most of her professed life Elizabeth Gwen has held
responsible positions, having been in charge at Darling and
Mission House, novice mistress and Assistant Superior.

In confronting the role of a contemporary Superior, she sees
an advantage in her moderation, neither 'an ultra conservative
person' nor a headlong radical intent on turning the cloister
into a thoroughfare: 'the Community's got to preserve certain
traditions, but I think we've got to sort out what are essentials
and what are non-essentials in our vocation'. She is aware that
some sisters feel that the Community has been contaminated by
secularism, but rejects the image implicit in this attitude of
CHN as 'a little ghetto that's untouched by the world in which
we live'. Like comparable communities, they must be able to
embrace the extremes of active pastoral ministries and the

solitary life, a diversity expressive of the Community's historic ethos: 'what is technically termed the mixed life...prayer and service...the one balancing the other...a difficult thing to explain, because in a sense all that we do is...the spirit of prayer'. She favours establishing new links with the diocese and has been asked to join the Ecumenical Affairs Committee, an affiliation that satisfies an old enthusiasm. The Community should be more visible: 'it's important [to] be *seen* at things, whether it's two of us or ten of us'.

The changed attitudes can be seen in the internal workings of the Community, where dialogue and consultation have replaced dogmatism and officiousness. The Community Council is no longer a cipher to give a democratic gloss to the Superior's will, but 'a sounding board' to assist decision-making: 'I'm the type of person that finds it helpful to check things out'. Sisters are no longer shuffled willy-nilly round the Community chess-board, causing personal distress and lingering resentment. Now no one is put in a position without consultation and an attempt to reach a consensus. In Faith's time, the contrast between past realities and future possibilities was stark, the dissonance between generations was explosive, and dependency was deeply ingrained in some sisters. The older generation has dwindled and some of its survivors are resigned to change. Dependency can be more easily tolerated in the die-hards and briskly discouraged in those who ought to know better. Many practical problems connected with change have been resolved.

All this seems to make the Superior's life easier, and yet there is still a mystique invested in the role, and no one would question the necessity for leadership. The Mother is still the symbolic focus of the Community's struggles, hopes and aspirations, 'no sinecure', an isolated position requiring a delicate sense of the points at which confidentiality should be maintained and openness tempered. Interaction between personalities continues to be complex and mercurial, while self-discipline creates problems of balance and demands discriminating awareness of the points at which one sister's concept of self-determination outrages or impinges on another's sense of propriety. It is the ancient problem of freedom and licence that every family knows, made more acute in the Community by the demands of its gallant ethos.

8

NOT SAINTS OR ANGELS

I can't explain it to you. People talk about conversion... From that moment on, I knew...everything fell into place...my commitment to the Church became complete... Everybody said I had religious mania, it was terrible...the hand of God was upon me, you just feel it... I was *absolutely* devastated. It wasn't what I wanted to do at all... It was just like a bolt from the blue, it was so loud and clear... It was like a flash. I can recall it now, talking about it.

The sense of vocation is the core experience of the religious life. To the secular world, this compelling urge of commitment is the most mysterious component of a mysterious way of life, and can attract a scepticism darkening into ridicule. It is dismissed as self-deception, sublimation, or the cruel quirk of a disturbed psyche.

If vocation is impenetrable to the outsider, even those who experience it find the sensation hard to articulate, and resort to exasperated cliches or shoulder-shrugging admissions of defeat. Although metaphor and symbol permeate religious life, vocation seems to elude even their illuminating force. Through paradigm, analogy, transformation, the irradiating likeness remains inaccessible. Perhaps the closest parallel is the artist's vocation, the impulse to act as a medium for abstract forces and more-than-personal emotions; but the parallel is limited by the different relationship between the self and the forces which work through it. While the artist occupies the universe as an interpreter, the religious is occupied as an empty vessel by the creative principle. Given that vocation invites a relationship between beings with limited expressive powers and an incomparable power of creation, it is quite literally unspeakable, and language that tries to capture it can only cast its net out into silence.

The sisters do not talk of blinding and dramatic conversion experiences in the manner of early Christian eschatology or medieval mysticism. The voices that issue from the void, the irruption of consuming fire, the searing pain of bodily possession, the standstill of overpowering weakness, the revelation beyond the dark night of the soul—these stock images of mystical experience are absent from their accounts. Indeed, one can imagine the pragmatic Superiors of CHN would scrutinize such talk with saintly shrewdness and a rigorous, even sceptical eye; for no community, especially not one as historically vulnerable as this, could afford the scandal of exaggerated vocations ex-pressing themselves in maudlin eccentricity or folding up with a melodramatic loss of faith. A stable constitution seems a better qualification for the religious life than a poetic spirit.

While supernatural phenomena are absent from the sisters' descriptions of their original call, they frequently mention an instantaneous sense of inner certainty, or a directorial undertone to their daily lives: colloquially, a 'niggling feeling' that recurs and refuses to be suppressed. It is a common enough human experience, exceptional here because so majestically durable and so suddenly articulated. Sometimes a sister has found herself simply announcing that she intends to become a nun. The statement is often deeply surprising, even shocking, to herself, and the setting can be almost absurdly mundane—not in the solemnity of a chapel or before the heart-stopping serenity of a masterpiece of sacred art, but perhaps in a seedy haunt in Melbourne, or on the summit of a hill outside Oslo, the unbidden reply is blurted out: 'without any sort of hesitation, and I was staggered when it came out and I said "Oh, I think I might be joining a religious community", and I thought "What have I said?"'

Most of the sisters' stories are characterized by the touchingly individual, the apologetically homely, the long-standing query

as to why one has been singled out. Even the most dramatic-
seeming is unexpectedly down-to-earth: 'I had what you'd call a
conversion experience... You wouldn't understand it, would
you? Have you ever had a blinding flash and known for certain
where you ought to be going next?... I was with a friend in a
low dive in Swanston St'. Into the ritual discussion of the
future, the friend interposed the idea of joining a religious
community: 'when I said, "It's one of the things I never think
about", I was gone, because it was the first time of opening up
and admitting there were areas I wasn't going to look at'.

As most sisters confess, these moments of spiritual certainty
are offset by the vagaries of circumstance and twists in motivation; 'to be honest, I would think that motives are quite
mixed'. Nor is the response to the impulse immediate and
unshakable. It usually becomes part of a protracted process in
which subsidiary decisions with seeming inevitability impel the
individual towards an answer, however belated, to the first call.
In the sisters' backgrounds and some of their life patterns similarities can be found, but the temperamental, experiential and
intellectual differences between them are vast. Ranging from
the hard-headed, bustling and managerial, to the flighty, fragile
and scarred, these women share an experience that escapes
categorization.

The initial sense of calling often takes place in adolescence,
often as an unprompted extension of the solemn new start made
at confirmation, but CHN has had many mature vocations.
The spread of ages of those entering the Community ranges
from twenty-one to the mid-forties, and in a few cases even
older. Particularly over the past three decades, few entered at
twenty-two, which for many years was the earliest allowable
age; almost half the former and present members of the Community entered the religious life when they were twenty-nine or
older.

The more mature woman was just as likely as her younger
counterpart to respond to the influence of a spiritual mentor. A
few key High Church Melbourne parishes, less often female
teachers or religious, had exerted a gravitational tug, but experienced ecclesiastics, including some CHN sisters, were adept

at detecting in girls who came within their orbit the sense of dissatisfaction with things as they are, the unformulated aspiration, and the dedicatory spirit that often combined to make a likely candidate for the religious life. One sister went on retreat and subsequently received a message from the officiating priest, ' "He wants to know how long will it be before you come to live here?" and I said, "Is he a mind-reader?" because I had always been drawn towards the Church'.

More importantly, perhaps, precept was a powerful force. Almost every sister cited some mentor; most often, a priest, but in a significant number of instances, a woman within or outside the religious life was mentioned. In her twenties, one sister was employed at a children's home run by the Order of the Good Shepherd, where she observed the unstinting generosity of the nuns, and thought:

they really don't hold back anything. They really make a total self-giving... They even give up their right to pretty clothes, and their money and so on. It appealed to me, so I was dabbling with it even while I was horrified... That was the beginning of the end of me, because I was right in with the Sisters and their life, and that was where I decided to take the plunge, you know. I was confirmed on my birthday in 1944, and made a postulant.

Another sister, who joined CHN when she was almost twenty-two, had worked at the Children's Home at Goulburn:

I saw the sisters praying there, and I think that was a tremendous example... Just before I left I thought that I was perhaps being called to come to the Community, but I ran away. I wasn't going to do that, thank you very much...but then I knew I had to come; it got to a point when I knew I had to come.

Her resistance lasted four years. On a more intellectual level, the pull of a powerful example can be resisted just as well. One young woman was influenced as a university student by a Roman Catholic sister who shared some of her classes:

I was saying to myself, 'No, don't be stupid... You're just thinking this way because you've been influenced by this Sister'... I still had this sort of niggling, drawing towards the religious life... I didn't think of it at all as being the genuine thing...but it wouldn't go away.

Occasionally, the propaganda was blatant and unrestrained. One sister recalled a Sydney church school where the incitement was so intense that the instinct was to resist fiercely. '"When are you coming to join us, dear?" And I used to say "Never, never, never... I've just come for the ride".'

Although the conviction of some parents that their daughters had been Svengalied was misplaced, CHN had a contingent of propagandists who used to exert their eloquence at youth meetings, or even spot a likely looking candidate in an unlikely setting. One sister was first proselytized by a female church organist: '"My girl, you've got to do it"—and I'd never mentioned anything to her. I said, "Do what?". She said, "Join the Community". I said, "What are you talking about?"'. She feigned ignorance, although she had been 'secretly thinking about the Community and putting it off, but it kept coming back'. She broke her engagement and moved from Tasmania to Melbourne. The fateful moment came when she was ensconced in a shop window demonstrating an accounting machine and was suddenly approached by Sister Elizabeth who put the classic question. 'I took the wind out of her sails by telling her that I was hoping to test my vocation the following year.' Being on the spot in Cheltenham also made one vulnerable to the sudden 'When would you like to come?', 'and of course I was a bit startled, and I said "Oh, well, I have to finish the year"'. Generally, these fully fledged sisters were perceptively tuning in on a nascent vocation, rather than shooting arrows into the blue.

A few admit to a period in which they were indifferent to religion—chiefly that time of dawning independence when life seems to offer kaleidoscopic attractions; but the majority never seriously questioned or doubted the fundamentals of the Christian faith, and only one sister described a period of agnosticism. Predictably, in most cases the young women who entered the Community had temperaments predisposed towards religious feeling, often from an impressively young age. The sensation of precocious piety can be conveyed with comic self-awareness.

'I've always been drawn towards the Church', one sister commented, her face crinkling into lines of relaxed self-mockery, 'because I received a prize at Sunday school when I was about three years old for attendance'. Another referred to the apathetic Anglicans in her background, and laughed: 'I was more or less the black sheep of the family. I couldn't get enough...looking back, you can trace how God's calling you, right back from a little girl. I can remember I was always very much God-centred'. She added that her two engagements foundered because her fiances could not match her ardent church-going habits. A rare example of the procedure working in reverse, with an enthusiast inciting God to endow her with a vocation she did not yet have, was the teenager who, having been inserted into a Roman Catholic school by her Anglican parents, knew of the Mission in Spring St, and 'used to pray coming down from the convent under the pine trees that God would lead me to it'. Though few would claim that they consciously considered their religious leanings all through their early years, the first realization of them usually retains its freshness—perhaps the child 'sitting on a form' at the age of nine or ten, hearing a particularly fervent group of Christians, like the Plymouth Brethren or the Salvation Army; or a solemn-faced six year old's desire to be a missionary nurse.

In fact, the glamour of a missionary vocation, the dispensing of care and enlightenment to those who would otherwise be lost, was often the first manifestation of a call that might end at CHN. About a quarter of the Community's current complement said that they had been animated from an early age by the exotic rigours of the mission field, China and India after decades of imperialist propaganda being the favourite locations for this childish romanticizing. Otherwise, more prosaically, the call might relate to the home mission field. The particular requirements of the missionary vocation led several of these young idealists towards teaching and nursing, as the professional adjunct to their plans, though in one self-confessed case it provided a cover for the real impulse, which was to secure an amiable outdoors job. Many of these missionary yearnings were not fulfilled, although several sisters did work in the mission field before coming to CHN (notably in New Guinea, which in the post-war decade was an expanding field for duty-conscious Australians); and one sister who had realized an ambition to work in India relinquished a chance for more permanent involvement there by deciding to join the Community.

Although the Community has learned to be wary of vocations which seem to manifest themselves like the stroke of a gong, many sisters can identify a precise time when vocation asserted itself imperatively. Religious observance beginning as a fairly routine obligation can be transformed into an experience imbued with meaning, accompanied by the sense familiar to the religious of a cleansing renewal of being. One sister experienced an all-encompassing change in her early twenties while on retreat: 'It was as though God had suddenly cleansed me, and had made me empty for something that was in His plan. That's the only way I can describe it... I felt very strongly that God was calling me to the life of a religious'. Uncertain though she was of the direction in which she was being impelled, her response was immediate. She thought, '"I suppose I've got a vocation to something, but I don't quite know what it's about"... I gave up dressmaking almost overnight, and went to work for the Church at the Cathedral'.

By contrast, the transforming experience could take place quite against the grain. One sister, who had been brought up in a brilliantly Orange school, recalled her feelings as a secular nurse at St George's, and how her contempt for the sisters was dramatically and somewhat bizarrely altered:

One day—it was a strange experience—I was sitting at the window...and I could see myself coming towards myself dressed in the habit, and I flung my book on the bed and got for my life, but a few weeks later I went and asked Sister Lily of all people—she was one of the Truro sisters [who were around only because the Japanese branch of their order had been stranded when war broke out]—would she prepare me for confirmation... Why I asked her, I've no idea, but I did.

An older woman, who entered the Community when she was forty-four, called in unexpectedly at a church after visiting a relative in hospital. She vividly remembered hearing music

being played on a harmonium: 'I had the most extraordinary
experience in that church of absolute peace, I can't describe it.
I mean, you couldn't describe it to anyone else, and I remember
thinking to myself, "Oh, this is where I want to be" '. She
carefully monitored her own responses ('I know I'm a very
impulsive person. I know this is one of the times I can't afford
to be impulsive'), until deciding that it was not religious mania
she was experiencing, but the reality of vocation.

Only rarely did the call manifest itself through a dream, and
even the compelling imagery of the unconscious can be resisted,
of course. One sister offered to do anything that God requested:

I had a dream a couple of nights later, and saw myself in a black
habit. I went berserk. I said, 'Lord, I can't do that'. . . It was so real.
You can only interpret these things by your own experience and
understanding, and in the secrecy of your heart make decisions on
them. . . For the next seven years I ran. . . I kept saying, 'Lord, give
me a bit more time'.

Sometimes the seminal point came in an unsought-for period
of reflection. While recovering from an illness, one sister heard
a nearby church bell, 'and I just knew I had to answer it'.
Another found herself stranded at CHN for an extra week
because of an illness that struck her during a training course
held at Retreat House. 'Very shortly after that I was aware that
this was where God wanted me.' A third was alone recovering
from mumps when she happened to read Patrick White's *Voss*:
'I don't know why, but that seemed to have a sort of quite
profound spiritual influence on me, and that sort of connected
up again with my idea when I was eleven and confirmed, of
really believing that I wanted to commit myself in some way'.

Not unexpectably, a combination of illness and death could
prove overwhelming. As an adolescent, one sister found herself
hedged in by crises: the death of a brother, the absence of her
mother for an operation, the serious continuing illness of a
sister:

That particular morning, my sister had been very unwell and I was
trying to cook a hot dinner, and I was just feeling desperate. It was a
beautiful day, a beautiful spring day, and I went out into the garden to

do something, and while I was out there I said, 'If my sister gets better, I'll give my life to the Church'... So I made that vow then that I wouldn't marry, and they used to laugh at me, and say 'You'll get over that'. Anyway, I felt I was *not* meant to marry.

The recollection of this touchingly desperate pact came as an afterthought in describing a vocation that took its final compelling shape only slowly and through less dramatic occasions.

The death of a parent, particularly a father, for an adolescent girl could precipitate a remobilizing of the entire personality—although few objectify the situation so thoroughly as the sister who admired her father's verve and competence and was unconsciously convinced of her mother's ineffectuality:

I think partly why I'm in a religious order where we're celibate is that my father died when I was sixteen... When you're in your teens you tend to sort of relate again to the male member of the family. You start noticing that they're around, and suddenly at the age of sixteen he wasn't. And because I saw him as a kind of ideal and I thought of myself as being a personality rather like my mother, I didn't like myself terribly much, because I saw her as just being a person who rushed around and chattered away, and I know now that she wasn't, but that was my picture of her; and I had this idealistic picture of my father, and that was encouraged by my mother, because she didn't cope terribly well with his death. People then didn't worry much about grieving... I kept on looking for my father, really...just from listening to different stories about other sisters' lives...there are mixed motives... And some of those things are reasons why people's marriages break up, because they want that person to be either like somebody they've known, or like their father; so it's not a totally alien kind of thing. It doesn't just apply to women, either.

This unusually introspective assessment of the sociological and psychological elements that helped to predispose the woman towards a celibate existence in no way negates the essential spirituality of her calling.

For several sisters, death came not as a precipitating crisis at an impressionable age, but as a liberation into their own maturity. Many had been obliged to nurse invalid relatives, particularly mothers. An extreme example was the sister who entered the Community in her mid-forties some time after the death of both parents within three days of each other:

You could've said I was free at last... When my parents died, it opened the way up for me to become a communicating Christian... For the first time in my life I could breathe. It was a growing into myself... Although it looked wrong, I think it's proved that it was right...but as for becoming a *nun*, that had never been a thought in my head... It had just been *there* without me sort of asking the question.

Like the sister who found compelling spiritual signs in *Voss*, several others were influenced by literature: the story of St Therese of Lisieux, for example, or G. K. Chesterton's life of St Francis, could lead to the readers seeking in their own lives parallels to these saints. Most of these literary influences are pietistic and intuitive, rather than intellectual-aesthetic, but one highly educated sister entered into her own bargain after reading Pascal, the French philosopher 'who had said "Make a wager that there is a God. If you lose, you've got nothing to lose, and if you win, you've got everything to gain", and I decided to try it... By the end of my second year at university I was a committed Christian'.

Even more unusual was the example of an aesthetic but non-verbal influence. One sister who worked in a bank before joining the Community, but whose real professional dedication was dancing in an amateur ballet company, sees lasting significance in her favourite *Les Sylphides*: 'I'm still seeing relationships between that ballet and the life of prayer... That was a great blessing and a leading really'. For another, who worked in aviation for many years, the imagery of flying always connected with her perceptions of the metaphysical.

In responding to a vocation, many sisters were also reacting to an urgent need to establish a framework of meaning in their lives. Sometimes, a secular impulse towards personal renovation could suddenly and disconcertingly reveal its essentially spiritual bias. 'I was really looking for some sort of purpose in life, but I wasn't looking for it in the direction of God at all. I was looking for it in a more wordly direction... I thought, "she [a

Roman Catholic nun] has got something that I want". One day it suddenly dawned on me that that was God.'

Sometimes the response is centred in exhaustion with a comfortable existence whose pleasures seem to be leading nowhere. 'I got so sick of having all the good times that I was really glad to come': the sister who said that was not the only one to experience the 'emptiness' of self-gratification.

The progress of each sister towards CHN is strikingly individual, but the patterns that exist do mirror the restrictiveness of Australian social conditions during the forties and fifties, when many of the sisters now in the Community were young women. The majority came from lower-middle-class backgrounds, and were educated to lower-secondary standard. None had working mothers, even when the mother was widowed at a stage when there were still children to support. Practical limitations therefore restricted girls who yearned to do something significant with their lives, but came from poorer families and were further confined by their sex. 'There wasn't a lot of choice for people with our kind of lack of funds... We automatically looked in the direction where scholarships were available.'

For girls whose ambitions stretched beyond a bout of office work before marriage, the available options were usually nursing or teaching. A third of those now in CHN had been trained for these professions. For some, a stultifying job was one element in their search for significance. Nearly half worked in offices (being 'bored stiff in the typing pool') or the retail industry before joining the Community, and the working lives of many were interrupted by stints of caring for relatives. Several had responsible secretarial jobs or were otherwise moderately successful; one was auxiliary organizer for a major Melbourne hospital. But whatever the occupation, a gnawing sense of dissatisfaction was common: 'there was something lacking in my life, you know, and I never could pinpoint it'. Or:

When the call to this life began... I didn't identify it with being a vocation really. I just thought it was a bit of joke. I was preparing for stocktaking and I just said to one of my staff members, 'There has to be a better way of earning a living'. Words to that effect. 'There must be more meaning to life than this.' And I said, 'Perhaps I'll become a nun'. And it was purely a joke at that stage, and we both laughed about it, but for several months later I began getting jolts, just little pokes about becoming a nun... For two years I avoided it, until there was just no choice.

The initial sense of vocation is often followed by a period of rebellion, brief maybe but in some cases postponing for several years the decision to join the Community. Many sisters speak of a sense of disturbance, bordering even on resentment at having to relinquish active social and working lives. One humorously described the sleepless nights in which she wrestled with the bedclothes and fulminated against a call that had struck as suddenly as a blow from the dark: 'I spent the next week fighting... At the end of the week, I said, "OK, Lord, you've won. All right". So I was so gracious, and so sort of furious'.

The frustration of having one's plans interfered with in this arbitrary heavenly manner was sometimes exacerbated by contempt for the life that was being insisted on:

My association with God had nothing to do with the Community... the only time I saw them I had no sympathy for the Sisters, because I imagined they were people who couldn't make it in life...so when the Lord asked me to join, that was an absolutely horrifying thought, because I was happy where I was.

One sister's flight from commitment lasted twelve years: 'He gave me a big line;...nuns aren't everybody's cup of tea...who wants to live with a batch of women?...it was a vocation that never went away, hard as I tried'. One sister who, like several in the Community, had been engaged before joining, felt an undefined vocation and discussed all the options with a priest: 'the only thing I couldn't definitely say no to was the religious life, for some reason. It had a pull on me... It wasn't something I naturally wanted. I fought it...it was very much an unknown... I just had an obsession with it. I couldn't get it out of my mind day and night'.

For the majority of sisters, a complicating factor was the reaction of their families, varying from sympathetic resignation to unhelpful incomprehension, to bitter hostility. Anguish was often the mothers' response, while the fathers were more prone to anger. Sometimes the whole family dissolved: 'he cried, I cried, Mum cried, we all cried, and Mum *never* recovered, never forgiven me, ever'. This sister's father, who had been a strong intellectual influence in her life, didn't speak to her for five years and refused to come to her profession, although her deeply distressed mother did; family relations dwindled to simple matter-of-fact transactions. Another sister's father threatened to disown her, while her mother said bitterly that if she'd foreseen the outcome the girl would have been brought up Methodist, a system that did not offer the celibate option.

Persistence in the face of a parent's deep distress often produced almost intolerable emotional strain. The response was likely to be more severe in small families, especially where the candidate was the eldest in the family or the only daughter:

I was the girl, so I was the one who was expected to take the responsibility, and I just felt as though I was walking out on them... Mum said, 'It'll be just like burying you'... A terrible fear of it... I surreptitiously got my black things together in the bottom drawer, feeling absolutely terrible about it.

This girl was the eldest and the only daughter, and both her parents were ill when she finally decided to come to CHN at the age of twenty-seven. Although her parents were eventually reconciled to her choice, she endured a conflict of responsibilities again much later, when her mother once more fell ill. Another sister, the elder of two girls, found herself confronted by a furious father, a furious sibling, and a furious employer. Her mother 'could understand what I was saying, but she didn't want it to happen'. She went on holiday, and arranged to be dropped off at CHN on the return journey: 'I knew that if I didn't follow that calling, I'd be sorry for the rest of my life, and that the only way I could do it hurting people the least was just to disappear, and that's what I did'. She had no contact with her parents during her novitiate, and there was no response to the invitation to her profession: 'I was ill during part of my novitiate, and I think that is probably why. It was ostensibly 'flu, but I would think it was a sort of grieving'.

Sometimes the reaction to a daughter's vocation was so extreme that it cast a blight over the novitiate and beyond. One sister, whose family was strictly Congregationalist and adamantly anti-Catholic, experienced 'a dreadful flare-up' that developed into a prolonged period of ostracism, when her father died three weeks after she entered the Community. She was held responsible for his death, and a campaign of abusive letters prosecuted this view. For years, her visits to her mother were permissible by back-lane entrance only. The Presbyterian response was no more accommodating, and could be complicated by anti-feminist feeling:

Until my father died, I really wasn't the most popular member of the family. Since then I've been quite popular... If I'd done what my father had wanted me to do, I might have been a check-out girl at Woolworth's or something... Although he had an excellent education...the girls didn't matter so much...but I got on with it.

Sometimes siblings reacted more strongly than parents. One sister's parents were 'absolutely stunned' to start with, but mellowed into acceptance, while her two brothers were 'totally devastated' and were permanently alienated from the Church. Another brother, the only sibling, was so enraged that for years he prevented contact between his sister and his children. One father's calm response was offset by that of the mother who 'practically had a nervous breakdown'. Not even peripheral relatives could be relied on for restraint: 'my aunties were shocking', one sister recalled. While the immediate household was absorbing the news, they traipsed onto the scene laden with affecting photographs of the past and loudly lamenting the prospective loss of their niece's hair. Three sisters who, before entering the Community, had had symbiotic relationships with twin sisters have had to withstand their twins' inability to adjust to the drastic separation. In both these cases, the violent reaction of the twin who felt abandoned adversely affected the parents who were already doubtful enough.

The anxieties of parents, particularly of mothers, often focussed on the life of drudgery and unfeminine austerity they believed their daughters were about to embrace. One mother lamented 'it seems that you're not allowed to have any colour in your life, and I said "Oh, don't worry. I'll put green bubble bath in the bath"'. Black, the colour of incarceration, sacrifice, nullity and death, aroused almost primitive fears. One sister's mother was horrified by the kit for a CHN novice, which was black and more black, including the gratuitously sombre item of a black dressing-gown. The analogy of living death often came to mind. 'She thought I was going to be more or less buried alive', one sister commented, adding that she herself was over-ready for the worst, expected a diet of bread and water, imagined looming austerities, and made sets of board-stiff calico underwear for her future life.

But some parents managed a much more moderate and pacific reaction: 'They thought I was a fool, that was all'. Still, the pliant response could be in deference to the daughter's own aspirations: 'They didn't *want* me to come, but they also thought that until I tested it out, I wouldn't be happy. Neither of them felt they should stand in my way'.

A common pattern was the gradual reconciliation of parents, even some who at first were bitterly opposed, and the dawning of a glow of pride that sometimes extended to the benign assumption of responsibility for the whole course of events: 'after a few years you'd think they'd engineered the whole thing'. One sister knew that her father had finally been reconciled when, without declaring its significance, he gave her a fob watch that had been in the family for generations.

When a young woman decided to test a religious vocation within the Anglican Church, she was faced with a very limited choice of communities: the Brisbane-based Society of the Sacred Advent; the English-founded Sisters of the Church, who had branches in most Australian states; more recently, a small group of Franciscan nuns in New South Wales; and CHN. For some, the choice was a rational procedure capped by an intuitive sense that one's destiny was linked with this particular institution and place. One sister worked her way through a book on Anglican communities, and gave each an imaginary approval rating. Apart from looking good, CHN was on the spot. Another weighed up the merits of various communities, but sensed that the choice of CHN was a foregone conclusion: 'I remember writing back to my sister before I even got to Cheltenham, and

'A community of being': a group of sisters in the garden at Community House, Cheltenham.

A girls' Friendly Society function at Retreat House, *c.* 1950.

'The work got done and the people who needed help got helped, and in some ways it was a much more *sensitive* organization because we were very *close* to it all': Mission House, Melbourne, 1950s and 1981.

just saying, "Even before I get there I just feel I'm going to be coming back anyway"'. With its good government, broad-based mission work, and lack of obvious eccentricity, CHN was likely to appeal, but bizarre elements could intrude on the rational decision-making programme. One sister who worked as an airline hostess organized her flying schedule so that she could vet all the Anglican communities. While the Sisters of the Church appealed because they were not in traditional habit, CHN's black garb was portentously significant: 'I was horrified, but I knew when I saw them in black that that was the dream I had. I was in *black*; this was the only crew in black; *so* this must be the place'. Given our storehouse of primordial images, the chance of dream-nuns appearing in anything other that black was fairly small.

Various factors, though, brought individuals to CHN. Its own diversity and the swag of involvements it had shouldered gave a range of opportunities. By contrast, CSC's work centred on teaching—a commitment that often failed to appeal even to those sisters who were teachers already—and its English cast seemed like restraint, even coldness, to some prospective applicants who preferred CHN's Australian origins and 'its vitality, enthusiasm'. Often, CHN won by being there without rivals in the field—though the whole platoon of OGS sisters, in the process of re-establishing their corporate vocation, settled on CHN by employing a unique blend of climatic and dietary considerations to supplement their sense of this as the one Australian order to which they wanted to belong. In rare cases the Community was the solution to a challenge provided by the much more formidable edifice of the Roman Catholic Church. Predictably, several sisters went through periods when they were infatuated with Roman Catholicism—an attraction that in one case lingered until profession. Another sister was directed to CHN by her appalled brother after she had announced her intention of joining a Roman Catholic order.

The first visit to Cheltenham often sealed the choice with a sense of homecoming, an intuitive empathy with the place. The expectations roused by the leisurely but potent drive, the austere but welcoming certainty of Community House, the sense of extensive vistas in every direction, every element

seemingly invested with a spiritual dimension, must have combined to assist many a prospective novice towards heart-felt
affirmation. One sister came to a retreat at Retreat House in its
corner of the grounds, and 'knew then that this was it'. She
added that she was not expected to last in the Community,
because hers was 'one of those sort of instantaneous vocations'.
Again, the powerful influence exerted by the atmosphere at
Cheltenham could merge with a sense of individual crisis: 'it
was while I was here that I was knocked on the head and
realized this was where I was meant to be. I knew that God was
pushing me into it. I didn't want to come'.

Once the initial step of entering the Community had been
taken, a revolution in life patterns had to be confronted. Until
recently, entering the novitiate meant not only a drastic alteration in daily modes, but relinquishment of even minor decision-making on one's own behalf, and adherence to a timetable
that left almost no room for self-directed activities or even the
luxury of being alone. Novices in those days were also treated
as a separate and subordinate class. The prescriptions were
particularly burdensome to those whose life before entering the
Community had been notably independent. One sister found

A very big gulf. There was a great wall built [between novices and
professed sisters]. I found it irrational and stupid. I found many things
quite irrational. We grew up with a lot of responsibility as young .
children, and we didn't have anyone checking when we did things,
then you come to the Community and you go back to infancy and
everything you do is questioned and checked and you're always junior
until you're about fifty, then you're old.

Many complained of the devastating effect of the 'wall' behind
which the novices were segregated. Occasionally, the reaction
is even more severe than this brutally frank statement:

Before I came to live here, I'd lived for twenty-nine years, and I was a
reserved person, and quiet, but I'd *lived*, and it was a *terrible* time,
because we didn't even *sit* with the sisters... I think it was unconscious
mental cruelty. Some people weathered it better than others, but I

didn't weather it at all, because I wasn't used to that kind of thing. The people I'd worked with, we were all *equals*, we were all grown-up *people*... It's been hard for me to cope with those who've been more rigid... It was a three-year probation... I used to walk to the gate and think, 'All I have to do is take a few more steps out, and I'm free'.

The sister who made this painful statement also reflected ironically that when she entered the Community she was required to relinquish religious books which the Retreat House now recommends to retreatants. Even those whose sense of vocation became a convinced certainty once they'd entered the Community, observed 'a very very rigid separation of the sheep from the goats in those days'. Novices were 'a sort of race apart... less than dust'.

The withdrawal of personal responsibility was particularly galling if you joined the Community in middle age. One sister who entered when resignation has usually lowered the flag of change, thought 'What am I doing, a mature woman, putting up with this?'. She emphasized that the problem lay, not as outsiders imagined in the impress of conformity and the suppression of individualism, but in the mind-numbing obligation to 'a lot of traditional rules and regulations that had been handed down from medieval times... there were things that were just absurd. I realize that now'. Insidiously, many of these, such as curtseying to the Superior at every encounter, reinforced hierarchy and dimmed the expectation of change.

'Not being able to make decisions any more' in a situation 'very much more structured than it is now', was compounded by the necessity for 'perpetual motion. And never having any time to yourself'. There was also the challenge of the binding vows that lay ahead:

[A priest] talked to me, and he said, 'You're not going to find poverty hard, and you're not going to find chastity hard', but he said 'You are going to find obedience hard, because you've always been a free lance'... It was very difficult in many ways. It was *very* closely regulated.

This sister's story suggests that with machiavellian shrewdness and inventiveness she found ways round the regulations; but the strictures could seem demeaning. Those sisters whose education had accustomed them to intellectual freedom were disconcerted by embargos on books, the monitoring of reading, the sudden withdrawal of access to information.

The personality of the novice mistress was also obviously crucial. One sister felt that during her novitiate she had been singled out for prejudicial treatment, and discovered much later that the novice mistress had most likely over-estimated by several lurid degrees the amount of worldly experience which needed to be counteracted: 'She'd bounce me at every turn. I used to hate going down to Community House for class days... When I look back on it, I think [the novitiate] could be improved 500%'. A calm novitiate also depended on the work allotted the novice. Some accepted being shunted around without demur, but others resisted being slotted into positions unsuited to their individual abilities, experience and predilections—particularly the assumption that aspirant nuns were naturally maternal, and thus candidates for a stint at one of the children's homes. The worst resolution was to internalize the misery that came from submitting to roles which were personally intolerable.

In some ways, the reaction to relinquishing talents and allowing training to lie fallow is surprisingly muted, partly because the traditional view—even though drastically modified over recent years—still has residual force: talents, it says, are left on the conventional doorstep. One sister, who believes in the superior calibre of previous generations of CHN, drew approving attention to the example of an earlier sister whose experience of finishing-school gave way to thirty-eight years in the House of Mercy kitchen. But few sisters nowadays would endorse the stereotyped self-denying view: 'The talents are actually God's gifts, and if He chooses to take them back He has the right to do so. None of them belong to us'. A more moderate reworking of this philosophy employed an engaging if not entirely apt domestic metaphor. 'You don't go through life letting out all your gifts because you've got them. They must be used as they're asked to be used...you don't use them willy-nilly...

anymore than you use all your kitchen appliances'.

The new mood in the convent would opt for more personal choice. The line that nuns should be totally self-abnegating was put to one of the younger members of the Community, who rejected it in a spirited if not spiritual manner, making it clear that her notion of religious living did not include the pointless and defacing suppression of individuality.

Given that a proportion of women who entered the Community either were turning their backs on unstimulating jobs, or envisaged this new career as the crowning move in lives already professionally dedicated to the Church, nostalgia for abandoned careers was uncommon. In a rare case, regret for the past was heightened by a sense of constriction:

My most difficult time came when I was a postulant. When I first came to the Community, I wanted to go back to [Forrest River] Mission. I loved the aborigines, I loved them, and I wanted to go back, and I felt I was in prison. I used to look out the window and see the rabbits frolicking on the lawn, and I spent a lot of time weeping. [Laughter] But as soon as I was clothed I never had any more doubts.

There was remarkably little resentment when the Community authorities had decided, seemingly irrationally, not to take advantage of professional training such as nursing. One sister who had been a teacher did not regret not teaching, but found herself committed to seemingly endless housework: 'I really hated it, and I wouldn't admit it to myself, and that was part of my problem when I got really down'. Sometimes regret is expressed on another's behalf; a sister who has left the Community was described as 'one of the best pianists in Australia. . . she almost wasn't allowed to use it. She was put in the laundry and her hands got all rough'. Similar laments are made for another sister whose musical talents also fell into a partly self-chosen abeyance.

Suppression of talents and training was rarely a factor with many of the older sisters who came to the Community with a world-view that accepted truncated possibilities and menial status for girls of their class. They were glad to find practical and compassionate work, often an outlet for the 'Martha syndrome', and could look with hard-headed dignity at the forces by which they'd been shaped:

I was and many of my own age were all products of the depression, and my mother was left a widow with us three, two brothers and me... We just struggled along... I knew poverty all my young life. You didn't think anything of it, because everybody else was in the same boat... I knew what it was, the humiliation of lining up with two hundred after a job, and the fortunate people who were in the job peering out and eyeing you up... It never occured to me to feel sorry for myself. It gave you a philosophical approach to things...you just didn't have the opportunities in those days.

Whatever satisfactions could be found in the community life, however, emotional factors were still liable to make the novice's experience painful. In particular, there was the withdrawal of affection in a situation where substitutes were disallowed: 'We weren't encouraged to have very close relationships with each other'. For those with demonstrative natures, or who had come from stable and loving families, the constraints were especially hard. One novice who hadn't been separated from her family before found Christmas 'devastating'. Coming well-prepared intellectually could likewise be followed by unforeseen emotional problems:

I'd read a lot of books about the religious life, and they were all the kind of pre-Vatican II sort of books. And therefore I didn't find anything that I wasn't *expecting*... I'd expected more outward austerities than there were, but I wasn't prepared for the interior kind of emotional difficulties of adjusting...to a way of life that's so different from anything you've lived before, and living at such close quarters with people. In the world you can escape from other people, you can escape from yourself, you can escape from your situation, and in a way you're doing it all the time without realizing it... In community you can't. You're just face to face with yourself and everybody else and God.

The learning process was all-inclusive and continuous: 'Profession was another ball-game too, because the novitiate was kept

apart... You began to learn the way of life, and then you began
to learn about things in the Community'.

Even under the more relaxed regime of recent years, problems
with the novitiate persist. An individual can be stranded without
contemporaries and with mentors who are no longer certain of
a teaching core: 'No one really knew what to do with me... I
was sort of wandering around at a loose end'. This novice
observed some surviving ritualistic mores, and thought:

'Oh, what's going on here? they're all mad'... They'd do things the
long way round...like deliberately standing over a bucketful of potatoes
peeling in a particular way... I had a horrific novitiate... I can
remember going out on Saturday afternoon and coming home and
saying, 'That's it! I'm leaving'...part of my conflict came because I
really wanted something that was genuine and authentic, and I wasn't
prepared to accept just things as they were, and I wanted a choice in
things. I didn't want to have to be just knocked into line.

The belief that the futile and eccentric elaboration of commonplace tasks is good for the soul—a quirk not confined to religious
societies—dies hard.

Another recent recruit had an equally extreme though less
pugnacious reaction: 'I came down here and I went into a state
of shock, and I remained in shock for four years I would say'.
This sister was allowed to retain civilian dress for a year, and
was granted other dispensations. 'Nevertheless, the pressures
were put on me to conform, and you're absolutely thrown in a
Community because you know you have to obey...there's a
difference between being led and being driven.' Like several
others, she felt that the blurred outline of the Community's
present expectations made it even harder to resist. Yet the fact
that both these recent arrivals have remained in CHN shows
that the possibilities of a pliant vitality are there.

Contrary to those who felt thrown back to childhood, there
were others who, admitting to dependent and conforming
natures, found the transition easy, taking to it 'like a duck to
water...thrilled to be here', 'very eager', pleased to hand over
management of their lives to a strict regimen: 'I'm an adaptable
sort of person, and I just took it as that's how the religious life

was lived'. This sister added that her novice mistress 'did treat us like children', and the protracted trauma she later experienced in her community life arose from submitting to requirements that seemed to disfigure her individuality.

Even those who adapted like the proverbial duck found the water ruffled at times, but it was smoothed by philosophical acceptance: 'I felt at home as soon as I got here. I'm not saying I didn't have hassles...[but] whatever came was just part of it, so I gradually learnt to adapt'. Another who joined CHN at thirty-three found her induction 'pretty traumatic' and 'really had to think hard about [her] vocation' during the first rest period of her novitiate, but she returned. As 'a person of routine', the discipline of community life suited her. Conformity however could be as problematic as rebelliousness: 'I think I *knew* I had to be *here*...but I really *wasn't* here... Various people find it easier to fit into a regulated sort of pattern but it wasn't very good for my type...it just fed my weaknesses rather than anything else...ultimately, things began to catch up with me'. This sister was disconcerted by the flexibility that stronger individuals demanded, and felt uneasy with the movement towards self-direction. For her, it meant a personal dislocation of painful intensity: 'I have come close to falling into the temptation of despair or hopelessness. Just the darkness, I suppose, not really knowing what's going to come next'.

The disciplined format of professional training eased the transition for some. A former nurse expected more severities than she found, and observed simply that the Community comprised 'a joyful lot of people'. The schooling another sister had had, hemming her in with traditional observances, facilitated her adjustment, and for many an old-fashioned upbringing left its mark: 'I was brought up at the table to be seen but not heard.... I was a very fearful person, and didn't realize it, and very timid and didn't realize it'. Probably, no one nowadays expects a cowed demeanour at the dining table to prove one's amenability to the religious life.

Even the negative-looking emblems and accoutrements of the nun could be attractive to certain temperaments. One very traditional sister 'felt absolute happiness that I was to be in a habit'. Release from the responsibilities of professional life could also be liberating: 'my postulancy was heaven, absolute heaven, nothing to do but scrub floors and no responsibility. . .absolutely bliss as far as I was concerned'. Even this sister's experience of 'one of my loneliest times ever' at St George's, where the separation of novice and professed was exaggeratedly maintained, could be welcomed: 'it forced me back on God'. Feelings of loneliness and homesickness, the gnawing confrontation with distressed parents, and similar griefs were mitigated by a sense that one's choice was right, while the isolation of the novitiate could help develop lasting friendships among the newcomers, even when they were widely separated by age. One sister who belonged to the largest novitiate in CHN's history found it a 'strong, stable and secure sort of environment'.

So, humiliating and grotesque though they sometimes seemed, the old ways offered certainty and promised stability. The vanishing of consensus about the nature of the religious life may have heightened the risk of friction and disharmony; and in any case there are always human flaws to contend with:

People outside sometimes think that a community ought to be a collection of perfect people, forgetting that we're just ordinary human beings. . . It's quite an irrational idea really, to take people from all sorts of backgrounds and throw them together, and sometimes at very close quarters. . . I think the sad thing is when we go on and on, and don't really see what we're doing ourselves.

As another sister put it, looking back over fifty years in CHN, 'the hardest thing about community life is community life'.

Belief in the validity of one's vocation does not mean that doubt and suffering are over. Although profession has a finality, it opens vistas of self-knowledge and understanding. Most sisters have experienced times when the life they have adopted seems too difficult, too agonising, even futile: 'It's a real stressed life, it is. Everyone keeps telling you how peaceful it is. . .you try and live where you get up every morning at 7 o'clock and you're in chapel, and in the end it loses its meaning for you. . .day after day after day'.

Even among the serenely conforming, there is little complacency. Several sisters admitted crises in their vocations, 'temptations' that usually focussed on regrets at the inability to marry and have children. The creative response was to confront such difficulties as a positive challenge: 'I don't think there'd be many Sisters who hadn't really gone through some kind of bad patch in their community life, and you either grow through it, or you spend the rest of your life being bitter about it, or you ditch it before you have worked on it'. On the other hand are vulnerable individuals who find it almost impossible to summon the emotional resources to survive. Questioned, one sister immediately replied that she'd experienced doubts 'hundreds of times', then added:

I'd have to qualify that. There have been times when I've quite literally hung on to the end of the bed to keep myself from going... It's hard to express, it's just something very *deep* within me that's kept me coming back, and yet I've still got a sense of not having found my heart's home. Now how you'd interpret that, I just don't know, and I don't know myself what it is... It's extraordinary, but so much is a kind of haze. I've just gone through the years. I wouldn't chose to do this all over again. It's been too difficult, more difficult than it ever should have been.

She tried to describe the painful interactions of what assailed her: 'My own personality, the people who were dealing with me, and—tradition. Their fears. The expectations that were placed on them to produce, and so the false expectations of you'. Perhaps in speaking of her own personal case this admittedly fragile sister isolated strains which have to a lesser degree affected many members of the Community.

Some crises are relatively minor and temporary: a difficult personal relationship with another sister or with someone in authority; a quandary over one's professional direction; a sense that the ideal and the reality of community life are glaringly out of step; a feeling of loss and fragmentation in the face of vanished certainties; for some whose vocation came late, the dislocation of switching from one life to another. Even the most equable explanations can be touched with ambiguity: 'none of it...was plain sailing. I was on very rocky ground, but...any questioning of my vocation has been superficial and a surface thing. I knew jolly well what God wanted, and I knew that I wanted it too, but I think there's just a natural instinct to fight and have your own way'. But the introspections of some deeply divided sisters are haunted by contradictory movements of mind, more riven, more beleaguered.

The convent is no haven where religious can escape from the need to earn a living, substituting prayer for practicality and piety for active involvement. In the past, this insulation was available (though perhaps to seek this redoubt was not unlike the attitude of women who sought lasting financial security in marriage), but even by the mid-1950s when the Order of the Good Shepherd was in crisis, one now-elderly sister admitted that she had contemplated her revenue situation if she should be forced to go on the job market, and concluded 'I'd had experience but no training'. Outside her community, she was familiar only with 'shop work, being nice to people over the counter', and her own work within her vocation seemed likely to be unvalued. The outside world's view of the nun's life is of course a further pressure on that life itself. The three sisters who left the Community in 1937 when a secular was placed over them at St George's were responding to an intrusion of values and standards which both overtly and implicitly challenged their particular dedication and seemed to devalue it. In recent years, as some of the disruptive forces have moved to the heart of the way in which the Community perceives itself, those challenges have become ever more complex and painful:

People were beginning to question things...and I suppose I was in a smaller, lesser degree caught up in it... I felt I had to get out. Quite frankly, I was saying I'd have to get out altogether because I couldn't come up to the standard. We were just going through the stage where people were beginning to be called to more prayer and more silence... This was where Sister Faith was marvellous. I said to her, 'I have to get out, I just can't keep up with these standards, and I'm just—I'm a mission worker. I'm the Martha type'.

Advised to leave the Community for six months, she worked in a nursing home and had the novel experience of being paid, enabling her to dispense gifts to relatives and friends: 'I had a wonderful time, but I realized it could never satisfy me. I need the structure, the discipline of having offices to go to'. Like another sister, who spent six months of 'freedom' to find that she could not live without the Community, this member of CHN returned.

But doubts of all kinds surface and resurface. The imminence of final vows can be intolerable. One sister left for three years when profession loomed. Sometimes adjustment is hardest during the first years after profession when the contrast between life-styles is still relatively fresh, and yet the future as a totally bound person seems dauntingly long. 'I could have walked out at the drop of a hat'; but the same sister who said so has found the Community become the passionate centre of her life. Wistful periods, understandably, centre around the relinquishment of intimate relationships: 'there've been times when I've wished God hadn't called me to the religious life... I've thought it would have been nice to live a more normal in inverted commas kind of life'. Often, consequences makes themselves apparent only in a slow, lucent crystallization:

my sense of being called to something was not to any particular work or service. The sort of life the Community lived and the work they did never seemed to interest me. It was more a call to a relationship with Christ, and it always seemed to me in those, the early days, to be a call to sacrifice. And a sacrifice that involved loneliness more than anything else... It wasn't until as the years went on and I realized what it meant in the way of giving up of relationships that I realized just what the loneliness entailed. It was a mysterious sort of thing at first, and then, as the years went on, emptying... I was separated from people. It's like losing part of yourself...and yet, *beneath* that, there's always been the sense of being held, that sort of spiritual fellowship and companionship.

One of the newer sisters says that her vocation has been strengthened by the part it has played in locating and resolving a tortuous family relationship:

I'm feeling reaffirmed in my decision because I've been freed of an imprisonment...it's not until I came to this life and I've started to

---

learn the power of prayer and how much spiritual healing is again so powerful that I can start to understand a little of the freedom it brings. My own identity has been revealed, and that's understanding—self-understanding: looking at yourself and analyzing and so forth; and I think recognizing and accepting mistakes, being prepared to say that you're sorry...instead of getting resentful.

The new mood in the Community encourages individual value, verbally, professionally, or in the unfolding of unsuspected talents. This self-liberation is hardly more straightforward than it is for unbelievers, however, and the spectre of tradition lingers still. More disturbingly for some, although the sense of vocation is intact, self-discovery has deepened the gulf between individual and Community:

I've often said 'Stop the bus, I want to get off', but I've never doubted my vocation. A lot depends on how CHN goes... I'm on a track, and the Community's on the track, both of us are on the same track, but we're going in different directions. I'm moving in the opposite direction to most members of the Community.

Like an outermost planet wheeling in its own irregular orbit, this sister belongs only peripherally to the Community, though still held by its gravitational pull—as in her contradictory statements, that she both does and does not want the Community to change. But few can look back with the simplicity of one sister who averred that 'never, never' had she had any doubts. The more usual fact, mostly resolving difficulties though sometimes intensifying them, is that at the heart of vocation is the unerring aim of the arrow: 'It's sort of the verse "You have not chosen me, but I have chosen you", and there's just no escaping'. Some may say 'I've always known that it's going to be alright. If you can hang on long enough it'll be alright, and that's always been the pattern of my life'. Almost none would deny that religious vocation remains open to the tremors of doubt most radical life choices undergo. It's 'like any other life. Like marriage must be sometimes'.

'I had a stronger thing to keep me here, because I wasn't going to walk out on [the Community]...even though I had a break-

OUT OF THE SILENCE

down and just about everything went, the only thing that really stayed was that I was meant to be here'. Contrary to a fairly common suspicion, vocation is not a misguided and tragic second-best, a 'sublimation' that causes mental illness. It can instead be a source of strength in overcoming disturbances of the psyche. Another said:

When I was having that breakdown, the doctor used to keep facing me up with the issue, 'Are you sure you're in the right place?', but during those years that was really the only thing I had to hang onto—the fact that I was in the right place. I couldn't feel happy about it...it was really the *only* thing that I had to hang on to.

One of the oldest members of the Community described the debits and credits, the qualifications and sureties, the interaction of positives and negatives that has made up her long life in the Community:

I never found the life *easy*. I had lots of ups and downs. Not that I'd made the wrong decision, but that I was a fool to stay there. When things got on top of you...then I'd think to myself, 'Well, the Lord *did* call you... I've heard sisters say to me that they've never had [any doubts], well I find that very difficult to believe, because I don't believe in any walk of life, I don't care whether it's the religious life or married life...there *must* be times when everything gets on top of you... I did know that God had called me, and I knew if I ever left the Community I would not expect to be happy...because God didn't force me to make those vows... But I've never doubted my vocation, never, not at any stage along the line... I'm too much of an individualist, even though I belong to a Community, not to have some doubts.

The weave of the pattern seems impossible to unravel into separate simple strands.

As an Anglican community, CHN stands apart from the lofty hierarchies of Roman Catholic religious life. In many of its manifestations its development is unique, disabling some cliched assumptions about convents and those who live in them. For instance, the claim that nuns adopt the life only because they are snatched into it from school is cancelled by the average age at which this Community's sisters joined. Similarly the statement that girls become nuns without experience, and are therefore deficient or fearful human beings, is invalidated. Many CHN sisters relinquished quick-step social lives and relationships with men to follow their vocations. Moreover, the rarity of Anglican groups meant that families hardly looked forward to their daughters taking the conventual path. Several sisters had to delve rather deeply to discover that CHN even existed, and then had to endure parental disapproval of their apparently unprotestant choice. Almost as surprising is the drawn-out pro-crastination that for several sisters preceded their final com-mitment, and the equally tortuous progress of self-doubt for others: not dramatic show-downs ('I Jump Over the Wall'), but long-continued struggles, often capped by the discovery that fulfilment meant staying in the very place that the world was ready to identify as the source of their anxiety. Perhaps the least expected, if modest, surprise is the fact that of about forty sisters now in the Community four have twin siblings.

Despite its divergence from the classic patterns of nunhood in Australia, CHN has quiet symmetries and harmonies of its own. Although there is an odd classlessness about the Com-munity, it is largely made up of women from lower-middle-class or middle-class Anglican families, often rural. These unusual daughters are distinguished by an instinct for self-giving, a spon-taneous God-centredness, and the early onset of religious feel-ing—usually influenced by some powerful mentor, most often a priest, and further compelled by the incursion of illness and/or death into their family life. Muted symmetries can also be seen in the moderate educational levels and limited work experience of many sisters, which again—quietly but unerringly—reflect the constricted environment of Australian womanhood in the world they came from. Unrhetorically, the women of CHN have proved themselves exceptional by their exceptional choice. And when these patterns are gathered into the constellation of an individual life, the story is moving in its cumulative effect, perplexing in its twists and turns, rich in idiosyncratic detail.

Mostly, the language in which the sisters describe their expe-riences is homely, disorderly, even at times banal. Yet the low-key manner of the telling is sometimes uncomfortingly at odds with the dramatic nature of the outcomes. The overriding impression is of extraordinary events told in a disarmingly ordinary style. Even the arctic austerity of the solitary vocation, with its dense spiritual riches, may be outlined in commonplace terms, and its grinding routine organized with the pernickitiness of an over-anxious housewife. One of CHN's hermits, who is seventy-six rises at 3 a.m. and goes to the chapel at 3.30 to say an hour-long office.

And then I come out for just a little while to wash my face, and then I come back for Mass, and then I say another office. Then after breakfast—I get my own breakfast—then I have a short rest—about a half an hour—and then I do some work, ironing mostly, and then I have another hour's prayer time, and then there's another office to say. By that time it seems to be dinner time. They send my dinner up to me at one o'clock. And then I have another office to say. Then in the afternoons I do some gardening, or perhaps some more ironing, or whatever, and do some reading. I seem to take longer to do things these days. I suppose I'm getting older. And then at about half-past four, I have another hour's prayer time, and say vespers, have tea, and listen to the news. And then I say compline and go to bed. I should be in bed at eight o'clock.

This packed programme can be swelled by a night vigil. Her mesmeric repetition of 'then' is a refrain anchoring her to a vast obligation. The other hermit, who church-mouse-like gets her supplies from the kitchen 'when no one's around; usually at evening time when they're at chapel', described a similarly daunting apportionment of her days—then added apologetically and with a touch of wonderment, 'It sounds an awful lot as though you're thinking about yourself all the time'.

Like the rest of us, the sisters are victims of a socio-linguistic shift. The process is not a simple one of loss, but rather as though a discontinuity has invaded language itself, leaving uncertainty about what can be kept, what should be changed. In the past, even those who were not highly educated had access to rhythms, resonances and idioms that permeated daily life with a distinctive grandeur. There was the sermon, the Bible-reading, the gospel in church, the Book of Common Prayer. But now the symbolic tide has dwindled to a trickle. For

The Community tried to carry with it some of its most cherished effects: *above* the wood-lined Chapel of St Laurence was transported from St George's to the new Ellerslie; and *overleaf* a memorial window from the chapel at Brighton accompanied Sister Margaret Ann to Box Hill Hospital where she had become chaplain.

many older people in the world at large the time-honoured spiritual habits are kept alive only by an effort of will. For many of the young, the Bible is a foreign text, and the King James version a relic that at best attracts pitying acknowledgement. For the sisters, the change is great, and the attempt to rediscover connection and remake an approach is perhaps more fraught than for most of us in the secular world. It is not surprising they so often falter in trying to articulate why they are where they are and living the lives they do.

The outsider is likely to expect of them insights almost no one could deliver, revelations, illuminations; hands are cupped to catch some palpable spiritual presence, something as dazzlingly unholdable as a falling star. What the sisters most compellingly point to is an apprehension of absence: a sense that worldly lives which most people would find tolerable, even satisfying, are without sufficient meaning—in some deep sense, inauthentic—and the universe itself full of tantalizing disharmonies which surround and command the self, pointing it towards its own insufficiency. But beyond the emptiness and the dissonance, out of the silence, the force that impels the vocation exists, an immensity, an unstoppable flow. The experience is colourless and abstract, wordless and imageless, without sensual force—in Jung's words, 'a tremendous intuition striving for expression'; or else it is most fittingly described through a homely, tactile image straight from hearth or kitchen, whose sheer accessibility reveals a strangeness at the heart of the commonplace. In Julian of Norwich's revelations, the entire creation was shown as 'a little thing, the size of a hazelnut, on the palm of my hand, round like a ball' ('And I wondered that it did not instantly fall to nothingness, it was so small'). William Blake's 'Auguries of Innocence' 'see a World in a Grain of Sand/And a Heaven in a Wild Flower'. In both, the macrocosm and microcosm assert their inseparability, and this same awareness of the domestic entangled in the vast is familiar to the Community of the Holy Name. The mother foundress compares a person with an overactive conscience to a hedging turned up the wrong way; the novice mistress standing by the lily pond likens Christ's redemptive action to ducks diving and coming up again; the young nun sees God as 'the sea', an overwhelming oneness, fertile, awesome, surrounding the frail human being. 'You're responding to a mystery the whole time... The more you try and describe it, the more you tie it down, and you haven't got it.'

When the oldest member of the Community, Sister Agnes Mary, died in 1985 her funeral eulogy quoted a text from Ecclesiastes: 'For gold is tried in the fire and acceptable men in the furnace of humiliation'. 'And of course also acceptable women', added the speaker diplomatically. Despite the singularity of their experiences, almost all the sisters of CHN have felt something of the fire, the beneficent warmth that turns into savage conflagration, its transforming and regenerative powers, its destruction and refining. Some have merely been touched by the embers or survived a scorching relatively unscathed; others have found themselves seared by the fire, or have seen the dark core of the blaze. Many have spent a large portion of their lives in anonymous menial work for others and in gratuitous prayer for humanity, but all in varying degrees know the truth of Jung's adage, that 'a person must pay dearly for the divine gift of creative fire'. 'When a man is capable of being in uncertainties, Mysteries, doubts, without any irritable reaching after fact and reason', wrote Keats, the creative work begins. The will is in abeyance, and the logical faculties submit themselves to an order of reality in which the intellect assists without dominating. Such experience, whether in art or religion, is supra-personal, although it deepens personal awareness too. It becomes in Jung's words an 'innate drive that seizes a human being and makes him its instrument'. For 'the artist is not a person endowed with free will who seeks his own ends, but, one who allows art to realize its purpose through him'. The liberations of art and religion bring a freedom beyond the freewill of the ordinary self, and for one sister what best expresses the religious life is this transforming of the everyday:

Vocation enables a person to respond to love and grow into a loving and freeing relationship with God and others...you grow into the person God has created, [becoming] more aware of the potential in yourself. It is a journey and an exploration into the unknown...an ultimate confrontation with yourself, a stripping of all that is false and an openness to the spirit and fellow human beings. Thus you experience liberation from the restrictions you put on yourself. It is a discovery of the vulnerability of our human nature, our frailty and the loving mercy of God... But it's not all stripping and confronting yourself. It's experiencing joy in your own being, the joy that you discover in being in the presence of the heart of God and the heart of Jesus, and that joy is God's life in you. Every part of your being is illuminated by light, heightening the senses and the perceptions. When the sun sets behind a person, and every part of the person is accentuated—the eyes, the fingers, the hair, you can almost see the hairs on their hand. It's that fine.

9

FREE TO BE PROPHETIC

For the first time in centuries religious *can* be what they want to be, they *can* be *free*, free of all the clutter, free of all the junk, to be what the religious life was *intended* to be right from the beginning. . .free to be prophetic.

Alan Harrison

If many of the individuals who make up CHN have paid 'dearly for the divine gift of creative fire', the same taut and transparent comment could be made of its collective experience. Through all the cadences of the Community's life, the accent that overpowers every other modulation is consciousness of the duality at the heart of all its experiences. Some of the contrasts are muted and whimsical; others are turbulent and violent: inner/ outer; idealism/pragmatism; permanence/change; stillness/move- ment; liberty/authority; unity/disparity; the one/the many. This comprehensive series of opposites leads back to the dichotomy that is the source of all creativity and all finality: the tension between the macrocosm and the microcosm. It resides in the Community's core and relates to Sister Agnes Mary's sure ges- ture on my first visit to Cheltenham towards the centrality of the notion of community, the one and the many, which may be seen working out their arduous contract in community.

Communities are chameleon or phoenix-like entities. Refer- ence to community suggests an assumption that a community is

a known quantity whose distinguishing characteristic is an attitude of common interest, common loyalties, common commitment to an often intangible ethos, a unity in diversity. In
practice, the concept is as elusive as a handful of air. Some
groups and organizations earn the label of community, while
others fail to make the grade. Communities exist within communities. They overlap, so that individuals can be aligned with
more than one grouping. Sometimes a community seems ludi-
crously vague from the inside, but under threat from the outside
it arouses passionate loyalties and coheres like an irresistible
force. Sometimes communal identity breaks down and the
community, like the individual flower and the species dinosaur,
ceases to exist.

In most communities the consensus is fortuitous and fragile.
It can be unhassled, relaxed, content to be an episodic union
that firms if a common approach is required or if its existence is
threatened. It is often taken for granted and aroused only when
outsiders criticize or invade. Or else the bond can be fostered by
vivid exhortations that attempt to dragoon wildly disparate
forces into unanimity. The tenuousness of the community label
may be seen in the often painfully self-conscious use of the
word and the spawning of a compendium of crass dependent
phrases.

A religious community is a very special kind of community,
but it shares several characteristics with other communities in
that it is a chance assemblage of individuals with disparate
abilities and interests, bound by more than physical bonds and
joined to the wider community of the Church. However, there
seem to be fewer qualities that a religious community has in
common with other alliances than those in which it dramatically
diverges.

In a religious community, the self-consciousness of the label
reflects the reality. It is tighter knit, with a solider core and a
seamless ethos. Every detail of its life refers back to the core
and the ethos. Yet, despite its physical and ideological density,
its intent is diffuse, spinning from the expressible to the ineffable.
Its heady expectations are shown in F. B. Connolly's *Religious
Life* 'A Profile for the Future':

What is a religious community? It is a group of people where each one
has been touched and gifted by the spirit of God...a place of adult

faith; a place of heightened response within the Church. . . a place of Christian togetherness. . . a place of acceptance; a place of appreciation and yet a place of oneness. . . a place of luminous Christianity.

Even the obvious differences between a religious community and other communities in terms of gender composition, concentration of physical location, communal ownership and self-consciousness of community status, set it apart. Moreover, its members are devoted to the service of others through work and prayer and aspire to perfectionist standards of behaviour among themselves and towards others. They are united by the principle of love and defer to a core of belief that is expressed in a corporate spiritual life. They are subject to vows of poverty, chastity, and obedience. Of course, as any CHN sister will wryly say, these factors are regrettably subject to human fallibility.

The implications of these clear differences are so vast that they suggest a qualitative distinction of community. The balance between the individual and the group has lines of authority and significance that extend beyond the material and the utilitarian. Symbol and metaphor are integral to the daily lives of the individual and the group. Religious vows must be expressed not merely outwardly, but inwardly, and must be sedulously re-examined. The sense of community reaches towards a sublime unity and insists that the members of the flock should constantly rethink the meaning of their association. The interaction between the real and the ideal, time and eternity, the visible and the invisible worlds, brings the community into the orbit of mystery: 'We need a theology of community—we need to know it as a mystery. . . We are so action orientated that when we *do* come together, we feel we have to *work at* something or *decide* something, to justify our being together. The *element* of *mystery* in community life is passed over lightly'.

CHN's flighty and poetic ambitions as a community seem to cast it into the empyrean, a realm of the peripheral and atypical, a darkness of impenetrable mystery; but its heightened sense of the function of community and its precious qualities as a group highlight the fundamental stresses in community, the way in which communities confront and manage inner and outer change. In talking to the sisters, one is acutely conscious of the dualities of human existence that affect the equilibrium and continuance of communities.

The importance of the community structure and the centrality of the community ethos have been constantly reiterated over CHN's one hundred years. Like many of its English progenitors, CHN incorporates the word 'community' in its title, and the notion of the Community as a rare and responsible entity is enshrined in its key documents. Unlike non-religious communities, the entity is sacred and subject to the ceaseless pull of an ideal manifestation. The existing Community is like a partly developed photograph; the full image can always be seen hovering within the frame, oscillating in and out of being. Its outer life is matched by an inner life that aspires to daunting consistency and integrity. It exists on earth and anticipates continuance in heaven.

In 1914, Esther wrote her lengthy instructions to novices on the rule in which she referred continually to the special community-consciousness of her group:

The Rule of a Community is prescribed in order to be a means and help to our perfection. . . Some rules must be made when a company of people band together for the mutual good of all. . . By using a Rule, the private personal life of the individual is merged into a stronger, fuller, better, grander life of a company banded together for the love of Jesus.

When the foundress defines a religious community, she isolates love as the pivot on which the whole structure depends:

Consider for a moment what a Religious Community is =
It is a threefold cord—& is not easily broken for its members are bound by a three fold love:—
1st the love of Christ for His own sake
2nd by the love of all in need, for Christ's sake
3ly by the love of one another for the sake of the work to which they are pledged and the object they have in view. . . . The Religious Life is an associated & also a family life—all wrapped round with love— That is what God means every Community to be.

The relationship between the individual and the group puts overweening emphasis on the submergence of the individual interest in the common interest and requires imperiously vigilant loyalty: 'Let your Community be more than any member of it— more than yourself...in work, in speech, in action, in the letters we write'.

Although there is a recurring imagery of challenge in references to the similarities between a community and a military camp, in strictures about method, order, promptness, regularity and punctuality, the central image that Esther and her successors evoke is that of the family as an association of sometimes conflicting individuals, bound by affections that transcend the tight-rope of human variety; 'different in characters constitutions and tempers...they come for the love of Jesus'. The obligations are never allowed to lapse and the Community's regular prayer includes a supplication for the well-being of 'a society bearing Thy Holy Name... For each and all...'

For decades the message assumed a fixed ideal of community; the performance might lapse, but the goal remained constant. The main mechanisms for its achievement were the willing suppression of individuality and deference to authority. With the years, as Ida recognized in her 1943 address to Chapter, the tight-knit 'group of contemporaries' had been superseded: 'The generations space themselves out...the old family bonds are less easily maintained. The great dominant personal influence of the Mother Foundress has gone...there is the delicate task of combining faithfulness to the Rule...with readiness to appropriate fresh inspirations'. Yet the traditional admonition has barely altered: 'It is to a *super*-natural life we are called, and we can only live it by supernatural means...we are building the Community for the future, and for Eternity'.

By 1969, however, a revolution has taken place in CHN's position, a transformation painfully confronted by Faith:

We can't live in a vacuum; we have to live in the world, and face facts and in fact our world is hurtling forward at a giddy pace... We christian religious must hold firmly to the rock of our basic ideals, adapting the incidentals as fast and as flexibly as possible, or be swept under in the vortex...change is just the one thing that has come to

stay. . .christians have leant too heavily on the traditional structures
of church life and government and that means for us religious, on
those of community life and government.

Five years later the icy stability of tradition and form have
nearly melted in the bright flow of change and challenge:

A nostalgia for the past is natural; the past is important for our
present has grown out of it and can only be understood in reference to
it but the present and future must predominate in our living and
thinking. . . God's time for us is always now and if ever Christians
have been called to ride lightly to everything but God it is now. . .
C.H.N. is all question marks today and few answers.

For a religious community, change provokes acute and rava-
ging sensitiveness. The fact that its belief system enshrines a
stone-henge of monolithic certainties makes the pressure to
change tortuous, aggravated by the fact that authority in the
Community is divinely sanctioned. Even minor modifications
to structures, procedures or the liturgy can be interpreted as
tampering with the divine will. Several sisters concede that
CHN has been endemically cautious: 'definitely we don't rush
into things. . . We tend to look on the negative side. . .in
relation to change. What it's going to *do*, and how's it going to
effect *me*'. While there may be wide tacit agreement that CHN
has been conservative, the question of whether the Community
has changed too little or too much has sparked off terse debates
or leached into bitter undercurrents of stoical dissatisfaction. A
couple of sisters even feel that for them the frail consensus that
exists is no longer viable and that they live in an outer circle
where the links with the centre have worn dangerously thin.
Age is a predictable determinant of flexibility, although the
division of attitude by generation is not absolute, and a few
relatively young sisters class themselves as conservative. Some
older sisters look at the dynamics of human relationships in the
Community at present and lament the isolation and seeming
indifference that a relaxation of patterns and controls has
brought.
   Much of the metaphor used by the sisters to describe their
sense of the undermining of community repeats the imagery

embedded in the written lore and revolves around the analogy
of the family. The demise of a traditional familial structure,
essentially Victorian in its all-embracing authoritarianism, is
regretted:

it was more of a family atmosphere...everyone does their own thing
now... Some of the sisters just can't see how this generation ticks at
all... There was a more caring attitude I feel...it's a more individualistic ministry now, it's got to be, because the government's taken
over so many of the ones where T[ender] L[oving] C[are] was the main
thing... I find it very difficult to reconcile the fact that we're diver-
sifying so much... I don't think it makes for a harmonious household...there was the common life which doesn't exist any more.

The old family structure was characterized by a benign ma-
ternalism which, in one sister's opinion, began to be fatally
eroded in the difficult years of Ida's decline.

The old way meant stability that seemed to be a guarantee of
permanence. One of the oldest members of the Community
looked critically at the changed mode, 'the modern thing', and
reflected 'if you'd been through it the other way, we knew
exactly what to do, we knew exactly our place'. Religious
communities harbour a proportion of people who bask under
the umbrella of authority. Even those elderly sisters who are
more flexible and detached in their attitude to alterations in
'the *domestic* life of the house' see a disciplined family life as a
prerequisite of harmony because of the fallibility of human
nature.

Relaxation of structures, combined with the Community's
withdrawal from the institutional work that required a corporate
response, has had another result that is seen as a threat to
community stability and identity. Dialogue has replaced the
non-negotiable directive of the Superior, and in this consultative
atmosphere a rich diversity of vocations has developed. Where
activities are disparate, diversity can be perceived as a violation
of past values, a disruption of the corporate sense and a force
for disintegration. One sister observed that diversity 'just does
make it very difficult at the same time to remain a true community' and characteristically, given her rarefied values, inter-

preted the shift as an adjustment to secular demands that became a compromise with wordly values:

It's sort of the pendulum. The thing goes round and round and you become too isolated from the world, living a pie-in-the-sky kind of life, and that happens to the Church, but then you try to redress the balance and become involved in the world and then you suddenly find in fact that it's the world that is calling the tune, and I think we're going through one of these periods now.

Sisters who make comparisons with the past that disparage the quality of community life now assume that the clear perception of the nature of community that formerly prevailed is still available. Others recognize that the Community cannot be a fossil rock in a molten world and accept that, when the external situation of the Community alters, repercussions in its internal existence are inevitable. The reaction is sometimes confused, faltering and tinged with fear:

community life is part of the work and it's a very exacting part of the work, and I think we've tended to take it for granted in the past... We can't go back, nobody can go back to what it *was* like in the beginning, and I'm certain the world is an entirely different place now than it was when I came here and therefore the whole structure has changed... [The Community] is part of the world, it's going to be *more* part of the world...change for change's sake, that's wrong.

Humility in contemplating change is a response that can straddle past and future, although it may be tinged by existential helplessness, even when the observation comes from a hermit:

I think it's not altogether *good* for them to be too individualistic, but I don't think I can judge...because times are so different...wherever we are and whatever we're doing, we're in a state of transition and I think we can just go along. I don't mean we should accept everything, but I think we have to be very careful about judging.

Sisters who arrived in the Community in the 1960s when the religious life was experiencing its post-Vatican II upheaval are undisturbed by the prospect of further change: 'I think it's

changing, that's all. . . I came into the Community when it was
in the middle of change. . . A lot of things that some older
sisters find difficult I don't. I try to understand their point of
view, but I do see it from a different point of view'. The
youngest member of the Community is aware of the jolts that
attend the erasure of old ways and concepts, the fear that any
alteration to the lie of the drapery may lead to stripping of the
torso: 'once you're brought up in something. . . anything that
challenges it is automatically threatening, so that if you give up
anything externally that appears to be right then you're in
danger of threatening the basis'.

The bland response that sees change as inevitable without
confronting its role as an incubator of destruction is fortified by
reactions of creative enthusiasm for the outcomes of change. In
contrast to convictions that the Community's family life has
foundered and the isolation of individuals has increased, other
opinion claims that a more natural sense of family has developed,
mutual consideration has increased and possibilities for loneliness have been reduced. The benefits of encouraging self-
awareness, fostering open relationships and coming to terms
with the Community's suppressions are also applauded: 'more
and more we're beginning to understand ourselves. . . [individual]
people are becoming more looked at and their own particular
problems. . . it does mean a *change* in the way we approach
living together'.

At the other end of the spectrum from those who are permeated by nostalgia, some individuals consider that any change
that has taken place is timorous or insubstantial. They react
with impatience, believing that, although the Community has
altered its structures by devolving authority, emphasising personal
responsibility and dispensing with the old, almost pathologically
rigid distinction between professed sisters and novices, change
has been more apparent than real:

by word of mouth it may have [loosened up] but in tradition it
hadn't. . . in fact it still applies in many areas. You can say one thing
but tradition has such a strong hold. . . in the areas of individuals who
may be able to influence or who are powerful people. . . I imagined
the Community to be, I still hope it will be one day, a place where

people can feel completely free to come in and find the Lord, at their own pace, and may be there are rules and regulations as far as the Community is concerned, but that nobody's forced to obey any of them.

The undertow of conformist expectations has drawn one sister into the depths of alienation:

it's the individualism that's been suppressed. Attempts have been made to suppress that, and it's worked in many cases, and it's very damaging... Somebody said 'Why don't I leave?' And I thought well that's a funny thing to say, because they see me as not conforming. Therefore I shouldn't be part of the Community. And yet I think I *am* part of the Community.

Another sister who feels that the exercise of individualism has edged her onto a limb is tough-mindedly defiant:

I still feel that the Community is a sharing of adults, and I still don't think we've arrived at that... I used to think... I had to be what other people expected me to be. I gave that away some time ago... All communities were so suppressed for so long, and you didn't say what you thought or felt...like many clergy today, religious try to justify their existence, they're not quite sure who they are or what they are. I think you just have to do whatever you're led to do. And what community is, I really don't know.

Over the last twenty years, CHN has had to accept a metamorphosis that has demanded courage, sensitivity and will of all its members, but that has been particularly harsh on its Superiors. Faith carried the major burden of changes that not only saw the Community divested of its special place in social welfare, but also required a painful transformation of its inner workings. She reflected on the anguishing role into which she was cast:

people wanted to tell you what to do, but then they wouldn't want to take the responsibility of making a decision that might turn out to be wrong. That probably sounds a bit harsh, but people were not used to being consulted... People hadn't grown up, they hadn't made their mistakes early, and they didn't want to face making mistakes now...

There were certain realities that nobody wanted to face, and yet obviously ultimately we were going to be faced with them, whether we liked it or not, and the sooner we *did* look at them the better, because we'd be that much better prepared... There was considerable conflict in the Community. It surfaced, I suppose, as fear, on the part of the more actively inclined, of the people whom they saw as going in an opposite direction, not an opposite, but it was a different way... I felt there was something going on in the Community that was leading us somewhere, but I couldn't identify it, and I wasn't enabling other people to live with it, or perceive it, or do something with it.

The outcome of the unclassifiable but insistent pressure towards an obscure change which Faith sensed, she did not survive to see. While religious communities have been declining or disappearing, growth in the religious life has been concentrated in the contemplative groups, and CHN conforms to the general pattern within the Anglican communion, where, in the last ten or fifteen years, some active communities have been drawn towards enclosure.

An obvious reason for this movement is that the welfare state has occupied their old charitable ground. There is even a mood of retrospective condemnation that religious people ever dared to manifest Christ's injunction 'To suffer the little children...' Although these trends are clear to CHN sisters, they emphasize the intrusion of worldly values into spiritual places, an invasion that produces a reaction in the opposite direction and an attempt to eliminate profane influences. At its most extreme, this response is expressed as an impetus to provide a different model within the Community itself:

I...see it as a reaction against the secularization of the Community which seems to be happening at present... Less emphasis on community. Less emphasis on prayer life...there's not very much difference now actually to my mind between the world and the cloister... What the world needs is silence and prayer...[to] balance this mad rush towards paganism.

Understandably, few sisters would endorse such a hard line on the Community's deterioration, while to the outsider the

Community still seems an astonishing example of the power of a dignified and rigorous philosophy to preserve values that the world has squandered or suppressed. However, almost everyone agrees that a state of perilous tension in the world's political and economic viability and moral stability has reinforced the determination to affirm selfless—even reckless and power-less—values in the world's terms and to provide a contrasting witness.

The debate involves questions of terminology and definition that tend to be resolved by unconscious reference to individual sisters' decisions about the way they feel compelled to exemplify their vocation. Nobody is quite sure what a contemplative is, although one sister was given a tantalizing if unhelpful insight in the comment that she said '"Amen" just like a contemplative should'. This sister made a distinction between those who, although not 'natural' contemplatives, have been called to the life of prayer, and the visionary few who are assailed by mystical insights and illuminations. The centrality of freedom is em-phasized, an underscoring that revives the thorny paradox of freedom through self-relinquishment. The diversity of the con-templative life can be seen in its various strands within CHN. Two sisters experience a remote and special vocation as hermits. Another sees herself as a solitary who would like the convivial option of involvement with an outside group providing accom-modation where married couples can be temporarily relieved of pressures. A radical departure is represented by those who feel an increasing urgency in their long-standing desire to form an enclosed group, a move that would reduce the number available for practical chores and institutionalize a division within the Community.

Although there is a reflex that scorns prayer as self-indulgent luxury, the contemplative life is not a soft option, but a rigorous regimen that most people would find intolerable. Solitude offers a terrifying freedom, and the 'white martyrdom' of the solitary life demands a rare balance of will, conviction and stamina, especially given that the Cheltenham hermitages are so basic that Spartans might blench. One sister who spent time in one was sardonically objective: 'I was so cold I couldn't pray, I couldn't read, I couldn't think... I got out and hoed blackberries. I don't know what God had me there for'. Enclosure can be seen, even by those who are not personally drawn to it, as 'in a sense preserving and protecting that aspect of our life which is *essential*, because there's no meaning in our life if we don't maintain that individually and as a Community'. Or it is consistent with an unbroken thread of vocation, 'a continuation of what I came to do in the *first* place, to give myself wholly to God, and I'm seeing the expression of it differently to what I did initially'.

Sisters who desire a more outgoing active existence contest reservation of the 'contemplative' label to those who are 'enclosed' and reject the implicit dichotomy between prayer and works. One of the older sisters added that for most of the Community's existence the luxury of withdrawal was hardly an option: 'to me our work sends us to pray for people and our prayer sends us to work for people and they're both together... I said once... "if I felt God had called me [to] the contemplative life I wouldn't have had the courage to ask because we were so flat out". And I was told "it's quite obvious you haven't got it", which is true'. Some sisters are frankly happy to embrace the Martha label, even if a tinge of unauthorised superiority attaches to the Mary role: 'I'm a real mission-hearted sister. I love Fitzroy and I love the old dead-beats... I like physically caring for people, rather than just going about talking... It's not my idea of serving God. I know it's heresy to say so, but it's completely foreign to my sense of vocation. I said "I pray with my hands"'.

Another reaction is to play down the decisive nature of the change by denying any conflict between the two different expressions—'I think all Christians are both contemplative and active'—and claiming that the two have long been coexisting, even if obliquely.

On Christmas Eve 1985, the chapel at Community House was the setting for a wordless, slightly tense demonstration. It was as if two rituals were taking place simultaneously, one that centred around the office and this rapturous service in the Christian year, and a second that focussed on the way the Community perceives itself and its attitude to change. This silent demonstration was conducted through the medium of the habit. Looking from sister to sister, one had the sense of being subjected to a quick-fire series of photographic images that represented the transformation of a living symbol. One of the solitaries is clamped like a squirrel in the old habit, a medieval hangover, black from tip to toe, the face squeezed into a constricted oval by a stiff, white-linen wimple. The other solitary, who spent two and a half years as a hermit in New Guinea when she was in her early seventies, also sports the old style, although she manages to look amazingly outgoing in the all-encasing black. A third sister of arguably solitary inclinations is wearing a shortened and blatantly patched old habit, her way of showing contempt for all superficialities of dress and appearance. Several sisters are wearing the dark blue habit that has been more or less standard, although not compulsory, since the early 1970s. Some of the more conservative deny that the inky dress was ever 'brought in'; it was merely offered as an alternative. It consists of a wide-collared tunic that reaches mid-calf and has wide panels back and front, with a dark blue veil to mid-back, whose white band frames the face without giving the impression that the features are being compressed in a vice. In summer, the dark blue may be replaced by a white version of the same garments. In New Guinea an early concession was made in the adoption of seersucker habits and nylon veils, and, as the sisters who worked there say, modern fabrics, often topped with a vast sun hat, did represent a more relaxed way of life.

For years the dark-blue habit has been the norm, and those who wear it this Christmas Eve represent a wide cross-section of attitudes within CHN. Apart from the old black and the recent blue, variety proliferates. Like dental nurses of a decade ago, two sisters are dressed in white uniforms. Several are wearing the recently introduced dark-blue skirt, golfing-style, topped by different blouses, mostly short-sleeved and softened with frills and ruches around the neck and yoke. None of these sisters, including the Mother Superior, is wearing the veil, an omission that means more attention to the horticulture of the hair.

In striking, even comical contrast, the chief actors at the service, the clergy and their assistants, all male, are decked out in the gorgeous historic panoply of the Anglo-Catholic church, like beached flying fish, floor-length white albs topped by gold chasuble for the priest, dalmatics and tunicles for deacon and sub-deacon, white albs with gold amices for the servers. Male power seems to be operationally and symbolically intact. The Community's photographic collection beautifully encapsulates this fact in images of events where the clergy, embroidered and brocaded, preside in the forefront, while the sisters hover in the background like a shy array of fairy penguins. Except for informal moments, in the presence of the hierarchy, even the proud Mother Superior is tucked to the side of the central action.

When the Community was formed, the habit was thought to be unwise provocation in a volatile ecclesiastical mix where, to some, nunnish garb was tantamount to defection to Rome, and a more neutral deaconess uniform was adopted. Photographs of the original solemn-faced trio show them in sober, civilian Victorian dress, crowned with white pillbox-shaped caps from which append veils so truncated that they hardly warrant the name. They look like housekeepers or governesses in upper-middle-class households of the time. The only feature that distinguishes them as religiously committed people is a floriated Greek cross inscribed 'Melbourne Diocesan Deaconesses' Home'. Offstage, Esther had closeted away the black habit of the Wantage Community, which was discovered much later with note attached: 'My first (blessed) habit. To be buried in'. And so she was, with the wimple, veil, cross and girdle of CHN to signify her dual commitment.

The steps towards becoming a religious were marked symbolically by changes in dress, the six months' postulancy which formerly merited a pitch-black school uniform with cropped veil, clothing as a novice in modified habit with white veil and a large Easter egg bow under the chin, and profession, which came after two years' (later three years') novitiate. Surrounded by symbolic signs and gestures, the profession ceremony is the time when a sister receives the full habit, laid out on the altar, from a distinguished member of the hierarchy. The version of the customary that was passed by Chapter in July 1951 allots the habit full symbolic significance as an outward manifestation of vocation, overlaid with puritanical prescriptions that reflect lingering nineteenth-century notions of feminine modesty. The description proceeds from the general to the almost medically specific. The variants of the habit worn by postulants and novices are described, suitable fabrics for underwear are suggested, and sleeveless nightwear is proscribed. Sisters are never to be seen, even within the convent, without a cap covering their hair, that insidious symbol of seduction and vanity. With clinical exactitude, measurements were specified: the relationship between lengths of cloak, tunic and tunic panel, the width of hems, the length of indoor and outdoor veils to be assessed with the head held erect, the width and length of sleeves, the cord for the cross to be '2½ in below collar'. Amidst this arithmetical thoroughness, two dispensations are allowed, one to the Superior permitting changes for tropical climates, and a licence to all: 'Small changes of pattern may be made, provided the distinctive features of the Community Habit are preserved'. This concession perhaps explains the capacities for muted style and subtle difference that can be incorporated into the stencil of the habit, and the reputation that one Superior had for artful alterations that distinguished her as a swan from the rest of the paddlers. Only whim explains the skittish nightdress that Sister Bertha consigned to the depths when she and Esther approached England in 1927.

The habit as fashion has long been a Community preoccupation, a concern that showed itself in amused comparisons between CHN's mode and those of other communities. When the Superiors made their peregrinations around the English communities, a key subject of their letters was the astonishing permutations of the habit that had been encountered. This interest was not only a homely subject that struck a chord in the differing intellectual levels of the Community; it exemplified fashion as symbolic of ethos and identity. Comparisons also allowed the exercise of a decent spirit of rivalry: 'Wantage customs are very much like ours. One or two things I prefer about our ways... [Postulants] certainly are dowdy here...long black dresses with very clumsy grey collars and frightful grey veils with elastic under the chin. I suppose it is good for the soul'. The contrasts were given an edge of the bizarre in postwar England by austerities that hit the convents along with the rest of the population, enforcing an assemblage of rusty and

motley black at Wantage, the result of an appeal for black-out
curtains. To see Mother Superiors gathered for a conference was
to witness a fashion spectacle from another realm:

quite an impressive collection of starch and serge... The most picturesque of them all was a young Franciscan...known here as 'Mother
Brown Hat'...what a collection of hats!... How the East Grinstead
Sisters manage to drive a car or indeed to do anything practical I can't
think. It is quite a trial to have a conversation with one of them, they
are buried so deep in their bonnets.

Of course, CHN had only abandoned their own cumbersome
outdoors head-gear when the hazards of driving a car dictated a
more earth-bound approach. The comparison was two-way: one
CHN sister was inspected by the contemplatives at Malling
Abbey, whose curbed tongues were not matched by sealed eyes
and who 'were all very thrilled with our habit and I was asked
to take my veil off so that they could have a good look at my
cap and collar!'

Clothing was inextricably related to ceremony, so that comparisons often involved observing differences in key rituals. A
Wantage clothing was observed to be 'almost exactly like ours',
except for minor departures that were inevitably arbitrated in
CHN's favour. The English custom of crowning the newly
professed sister with a flowery garland always amused the perhaps
more earthy Australians, especially when the officiating digni-
tary was slapdash in his placements. The deviations of a profession
observed at Malvern Link were relayed home with critical but
indulgent attention to the domestic aspects of the event:

a much longer service than ours and more complicated—and those
wreaths— I wouldn't have them on my mind, let alone on our
heads... I did wish they could see our chaplain handing the vesture
bit by bit, instead of the N[ovice] M[istress] running around with a
handful!... The Refectory was *packed*, as you can imagine—we had
rolls, ham eggs butter marmalade tea and coffee and an enormous 3
tier wedding cake—done up with fresh flowers but not as nice as ours!

The fact that the original monastic habit survived virtually
unchanged for so long is perhaps symptomatic of the Com-

munity's lack of a diverse, planned structure of the religious life subject to centralized controls such as exist in the Roman Catholic Church and partly as a consequence of this isolation, its internal difficulties in accommodating to change. After Vatican II, when the Roman Catholic orders submitted to pressure from the hierarchy and disposed of habits, converting to an updated version of the habit or to civilian dress, CHN, which had felt the pressure of these august deliberations, especially in its attitude to authority structures, stubbornly stuck with its medieval-style habit. A few sisters made their comment on the incongruity of their wrapping by flapping along in long black on motor bikes or multiplying the panoply by adding academic robes, but a change towards something more amenable was not debated. Early in the 1970s, the blue habit that retained the features conducive to modesty and separateness became the norm. This stasis vanished, and the habit, which was revised in 1985 to include the option of blue skirt and individualized blouse just in time to enrich the Christmas Eve drama, assumed a dimension of vibrant, symbolic importance in the debate between the active and enclosed factions.

The position of the enclosed group is put by one sister with admirable circumspection:

those of us who are looking in this direction [of enclosure] are not the ones who are angling for a change in habit...my own feeling is that [the blue habit is] simple, it's practical, it's distinctive... The people who've spoken to me about it at all have all expressed the fact that it means a great deal to them to see the Sisters looking like sisters... I feel that [the change]'s to an outward extent changing the image of the Community.

Some of the more conservative element, which also includes several elderly sisters who feel that change puts gratuitous pressure on their declining years, are scathingly critical, putting the rush to be rid of the habit down to 'delayed adolescence' or the thrill of novelty for those who joined the Community young, without having experienced the pleasure of choosing their own clothes: 'When I started to see it I thought, they just look like I used to feel when I came off the wards after a hard day's work... It just happened all of a sudden... I said "Well, if I get out of my habit, I'm going to get into civilian dress and I've got expensive tastes"'.

There is a particularly protective attitude towards the veil, the feature of the habit that is most thoroughly charged with symbolic significance, and the current Superior has attracted some criticism for allowing an experiment in discarding the veil which is in fact a *fait accompli*: 'I *do* think that once they take the veil off they've lost something... I haven't the hair to go with it... The Sisters... with their veils look far superior to the others. The others look more like bowling ladies or nurses'. Disregard of the hair can become a definitely superior virtue in itself: 'I can't really talk for my active sisters... I have to trust that they're doing what they see to be right... To me the habit is my means of clothing myself with prayer every day. I couldn't bear going back to having to look after my hair. And the fact that I don't have to gives me time to pray'. Some see it in the context of outside pressures on the Community and regard submission as succumbing to an attitude that wants to strip the world of symbolic values: 'One can throw out too much and forget that there is a symbolism in things, and the world wants to throw out everything that's to do with symbols, and I'm not saying "Retain everything", but I think you've got to look at it'.

Most of the sisters who favour retention of the habit recount stories that endorse their own preferences and involve favourable reactions from outsiders. The habit is an immediately recognisable symbol of separateness and sacrifice, compassion and spiritual authority, that commands respect and invites confidence. Individuals will single out the one in habit from those in secular dress to approach for advice. In a rampantly secular world, the reflexes stimulated by this garment of sanctity are still embedded in the psyche. One sister whose initial reaction to the habit was one of stunned horror has changed her mind:

what I have found now is that hospital visiting in particular, where people are dying in terrible agony, physically as well as mentally, people have tried everything else and here is one avenue that a lot of them haven't tried, God, and so you appear with the cross, and they know instantly who you are, and I think the Lord then draws them to Himself.

The habit also retains some of its power as a protective device, a warning signal whose usefulness was familiar to the nineteenth-century sisterhoods: its wearer should be allowed to pass unchallenged and unscathed.

Yet the world is perverse, and the habit can be seen as exemplifying the senselessness of the spiritual, even as an impertinent claim to difference and separateness that can attract ridicule or provoke expectations of a readily exploitable naivete. Even the pious are perverse, for those who have a sentimental affection for the habit are offset by those who welcome change as evidence that the Community is not entirely fossilized and point out the acceptance of change by Roman Catholic orders. From this viewpoint, the symbolism works in reverse:

[Outsiders] are looking at us from the point of view of the habit. . . I know there are far more important things than what we wear, but just the same I've always maintained that the habit is symbolic of something. . . This symbol of the nun, all veiled from top to toe, it's no longer an image with which the world in inverted commas is familiar because you don't often see it.

Contrarily, the Community needs to be tactful towards its supporters, because the habit is 'something that gives *them* some sort of satisfaction and they can't see it from our point of view'. The expectations of friends are often more difficult to satisfy than the reflexes of the indifferent or hostile.

The importance of the habit is underplayed or even dismissed by those who point out that the habit does not make the nun, usually enlisting some terse spiritual writer or wry novice mistress to ratify this disarmingly self-evident point. The stand is often taken by individualists who say offhandedly that they do not care what they wear. Sister Francine, the solitary, retains the style of Esther because she was professed in it and adds that, if profession had taken place in a cartwheel hat and slacks, that would still be her mode. This stance evades the improbability that such an austere individual would be attracted to a group that indulged in such frivolities. She also offered the practical point that she can abstemiously work her way through the Community's wardrobe of discarded black, even though she is about half the size of many other sisters, both vertically and horizontally.

The controversy over the habit signifies that the Community has reached a crisis point in its relation to its own past and to the outside world and in its internal interactions. History can be enlisted to validate either position. The opponents of en-closure locate their argument in the Community's origins, 'founded as a mission community...you've got to keep the spirit of the *foundress* and the spirit of the foundress isn't that'. None of Esther's surviving writings hints at a community unin-volved in active works, an authority that still has force; CHN's current situation would be inconceivable to her.

The other court summons Ida as their Clio, claiming that she 'always felt that the contemplative life would grow out of this Community', but she was also the Nightingale of the Com-munity's institutional expansion. Ida's two successors are also abrogated by the proponents of enclosure, but Flora seemed irrepressibly gregarious, and Faith was characteristically detached, leaving an unanswerable question mark about her intentions: 'it's always been there in this Community because...there's never been the other kind...in Australia...there have always been very madly active people and others who stayed at home more'. Yet there are bold indicators in the fact that the Rule that she fashioned was siphoned from a contemplative order, her encouragement of contemplative experiments and the mel-ancholy drift of her addresses. The present move is usually dated back ten years when four sisters tried enclosure, but throughout the Community's history individuals have been sent to England for an exploratory stint in an enclosed order. These sisters now believe that they should test the spirit within CHN, feeling 'very strongly that they weren't being called overseas', but 'to an expression of this kind of life within the Com-munity...[to] provide that sort of *core*'.

Most of the reasons against enclosure related to its practicality, the uncertain attitudes towards a human mission reflected in the break ('I think the holier you are the more *human* you become') and the repercussions for the concept of community. 'Who's going to do the work?' is an obvious question, just as a lop-sided distribution of the practical burden, with mission work being left to valiant stayers, seems an obvious outcome: 'they're not being realistic in being an earthy sort of person. They've...lost contact with work and living'. The move is seen as fanatically unrealistic given the Community's precariousness and leaves a glaring question mark over the viability of the tradition-enfolding Cheltenham property. More personal reasons for scepticism focus on questions of compatibility and willingness to compromise, and the danger of a minority group galloping off on the bolting horse of its own enthusiasm, justified by claims to be acting in conformity with God's will: 'it's often very difficult to know what *is* His will. I'm never sure, Heavens above!... People who get this direct line to God...my goodness, it's dangerous'. In the face of a hectic debate, it is tempting to resort to the sense of a brusquely self-evident truth ('I was given a tongue to use') or to toss away the wilting weapon of rationality ('If they think God's called them that's all right... As long as he doesn't call me').

The justifications of the barrackers for separation are partly defensive, probably they are fundamentally aware that their intention represents a major departure from CHN's traditional orientation. This defensiveness often takes the form of denying any conflict between the two attitudes and underplaying the novelty of the move: 'We should be able to embrace the two strands...that's what we have been doing'. Vulnerable to the charge of dehumanizing, they offer their intention to care for guests as proof that 'in those ways we would be *open* to people'. Self-vindication can take more cosmic form as a force 'to counteract a lot of the sins of being too material', even as a last resort in a world plunging towards apocalypse. In this script, contemplatives are 'holding us together' when prayer is widely regarded as a spent delusion rather than a saving force. A more positive attitude is the flourish that the enclosed sisters would be 'launching out into individual vocations within the one vocation', an expression of freedom for individuals and the collective and a force for growth that fleshes out the Community's already rich diversity. As vocation is not a call to good works, a prayer-centred round represents the essence of the religious life, and the culmination can now be achieved because of the relaxation of work pressures and structures. By comparison

with enclosed English communities, CHN, with its dual heritage,
is robustly seen to be in a peculiarly advantageous position:
'There's one part of me that says [CHN] couldn't have survived
so long here if it hadn't been of God and may be we'll be just
one community in *all* the communities that can marry both'.
The prospect can arouse imaginative enthusiasm, using the
Pauline metaphor of the body, the separate parts combining
into 'the one wholeness', or the muscles acting in tension to
produce movement, or spilling out an excited catalogue of
CHN's colourful botanical variety: 'black and blue and white
and no veils, going to hospitals, living in hermitages, a group of
enclosed...walking the streets'.

These bright responses gloss over the possibility of schism of
which most sisters are suspensefully aware. In confronting the
potential for fragmentation, reactions range from the pietistic,
fatalistic submission to God's will, to a reprimand that puts the
onus on individuals to curb the spirit of opposition and the
desire to dominate, to act with generosity, commonsense and
sensitivity. To one sister, the problem goes beyond the niceties
of behaviour and involves fundamentally different perceptions
of the spiritual life:

I think it could be really schismatic because of the different types of
spirituality that are involved. If they weren't so extreme in opposites,
then you might have some hope of the two being together, but when
you've got some who are really into sacrifice and the others who are
finding God in different ways, it's a lot harder to get the two to meet.

Another sister believes that the theology of the enclosed group
is hopelessly backward-looking. These sisters are touching on a
question that is crucial to the outcome: whether the move is
inherently conservative, even reactionary. In relation to CHN's
past the shift is radical; it is also going with the tide in general
developments in the religious life. Yet one of the group involved
admits that most of them are 'amongst the more conservative-
minded', and conversation with them suggests that their motion
is more a retreat into the still waters of sanctity than an
advance into the tumultuous currents where the spiritual forces
are at their most clamorous and urgent.

The Mary/Martha dichotomy which is the chorus to the debate relates to another seething issue that divides the radicals and the conservatives and gives the fencesitters another matter on which options can be kept open. A reinterpretation of the story diverges triumphantly from the hoary action/contemplation thesis that served the patriarchal church like a dumb waiter:

You can take it as the adoring female sitting in submission to the male. Jesus is sitting there and Mary's just adoring him... or you can read what it *does* say... he is the rabbi, the teacher. In those days no woman was taught because they weren't considered worthy of being taught, and Mary is sitting there as a student and learning... That's a different relationship. Martha's tearing round like a lunatic... 'You're *too* much *hooked* up into the expectations others are putting on you, you're hooked up into the female role of serving'.

Religions have always institutionalized women's inferiority. The role of women in the spiritual dimension has not commanded much attention in a society that ignores the incorporeal in favour of the material, but it may be seen as the last and most significant bastion in the struggle to clarify the identity of women. If they are to be eternally subordinate in the domain of the sacred and excluded from the holiest functions, the issue has not been pursued to its logical conclusion.

Whether its members are prepared to admit it or not, CHN has strong roots in an early and important phase of feminism. Its inheritance can be seen in understandable pride in the Community and its achievements and in the fact that it was founded by a woman: 'it's an *Australian* Community of *Australian* women... it wasn't founded by a man... women's lib, I reckon, our Mother Foundress. She stood up to the men; she wasn't going to be bossed by either the clergy or the archbishop or anybody else'. There is also widespread if not particularly sharp awareness that for a century CHN has essentially been exhibiting competence and asserting authority in its own right. When the foundation of the Community's worldly involvement, the Mission to the Streets and Lanes, passed into other and male hands, the outcome was an affront to the Community's feminine self-respect: 'They resented a man coming in and telling them what to

do... because we'd always had authority... And I think perhaps
we felt a bit inferior'.

The fierce, often acrimonious, sometimes deplorable battle
over the ordination of women opened up to amazed Australians
a Pandora's box of vehemence in the normally placid Anglican
tribe. It has forced the Community to confront the issue of
feminism on home ground, even if none of its members anticipates being personally implicated, except those in chaplaincies
whose role shares many priestly functions. Although a strong
CHN contingent attended the first ordination of women as
deacons in February 1986, only one sister belongs to the
Movement for the Ordination of Women. Even given the age
group represented in CHN, the conservatism forced on it by
historical circumstances other than the nature of its foundation,
and the blinding masculinity of the Church, the Community's
conservatism on the issue is surprisingly strong and pervasive.
Contempt is a not uncommon reaction—'priestesses, I call
them'—and the question is often trivialized. Many attitudes are
ill-considered, confused and self-contradictory. One sister declared herself indifferent, then exploded impatiently 'Who are
we to say that God doesn't call a woman? We're judging God.
We're putting something on God that we've got no right to'.

Some sisters take refuge in the equal but separate position
without realising that this too has enabled the ecclesiastical
patriarchy to reserve the highest functions to itself, and that
the attitude is often based on sentimental assumptions about
the nature of femininity:

women have got more power in the world than they ever know and
here they are throwing it away... if our Lord had wanted women
priests, I'm sure they would have been ordained in the first century... especially when we're religious, we need the male... it's a
Jungian thing really... the expression of your womanhood is towards
God. That's the fullest expression of your femininity.

The 'rare vocation' of the priesthood has been honed by centuries of cosy expectation into an exclusively masculine facility,
leaving 'a lot more fields', splendidly unspecified, to women.
Another historical 'accident', men's superior knowledge of re-

ligious life and church affairs, is cited as a further impediment to women's participation in the supreme sacral entitlement.

Another refuge that evades the issue is the sincere claim never to have felt the weight of female oppression: 'I've never felt oppressed as a woman. . . the world was divided into men, women and nuns. . . I couldn't get excited either way. If women want to be priests, let them. . . women can hold their own without having to pretend they're men'. This sister's sardonic distinction between men, women and nuns is perhaps the key to her feelings of emancipation; as a nun, she by-passed the conventional situations where women's disadvantage was embedded. A favoured, well-worn niche from which to look at the question as simply a pragmatic choice, rather than a philosophical and ontological problem, is the view that the movement may be just an excrescence of 'women's lib' that encourages aggressive types and indulges in militant propaganda, with the proviso occasionally expressed that 'I appreciate that you have to have a few extremists to get things going'.

Except in a few cases, the positions are poorly articulated on both sides of the argument, a surprising lapse given the widespread expectation within the Community that women will be ordained. There are honest admissions of conservatism and ignorance, and those who say frankly that they are waiting to see which way the wind blows. Even those with strong negative views tend to confine their response to the current situation and to back off from final judgment, particularly given that theology seems capable of validating either outcome. Again CHN posture seems to be endemically cautious when confronted with the inevitability of change, but there is a strong if elusive creative movement in a disposition among those who are not personally interested in the priesthood to sympathize with those who are. Circumstances may well change this tremor into an unqualified gesture. Certainly, the outrageous threat to bomb St Paul's Cathedral during the first ordination of women as deacons toppled some of the uncommitted off the fence into a more vivid paddock. Recalling the furore, one normally violet-shy sister flushed paeony-pink with indignation.

Apart from the power of deeper emotional engagement, hope for an intensification of this creative stirring lies in the minority who have carefully thought through the issue theoretically and as it affects them individually, and can see its repercussions for CHN's vitality:

I think that women's communities should be more defined by women who are in them... We've been based on a fairly traditional mode for a long period of time, which has been defined really by monasticism, which has been male-orientated, and I think that's very *stifling* for women in terms of their understanding what their own spirituality is...women are seeking more of an active means of expressing their own system of beliefs, and I think we have to be able to incorporate that in *us* as well... As a group of women and a community we have to be able to allow women to explore what they think their needs *are* with the church, find the expression of it and also be able to help people with relationships that are meaningful and freeing and developing and growing and creative... I see [CHN] more as a nucleus where ideas could be tested and people could become themselves.

The possibility that the issue will cause a schism in the Church lies in the background, a possibility that to some seems too devastating to warrant pursuing the cause. When the potential schism within its own ranks is added to this wider scenario and a multitude of other problems, the future seems more daunting than it has ever been. The pattern of attrition and the rarity and maturity of vocations that has been experienced in English communities has been repeated in CHN, accentuating the familiar spectre of a dwindling, ageing community. Just as many English communities have had to consider the hard facts of real estate, CHN must ponder the viability of its Cheltenham property and, if it is viable, find ways of infusing new life into the activities there. Moreover, the Community faces a brutally secular world in which the problem of defining its own position in the world and within the Church and the need to communicate the relevance of its spiritual witness are intense. 'Being there' may be justifiable for individual sisters, but it is not for others and may not be for the Community as a whole.

Uncertainty for the group radiates into doleful implications for the unique personal certainties that the metaphysically ratified imperviousness of the whole offered to its individual parts. Many of the sisters are vulnerable not only in their maturity and lack of professional training, but also in the suspicions aroused by the incomprehensibility to the larger world of their chosen life. Most communities are terminated by a decision imposed from outside or by an imperceptible withering that reduces the pain. Some communities fade into the sunset of superseded opportunities and lost time. Other groups are disbanded by considered, but voluntary decision, a dissolution that usually results from recognition that the particular need that they fulfilled has changed or disappeared. For a member of a body committed to supernatural and eternal values, admission of the group's vulnerability to the ordinary processes of growth and decay and the onset of irrelevance requires a harrowing deference to chance and uncertainty, fatalistic rationalization, or mute submission to metaphysical intentions that are no longer understood. All of these variations of response involve deference to forces of nemesis and inscrutability that are supposed to have no place in the divine scheme, or represent only a temporary hiatus that revelation will illuminate. To admit that God's eternal work may no longer have a niche that entirely and reassuringly fits one's contours is a fundamental challenge to those whose lives have been predicated on these uniquely self-justifying certainties. If the Community withers away or changes beyond recognition, the prime cause will have to be located in the supernatural will.

Questions about the future of the Community produce a gamut of forceful emotions. One sister reacted initially with a heart-stopping pause during which her eyes filled with tears, followed by a series of tragic sighs of perplexity, before she eased herself into anguished speculation:

Just terribly sad. Awfully sad. We just can't, you can't see, well, we're probably not meant to see, but I can't see ahead anyway, it's as though it's just all going to fall apart... It *may* be that in God's scheme of things we were meant to flourish for a time, to meet a particular need, and to work at a particular time. And that something else will grow *out* of what's left of CHN. It may be that, it *may* be that there's got to be two or three different things grow out of it, a small contemplative order, a mission order, or something else... I feel that when that begins to happen that's when the *real* change, we'll *really* see what's going to happen. It's almost like a sort of *landmark* for the

Community. When that happens, we'll have to think about this house, because we'll have the older and the sick sisters to look after. There'll be so few of us here. There'll be some of the sisters still wanting to go out and do their chaplaincy work, and we're not going to be able to cope with it all. This house is going to be too big for us. It's all going to happen. And it's all going to happen at once... You can feel as though things are working towards something early next year [1986]. And you can't really envisage what's actually going to happen.

Another sister snapped: 'Well, it collapses, doesn't it? I think that I have worked very hard over the last two years to try and prevent that, but now I can see what I'm on about. It'll collapse because of people's attitudes and not doing God's will. And I mean that in the best sense, not in a pious sense'. This hard-headed matter-of-factness was belied by the convoluted impatience of many of this sister's other comments. A third faced the prospect of the Community's termination with a philosophical brusqueness that probably obscures less resigned attitudes: 'If it folds up, it folds up. I'd be sorry... Life goes on'. Defiant pride is the dominant note of another reaction:

I used to think if the Community closed down the end of the world would come, if we sold this place the end of the world would come, but I don't know. If the Community *did* fold, say in twenty years time, I don't think it will, but if it did, it's had a hundred years it's given to this Church. It's made its mark... With all its ups and downs, its [up]heavals and its disappointments, its record is pretty good.

   There is a fairly common inclination to retreat into the kind of spirituality that provides a protective, if sometimes thin covering against questions that relate to one's worldly relevance. This reaction is particularly prevalent among those sisters who wish to form an enclosed group, a move that has brought the Community's survival into contentious focus. Internal currents and external pressures seem indeed to have produced a momentum that is decisive for the Community's continuance. While fatalistic abandonment to some impenetrable divine intention may seem by pragmatic standards an evading tactic, it engages considerable individual courage and will: 'it's the Lord's community, and if he wants it to go on it will, and if it's done its work, well, then I think we just have to die gracefully. It's not an end in itself'.

While the Church and the framework of belief provide a sense of ultimate security that provides a cushion against crippling uncertainties, the Community's fragility within the wider context can be seen positively:

I see it as a bigger thing than just us, because I think the religious life has a purpose... [CHN's] a part of the wider church... [Religious life] has a contribution to make over and above the individuals who make up this life and because we're fringe-dwellers in a sense...we've got a lot of good things going for us. We've got a freedom in a way.

When the urbane and broad-minded Alan Harrison, an Anglican priest who acts as a travelling mentor for troubled or self-questioning religious communities, visited CHN in 1984, his vision for their future was sombre and daunting. He saw them as smaller, older, more dependent on seculars, less secure financially. These more fragile organisms would exist in a savagely secularised, technological world, 'challenged at the level of faith' because of the growing religious diversity of the surrounding society and the increasingly aggressive thrust of non-Christian religious expressions. At the same time, their institutional stability and internal processes would be challenged to find a balance as they moved from a Ptolemaic to a Copernican model, 'from a single-centred community to a multi-centred community...the way for the future'. Yet he saw no shortage of vision in the religious life and triumphantly advised that, as an eschatological community, 'we ought to be *ahead* of the secular world in living for the future'. Communities might be smaller, but their members would be more committed to one another. A new level of human association has been made possible by the changed structures and the dissolution of the old strictures. Individuals are now freed for the expression of deep feelings and the exchange of unmuffled allegiances. The crucible of change provides the possibility of new forms and new firings, new resolutions and new intuitions. The false dichotomy between being and doing can now be discarded. Above all, in Harrison's view, hope lies in the 'growing role of the feminine in the ministry' and the rediscovery of the function of the 'wise woman' that was lost during the counter-reformation.

This script may seem like flying in the face of more mundane realities, but the power of the peripheral should not be underestimated, if those whose chief preoccupation lies with the preservation of comprehensively human values and the integrity of spiritual realities could ever be consigned to the outer ring. In recent years, CHN has received advice, not necessarily very palatable fare, from several quarters about its future. In her address to Chapter in 1982, Sister Elizabeth Gwen referred to an earlier abrupt appraisal from a priest that 'if you don't open your doors, you will die', and to the equally discomforting conclusion from the archbishop's visitation that year that the Community's 'mixture is too rich, the resources too poor', a diagnosis that some sisters interpreted as 'a recipe for gradual death'. She even brought up a matter that was perhaps about as unthinkable as the disbandment of the Community: possible sale of the Cheltenham property. Yet these conjectures came up in the context of positive developments, increased involvement with the chaplaincy department of the diocese and the opening of the south wing of Community House for guests, a development that contributed to a conviction that Cheltenham should continue to be the Community's centre.

Advice came in a more buoyant form in Alan Harrison's imaginative injunction to 'live as a pilgrim people, travelling light, not burdened with inflexible regulations'. While many of the old pressures impinged, the release of sisters, death, reconsideration of resources, focussed this time on the viability of the retreat houses in Melbourne and Adelaide, there were positives to emphasise that provided the basis for a new phase of growth: quality of community, creative experimentation with the office, review of structures, personal growth. Addressing Chapter after her re-election for five years in September 1984, Elizabeth Gwen referred to two extremes of the religious life that she had observed on her trip overseas that year: the ancient Superior in all-encasing habit 'staggering up the hill' at the Mothers' conference in England, and the postulant at the Sisters of St John the Divine in Toronto who, as a widow, was talking fondly of her grandchildren. Although she does not necessarily anticipate an influx of grandmothers, she clearly finds the second image more relevant to a revitalisation of the religious life. Creative daring for the future, not a shuttered reverence for the past, is required to foster CHN's flexibility, to reclaim its authenticity and to seed its mysterious vitality.

On Friday 21 November 1986, one of those days when late spring tips its bird-of-paradise intensities into high summer, and the air oscillates between gold-tissue opacity and crystalline clarity, I visited Cheltenham to see an everyday mass and to discuss with Sister Elizabeth Gwen certain matters, all of them disarmingly benign, relating to the manuscript of the book. The day reminded me how vibrantly some impressions are confirmed, how quickly seeming fixities are superseded, and how defiantly fluidities can be transformed into amber.

Some of the impressions confirmed and the changes observed are small. I see with a tinge of regret that the new gardener has conscientiously tamed the woolly wilderness near the gate. I notice with joyous recognition how the unofficial gardeners at Cheltenham dismiss any hint of the geometrical in their layouts and prefer the vivid enamels of searing blues, scorching oranges, resonant browns, scintillating crimsons, pulsating roses, and the tousled habits of the more cottagey flowers. The garden is rife with these dazzling luminosities and supple intensities. Never were pansies made of such lustrous otter skin; never were California poppies so faithful to the many gradations in the apricot to orange ribbons of the spectrum; never were the stipplings on the foxglove a deeper violet. Or is it just that this is one of those days when spring tips its embroidery basket of wild colours onto the cloth of summer?

Some of the small changes relate to individuals. Sister Betty, who had earlier declared her firm attachment to the veil, has returned from Adelaide bare-headed. Sister Penelope, who had wanted to develop a mission to married couples in stress, is up at the old novitiate house, 'The Pines', doing just that. Sister Hilda has come back from America and is engaged in a chaplaincy with AIDS sufferers. Sister Lois, who was reconciled to disabling damage to her badly injured leg, is walking again.

Sister Sheila has been given leave and accepted as a novice at
Fairacres. Sister Maree's children's book has been printed and
lies, with a new range of pressed flower cards, on the table in
the vestibule.

In the warmth of this ordinary extraordinary day, the harmonious rhythms of the domestic life of the house wash around
one like the warm waters of a rock pool. A voluble former
employee arrives with a cake for afternoon tea and photographs
of her grandchildren. A party of disabled children, with their
mentors, is picnicking on the village green in front of Community House. While we watch them, Sister Helena tells me
how as a child she used to love to press the collapsible silk of
California poppies against her nostrils, and of the difficulties in
producing a response in her retarded foster granddaughter: 'I
keep telling her that one day she'll smile'.

Some of the changes are larger and less personalized. The
drawn curtains of St Julian's are a reminder that the sisters who
were moving towards enclosure have adopted that life, although
they are apparently wearing a track to Retreat House where the
healing ministry is in full swing. Their decision has removed
the harmful fractiousness of uncertainty from the Community's
life. One of the matters that Sister Elizabeth Gwen brings up is
her feeling that perhaps I have misjudged the Community's
attitude towards women and the priesthood. I agree that, yes,
the stirrings of a more thoughtful and challenging approach are
evident and that the Community, despite its problems, is in a
state of courageous health. Mass, where the priest and sisters
gather in circular formation around the altar, is a dramatic
embodiment of a shift in the liturgy towards redefining the
relationship between the priest and the congregation, between
God and the people. The ceremony lacks the well-rehearsed
grandeur of more formal occasions, but it breathes with the
simplicity that the gospels intend. It is as sharp and tactile an
efflorescence as the blood-red lily with bone-coloured rays on its
six petals that stands on the centre. table in the refectory.

In September 1987 the debate in the Anglican Synod on the
ordination of women was preceded by a slanging match more
reckless than the rumblings caused by any other doctrinal change.

The odd bishop sorrowfully forecast his departure from the Anglican congregation to a more polite elysium, presumably the Roman Catholic Church, which had set itself adamantly against the advent of women priests and had pragmatically shown itself prepared to countenance his deplorable married status. Some of the Church's more educated luminaries elaborated their justifications against ordination with a fervour barely papered over with academic objectivity, sometimes managing to make their more temperate adversaries look like weak-kneed shifters with the times. The press revealed the plans of one diehard, complete with organizational details and lists of likely parishes, to set up a 'continuing' Anglican Church, unruffled by the uppitiness of women. Given that Anglican churches in the United States, Canada and New Zealand have for several years been ordaining women and that the mother church is on the brink of accepting them, the ferocity of the opposition suggested that the Australian church was lingering in a reed-choked backwater.

After the vote in which the proposal was accepted by the Houses of Bishops and the Laity, but was narrowly lost in the House of Clergy, the defeated cohorts gathered outside St Andrew's Cathedral, Sydney, where synod had deliberated, singing 'We shall overcome', the theme song of 1960s civil rights movements. Posters were hung around the precinct, singling out the Archbishop of Sydney's failure to appreciate the implications of the biblical axiom: 'Your sons and your daughters shall prophesy'.

Although a few sisters are known to buoyantly favour the ordination of women, the Community as a collective has not debated the question at length and has exhibited a casualness that seems at odds with its essential call and the radical nature of its historic mission. Yet, as the Mother Superior says, the matter is not going to slip into the limbo of failed causes and 'it's extremely unlikely that we won't be affected in some way... We need to be sure that the Community would support any-body...who might be so called'. Different ministries, vocations within vocations, have been accepted since the move to New Guinea in the early fifties, and diversity, with chaplains, enclosed sisters and hermits, is now the Community's fabric. Most sisters are involved in pastoral work of some kind (even the conservative who delights in transporting the reserved sacrament for communion at Kingston Centre for the aged) and the four chaplains perform most priestly functions. Attitudes to all the sacraments have altered, and ordination is a sacrament like the others. At a deeper level, all sisters have had to struggle with the reality of vocation which they share with the priesthood. Besides, the Mother Superior, like the priest, has always been seen as a representative figure. She, not the chaplain or the warden, exemplified the intensity and validity of her group's witness. The image of the foundress, who taught priests to say mass, rises up: '[it's] pretty sad we can't get some of Mother Esther's spirit into things today... We of all Church people should be the ones who are getting excited about it'.

When the question of the priesthood was introduced at a recent Chapter meeting, an easy-going acceptance was evident, surprising given earlier hostility towards the idea among the older generation and the heated debate on more trivial issues in the past. Any sister who feels called to the priesthood is to be given full support. Although a gem-like hardness of response might be more appealing to the outsider, the matter-of-factness of the reaction does not signify insouciance. If a dispute had erupted, the eloquence of habitually calm demeanours might have jostled the air. As it was, the matter was introduced in a way that invited only a statement of intent and discouraged a forum. There are probably more reasons for parishes to be convulsed and divided, and the Community appears to have shaped an unbidden consensus in its understated, almost covert way. Although a degree of embarrassment over the sometimes crude rejection of the idea in the past probably assisted some ayes, an awareness of the depth of the group's involvement in the issue has prompted a process of individual reflection that has coalesced in relaxed unanimity. A few may have bowed to the inevitable. As well, the possibility that the Community could be used as a pawn in the highly politicized atmosphere may have counselled a mix of dignified detachment and quiet commitment.

Seen as part of a conservative stand on a wide front that found a maddening, accessible target in a potential woman priest, the extremity of the opposition has demanded a response and highlighted both the culturally based nature of the status quo and the flimsiness of the theological impediments. One sister, who inherited a prejudice against women priests from a background in the Plymouth Brethren and a 'spiky' Catholic tradition, found herself amazed by the white-hot feeling aroused. Women were powerless, she commented, because men decided the issue. Prejudice, the cult of male superiority and the desire to retain power were the operative reactions, 'part of a sacramental attitude where man is head by divine right'. She likens the proponents of ordination to the suffragettes, scorned as viragos in their own time, but now regarded as fighters for natural justice: 'We'll look back in twenty years and wonder what the fuss was about'.

The Community has been in a unique position to observe those women who are likely to be the first ordained. In February 1986 the sisters at Retreat House were hosts to the candidates for the first ordination as deacons and observed the suffering aroused by the terrorist tactics of some opponents. After all, breathless, ideologically inspired bidders are unacceptable in the gruelling selection process that precedes ordination. The sisters have had women priests living with them and have been able to observe a feminizing influence of their training on some women deacons. The blossoming spirituality of these women has been added confirmation. These changes have impressed some sisters with the positive feminine values that can be brought to the priesthood, qualities that are usually described in traditional terms as compassion, caring, the easy unlocking of confidentiality. One or two sisters would extend this to a belief that the priesthood is defective without the female and that women must become priests to provide a complementary mode to the male hierarchical structure.

In reacting to the ironies of the current situation (for example, the sanctuary of a pro-ordination local church crammed with the usual aquarium of men), a recoil against the whole system can emerge: 'Who wants to join the club? Who wants to lose their lay status?' The obsessive emphasis on the priesthood and the lack of interest in a lay ministry for women irritate a few sisters. Acceptance of a priesthood for women is not seen as a threat to vocations to the religious life, but the possibility cannot be discounted. Anticipation of a right outcome sometimes arouses mixed emotions and is shadowed by the pessimistic conclusion that the ordination of women will not alter the stratification of Church government in the short term, if ever, because the Church is embedded in the systems of the past. The most cheerless observation is that women will sacrifice more of themselves to become part of the power pyramid, accommodating rather than confronting the system, a buckling that is felt to have occurred in some women who have become deacons.

In the end of an age the garment of the past can no longer be patched into new clothes: it has to be unwoven in order to be rewoven, and in order that it should be rewoven, the loom must first be set up... In a day when so many either seek to patch or to weave bits of cloth of old patterns, it is hard to be occupied with the framework of the loom, but without it there can be no new weaving to bring in, not a patched, but a resurrection garment.

The ordination of women is only one facet of the call to spiritual renewal that confronts those who struggle with enigma and mystery. For one sister 'that hiddenness of God allows the spirit to become active... We may not see ahead, but we know that we're working in the new way and that the Church is being called to new life and that we're being called to new life within the Church...we're being called to exploration'.

And am I wrong to worship where
Faith cannot doubt nor Hope despair
Since my own soul can grant my prayer?
Speak, God of Visions, plead for me
And tell why I have chosen thee!

INDEX